BOOT

BOOT

AN LAPD OFFICER'S ROOKIE YEAR

WILLIAM DUNN

WILLIAM MORROW AND COMPANY, INC.

NEW YORK

To God, for being the best backup a police officer could have

It is the policy of William Morrow and Company, Inc., and its imprints and affiliates, recognizing the importance of preserving what has been written, to print the books we publish on acid-free paper, and we exert our best efforts to that end.

Library of Congress Cataloging-in-Publication Data

Dunn, William C. (William Carl), 1960–
    Boot : an LAPD officer's rookie year / William Dunn.
      p. cm.
    ISBN 0-688-14713-5
    1. Dunn, William C. (William Carl), 1960– . 2. Police—
California—Los Angeles—Biography. 3. Police—California—Los
Angeles. I. Title.
HV7911.D96D86   1996
363.2'092—dc20
[B]   96-12726
                                              CIP

Printed in the United States of America

First Edition

1 2 3 4 5 6 7 8 9 10

BOOK DESIGN BY MICHAEL MENDELSOHN OF MM DESIGN 2000, INC.

PREFACE

Southwest Police Station lies on a corner at the intersection of Martin Luther King Jr. Boulevard and Denker Avenue, about two miles south of downtown Los Angeles. A modest two-story brick and cement structure with a noticeable lack of windows, it was built in the mid-1960s to replace what was previously called University Station, which had been standing in the 1200 block of Jefferson Boulevard since the turn of the century. On the west end of the building there is an enormous cone-shaped communications tower topped by a flashing red aircraft warning light. This gives Southwest Station a resemblance to a lighthouse standing guard at the mouth of a harbor.

The area covered by patrol cars from this station is only nine square miles, making Southwest Division the third-smallest, geographically, of the Los Angeles Police Department's (LAPD) eighteen patrol divisions. Bounded by the Santa Monica Freeway to the north, Vernon Avenue to the south, La Brea Boulevard to the west, and the Harbor Freeway to the east, Southwest Division is populated by a rather stable number of African Americans, a rapidly increasing number of Mexican and Central Americans, and a small contingent of Koreans.

The first time I was ever in Southwest Division was over a decade ago, my freshman year at UCLA. At that time, UCLA still played home football games at the Los Angeles Memorial Coliseum, located in the eastern end of the division. Students would make the thirty-minute trek along the Santa Monica Freeway from Westwood to watch what that year was a pretty good team with All-Americans Freeman McNeil at running back and Kenny Easley at safety.

With the first home game of the season came football fever for me, so I made my journey to the Coliseum in a convertible sports car with three other freshmen. On the freeway we drank beer and talked about the chances for a Bruin victory, neither noticing nor caring about the changing cityscape around us. But when we exited the Santa Monica Freeway at Vermont Avenue, I immediately became aware of one thing: We had entered into some rather ominous-looking territory. All of the businesses seemed to have burglar bars pulled across their doors, the salespeople inside suspiciously evaluating any passersby. Even the small, storefront-style churches were built like fortresses against some invading army. And the streets themselves were filled with debris. Bag people, their clothing ratty and stained black from lack of washing, walked zombielike through the streets, checking trash cans. And the graffiti, sprawling letters shaded and shaped into the names and proclamations of gangs that had taken custody of these streets, seemed to cover every building wall, flat surface, and fence.

Although I recall no untoward event involving the populace around the Coliseum, I know I never felt comfortable driving there. While nothing could beat the pageantry and excitement of college football, the getting there, traveling through besieged neighborhoods surrounding the stadium, always left me feeling uneasy.

My feelings of uneasiness were further stirred by stereotypes developed from reading our local newspapers. At that time, there were two major papers in the city: the *Los Angeles Times* (now the city's only major paper), and the *Herald-Examiner* (now out of business). Reading those papers, apart from sporting-event coverage, I found nothing positive reported about the neighborhood surrounding the Coliseum. It seemed that robberies, rapes, and murders were the only nonsporting events worthy of newsprint. And those crimes, as reported in those two newspapers, had one common factor. They were committed by neighborhood males who were in local street gangs.

I first applied for the Los Angeles Police Department on a cold January evening a few years after my graduation from UCLA. At that time, I was a salesman for a company in the San Fernando Valley.

Looking for an employment change and steadier income than the roller-coaster earnings provided by commissioned selling, I decided to answer one of the many newspaper ads placed by the LAPD as they attempted to beef up their force to an unprecedented level of eighty-six hundred officers. I was told to go to Wilshire Division Station in the midcity district, where, together with about thirty other applicants, I signed up for the LAPD.

I easily passed the first of six tests needed for employment (a simple one that checked grammar and math skills), and was quickly scheduled for an oral interview with a police sergeant and a civilian employee from City Personnel. But I ended the process there, canceling the interview, not being sure if I really wanted to subject myself to the abuses and dangers I associated with police work.

It wasn't until almost two years later that I changed my mind. Still in sales, I had drinks one night with a coworker and her boyfriend, a Los Angeles police officer. Throughout the evening, he kept me on the edge of my seat, telling war stories from his fifteen-plus years on "the job." There were car chases at high speeds; kids found who had fallen into sewers; bad guys with guns barricaded in houses; and tales of bizarre criminals who pulled some very amusing capers. I was spellbound. But it wasn't exciting stories alone that led me to join the LAPD. What caught my attention was that this man thoroughly *enjoyed* his job. Every morning he got up and looked forward to going to work, patrolling the streets of Los Angeles. His enthusiasm was a major selling point for me, as my work at that time was simply a way to make money; it was not work I really enjoyed doing.

So I reapplied, and after passing a battery of physical and mental tests, I found myself marching in step around the manicured grounds of the Los Angeles Police Academy. For the next six months I learned criminal law and procedures, practiced tactics to subdue suspects, fired hundreds of rounds from my 9mm Beretta handgun, and was taught the rudiments of the Spanish language as well as basics relating to the cultures of various ethnic groups. I also ran an amazing number of miles—and all to the tune of full policeman's pay—which seemed like stealing, because I thoroughly enjoyed the training.

Being a member of the LAPD was something all my friends

wanted to hear about. I would receive calls daily asking me, "What is it like?" "How is it going?" "What did you learn today?" I had attained a sort of celebrity status. It was a remarkable employment change for me—and I couldn't wait to hit the streets.

But throughout our training at the Academy, instructors gave us veiled warnings with one theme: This job is for a special breed, and once we leave the Academy, many will become disillusioned—many did not truly comprehend what we were getting ourselves into.

"Police work is not something learned in a classroom," one instructor said. "Your time in the Academy is simply a time to familiarize yourselves with the workings of the *LAPD*, *not* the workings of the citizens, criminals, and situations you will come into contact with. You will have to learn those on your own. You can hear all the war stories and see all the videotapes of police incidents you want—but they do very little to prepare you for the *street*. Being a police officer is almost instinctual. And if you don't have the instinct for it, it's best to find other employment."

This book is about this individual officer's probationary period, my "boot"[1] year, as it's called in the LAPD, and what I came to learn about the streets of South Central Los Angeles and about myself during that first year as a police officer. I still enjoy this job—even after events involving Rodney King and the ensuing riots. But I enjoy it for reasons that could never have been imagined when I sat in that bar at a time that now seems ages ago.

At a party given for my graduation from the Academy, a family friend who retired from the LAPD as a homicide detective with twenty-five years of service draped his arm over my shoulder and said to my mother, "He's going to tell you stories that you're not going to believe. Well, I'm here to tell you something: Believe."

So read on. And believe.

---

[1] In most other departments, new officers are called rookies. But in the LAPD, new officers are called boots. The origin of this wording is unclear, although the two most common explanations involve a reference to military boot camp, or the necessity for new LAPD officers to keep their boots spit-shined.

AUTHOR'S NOTE

The majority of the individuals portrayed in this book are real people. However, to protect the privacy of certain individuals (including all of the minors) mentioned here, many names have been changed and, in some instances, composite characters derived from real people have been used. These pseudonyms and composite characters are indicated the first time they appear by an asterisk (*). The events described really occurred, or are composite scenarios of actual events. Opinions in this book are those of the author, and in no way should be construed as those of the Los Angeles Police Department.

CONTENTS

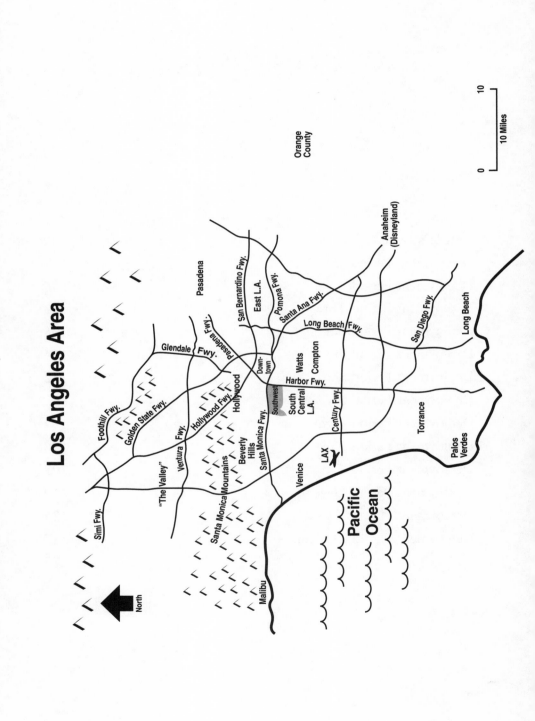

Los Angeles Area

Southwest Division 1991 (LAPD)

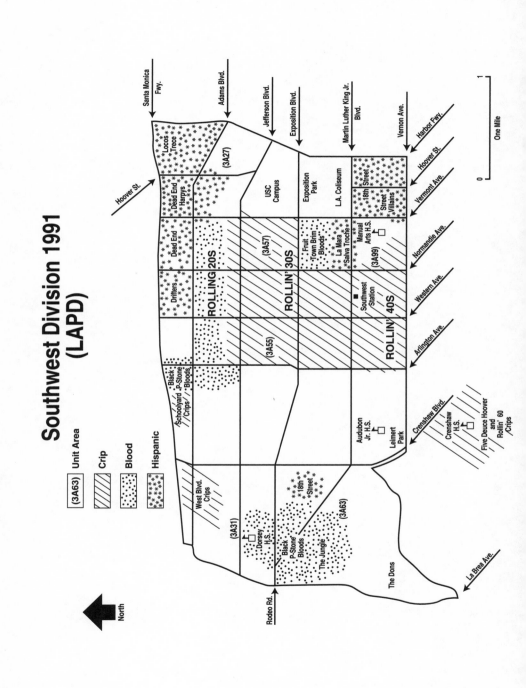

Legend:
- (3A63) Unit Area
- Crip
- Blood
- Hispanic

North

One Mile
0 — 1

Streets and Landmarks:
- Santa Monica Fwy.
- Adams Blvd.
- Jefferson Blvd.
- Exposition Blvd.
- Martin Luther King Jr. Blvd.
- Vernon Ave.
- Harbor Fwy.
- Hoover St.
- Vermont Ave.
- Normandie Ave.
- Western Ave.
- Arlington Ave.
- Crenshaw Blvd.
- La Brea Ave.
- Rodeo Rd.

Areas/Gangs:
- Locos Trece
- Dead End Harpys
- (3A27)
- USC Campus
- Exposition Park
- L.A. Coliseum
- 18th Street Villains
- Dead End
- ROLLING 20S
- (3A57)
- ROLLIN' 30S
- Fruit Town Brim Bloods
- La Mara Salva Trucha
- Manual Arts H.S.
- (3A99)
- Drifters
- (3A55)
- Southwest Station
- ROLLIN' 40S
- Black P-Stone Crips / Bloods
- Schoolyard Crips
- West Blvd. Crips
- (3A31)
- Dorsey H.S.
- 18th Street
- Black P-Stone Bloods
- The Jungle
- (3A63)
- Audubon Jr. H.S.
- Leimert Park
- Crenshaw H.S.
- Five Deuce Hoover and Rollin' 60 Crips
- The Dons

DEPLOYMENT PERIOD ONE

"**W**hat's up . . ." he says.

It is not a question, nor is it an attempt at conversation. The words, along with an accompanying nod of the head, are simply a sign of recognition. It's the first night of patrol for both of us, and even though we have spent the last six months training eight hours a day together, I still know him only by his last name, which is Dozier.* I nod a hello back, grabbing a seat next to him. I glance up at a clock hanging on the wall of the roll-call room; it's fifteen minutes before the start of P.M. watch, which is roughly the late afternoon into night shift.

"First night," I say, more out of nervousness than anything. Dozier's hands twitch on the desk before him. He's just as nervous as I am.

"Yeah," he replies. "First night."

Even though I've been training the last six months to be sitting here this day, I do not know what to expect. Our Academy instructors told us little about the actual proceedings at roll call. All I know is that roll call is where we receive our partner pairings and our unit assignments. But beyond that, I'm not sure; especially since it lasts forty-five minutes, and there are only sixteen officers working tonight who need to be paired and told their assignments.

The only other officers now in the room (about seven total) are also recent graduates from within the last year. We sit tightly in the first two rows, the other six rows behind us deliberately empty. Department etiquette dictates that probationary officers be at least ten minutes early and sit only in the first two rows—the rest of the room being reserved for seasoned officers. We have all adhered to these

1

unwritten rules. Violation of them could get a probationer branded as being "salty," LAPDese for being too big for one's britches. This label cannot only mean a cold shoulder from veteran officers, but it can also cause poor ratings, or even a physical challenge. Officers will not put up with a boot who cannot keep his ego in check. The thought is that if you cannot show a little humility in front of other officers, you won't be able to show any in front of citizens. A police officer cannot be without humility; it is a cornerstone to sound judgment.

Besides Dozier, two other probationers were also in my Academy class: a stocky Asian named Tanaka,* and a tall Hispanic female named Banderras,* who tacitly nods a *hello* from the other side of Dozier. She has dark brown eyes that attest to her Mexican ancestry. During training, there was a group of about a dozen recruits from my class who would regularly go out dancing at a nightclub in Burbank. It was during those nights when I discovered that Banderras has long, beautiful black hair that falls gracefully to the middle of her back. Now it is tied thickly and securely in a bun at the back of her head, LAPD regulations stating that no on-duty hairstyle may extend below the bottom edge of the uniform collar for women (the top of the collar for men). It gives her a compact, military look, a sharp contrast to the sensual woman I've seen off duty.

I spot another familiar face behind me in the second row, Kevin Riley, who had his gym locker near mine in the Academy. Being in a class ahead of mine, he would tell me when to expect "surprise" inspections and quizzes, each class having been run on an identical schedule. Kevin gives me a slow nod of recognition.

"Yo, Mr. Dunn," he drawls, his voice having a slow, almost southern cadence to it. He sits leisurely reading the sports page, in sharp contrast to the way my classmates and I sit, as if we were defendants awaiting sentencing. We four new arrivals are tense, and apart from Dozier's twitching hands, there is very little movement. We are all in the same boat; too much motion may cause us to tip overboard. The only sounds I hear come from outside, down the hall. Low talk and soft music emit from the locker rooms where "regular" officers, the P-IIs and P-IIIs, are getting dressed.

LAPD has three levels in the police officer or "P" rank. "P-I" is a new officer still on probation. "P-II" is the basic street cop rank (also called a P-II Dawg). "P-III" is a P-II who has passed a series of tests and can evaluate P-Is for job fitness. P-IIIs have two stripes, and the next rank above them is sergeant.

I scan my surroundings, having been in the room only briefly once before. The furnishings can be described as government functional. There is no style, no attempt to please the eye. A spartan environment.

Stretching to the back wall are rows of long, skinny tables with matching hardwood swivel chairs, all nicked and cracked by years of abuse, and all bolted to the floor. They face toward the front, where a huge old desk that looks as if it had been carved from a single redwood tree stump sits perched on a six-inch platform. Hanging from the ceiling above the desk are two ancient televisions, outdated models turned on by pulling out the volume control. Both are currently tuned to the same silent test pattern, the color shading of their screens being dull and fuzzy.

The room's walls, like its furnishings, are functional, without style. The front wall behind the huge desk holds a long chalkboard. It's been recently wiped clean with a damp cloth, its bold green writing surface having only a hint of white chalk dust around the edges. On the back wall are tacked dozens of WANTED posters with black-and-white photos of cold, hard faces. One side wall is covered by steel file cabinets while the other has a large, detailed engineering map of the entire police division. This map is used to target high-crime "hot spots." Using pins, the map identifies robberies with red pins, car thefts with blue, and burglaries with green. The pins seem to fill the whole map. Apart from a few pockets of resistance, the entire division is one swirl of color. Seeing this rainbow of crime and the need for policing so graphically summarized reinforces my decision to join the LAPD.

A wave of pride now runs through me. I finally feel that I *am* a Los Angeles police officer. Although technically I have been one for a half-year now, those six months were spent in the Academy, where I wore the light-blue uniform of a police recruit and accessories that didn't include either a badge or loaded weapon. But now I'm wearing the sleek, smooth, dark-blue uniform of an LAPD street cop; and over my left shirt pocket, a stainless-steel-and-copper badge with its depiction of Los Angeles City Hall. Resting passively in a holster on my belt is a loaded, blue steel, 9mm Beretta model-92F handgun, whose use by me, although possible, seems unimaginable.

ORIENTATION

My first official day at Southwest Division had been three days earlier, when I attended an orientational seminar in the roll-call room. Each division has one every three months. These seminars are basically get-acquainted sessions for officers new to the division (such as probationers or officers transferring in from another area of the LAPD), and are designed so that divisional management can lay down ground rules and expectations to their new underlings.

"I know you have chosen to work at Southwest Division because of our professional nature and attitude, as well as our commitment to our community," said Lieutenant Mike Ross,* the day-watch commander. A milky-skinned Caucasian with wire-frame glasses, Lieutenant Ross seemed to enjoy speaking before our group, his voice full of enthusiasm. "We have a tremendous amount of support from our Southwest citizens. And that is because we take the time to listen. We want to *know* what our citizens need from their police department. I call it an 'attitude of concern.' We as police officers are concerned about those citizens we police. We want to hear *their* concerns and then try to address them. They really *respect* us here because of this attitude of concern, and we really *respect* them."

Lieutenant Ross continued trying to build our "attitude of concern." He recounted stories he had heard citizens tell during community meetings—about officers showing concern by changing flat tires for the elderly, or stopping to talk with folks, just to say "hi." He let it be known that he liked officers who displayed this friendly attitude.

"There is a great deal of crime in this division," Lieutenant Ross concluded, his demeanor stiffening momentarily. "But we still manage to have some fun. I think you are all going to enjoy your stay here. I welcome each one of you." Then he nodded to two dark-skinned African-American officers who had been sitting quietly behind him at the front of the room, both of whom sported two stripes, an indication that they were P-III training officers. "These are officers Bobo and Horten.* They are two of our more senior patrol officers. They can give you a little insight into our job here from a patrol standpoint. I leave you in their capable hands."

Gathering up some charts and maps he had shown us earlier, Ross exited the room. Phil Bobo followed the lieutenant to the door, closing it.

"Lieutenant's gotta say what he said because of the bars on his collar," began Bobo. A large man, his voice was deep and thick, his forearms big, like a steelworker's. "You can take what you want from that touchy-feely stuff, just as long as you remember most of the citizens you'll be dealing with fall in that category known as criminals. And not every criminal down here cares how 'concerned' your attitude is, especially since he'd rather give *you* some attitude to be concerned about."

He looked us over, a pit bull examining a new playmate thrown into a backyard by its owner. He could just as easily make friends as eat you.

"He is right about one thing; we are a close station. It's not hard to get along here. The cops are *good* people, and there are a lot of citizens in the community who *will* back you up. But this is a working-man's division. You cannot sit on your ass here. A lot of shit goes down, and it goes down fast. On P.M. watch, you'll be chasin' the radio all night, going from one hot shot to the next. And everyone goes when there's trouble. This ain't a work environment for the fainthearted."

Officer Jackie Horten, a slender man, wore a long-sleeve uniform shirt with three hash marks on his left forearm, one for every five years of service and, I guessed, he was probably close to getting his fourth.

"We take backups seriously here," said Horten, speaking slowly. A pair of thin glasses bridged his nose, and he wrinkled his nostrils occasionally as if he were just getting used to new frames. "When your brother officers need you, you will go. Won't matter how far you are, or what you're doing. You go. If you're eating dinner and a backup comes out, you better dump your food and get in your car. If you're sittin' on the toilet, you don't even take the time to wipe your butt. You get in your car and you go. Ain't nothing, and I mean *nothing,* more important than officer safety here.

"Last month, we had two officers ambushed over in the Jungle," continued Horten, referring to a housing project in the western end of the division. "A bogus domestic-violence call, and some fool with a handgun lying in wait. Luckily, no officers were hit, just had some rounds go over their heads. But it reminds us there are people in this division who just flat out want to kill you. We have almost three thousand ex-cons living in this division, each one still burning up at *you* for puttin' *his* ass in prison. And that doesn't count their wives, sisters, and mothers who hate you just as much. Then we probably have another five thousand young gang members just waitin' to be ex-cons who also don't like you very much. There's a lot of hate for the police on these streets."

Horten paused for a moment, taking a short draw from a cup of coffee that had been sitting on the table next to him. I think he also wanted to give us a chance to let the numbers he has just laid before us settle in.

"There are over *twenty-five* identified gangs in Southwest Division, nine of which have more than three hundred members," added Horten for impact. "Four of those could have as many as five hundred-plus. And you're talkin' about a division four miles long and two miles wide. We have a major gang problem.

"You officers seated in this room will get to see a good amount of action. And if you don't watch yourself, *you* might become a statistic. We've had twelve officers[1] murdered in the line of duty in this little eight-square-mile piece of real estate you are sworn to protect and serve. *Twelve!* And if my words ain't enough for you, you go down to the lobby, because we got some of their pictures up on the walls."

Horten let this sink in for a moment. I had seen the pictures of some of them in the lobby two days prior when I had stopped in to get my locker. Nine of the twelve were there in medium-size portrait shots bolted to the wall behind the front desk, small brass plaques at their bases with each officer's birth date, years of service, and date of death etched in. A mix of black-and-white and color photos, they were probably taken when these officers were in the Academy. They all looked young; hair neatly trimmed; uniforms crisp; their faces cheerful and smiling.

---

[1] Since 1902.

"Those are murdered policemen down there! Each one of them shot dead. That's for a station that services two hundred sworn officers. That's a helluva lot of dead cops! I can't even tell you how many more have been pensioned off from here for serious injuries. These are some mean streets. There are police departments in this nation with more than two hundred officers that have never had even one officer shot in the line of duty. And we've had twelve murdered."

Horten surveyed the room, then continued, "Basically, you better be prepared mentally and physically. You better tell yourself right now that sometime over the next year some asshole is gonna try to kick your butt. Ain't no way you're gonna get out of here without being in a physical altercation. Fight's gonna happen. So you better get your mind in line. You better think you're a bad muthafucka. So keep your body in shape. Run your ass off and lift weights. And if you ain't good with that Beretta on your belt, you may want to think seriously about putting in some extra time. Lot of us go out to the desert. Take a cooler and a hundred rounds. We practice quick draw, shooting left-handed, shooting on the roll, reloading a gun if you've been shot—shit they don't teach you in the Academy. Take it from me. I've been in three shootings. In only one of them did I stay on my feet in a Weaver stance," said Horten, referring to a standing, two-handed shooting stance used by LAPD officers. "In this division, the most important tool you have on your belt is that handgun."

"You're gonna be here for a year," said Officer Bobo, summing up. "So, prepare yourself for some hard work. The average street cop in New York makes one felony arrest a month. In Chicago, it's also one. For all of LAPD, it's five. But at Southwest Division, it's about *ten*. *Ten* felony arrests a month. That's a helluva lot of hardcore criminals you'll be dealing with. A year at Southwest will be like a lifetime career at any other police department in this nation."

ONE MINUTE, ONE SECOND

The roll-call room is now full of officers. I sit in my chair, looking straight ahead. A spitball smacks Tanaka's ear two chairs away. I hear giggling from the back of the room. Tanaka does not scratch

his ear even though I'm sure it feels wet and sticky. A crumpled ball
of paper whizzes over my head, a bad shot, also from the back of
the room. More laughing.

All LAPD officers have had to put up with some hazing when
they were probationers, and it's accepted as standard behavior. It's
done not only as a rite of passage, but to toughen one up. If you
can't take a little teasing in the roll-call room, what happens when
the bad guys talk bad about your mother?

The front side door now swings open, and in struts Sergeant
J. J. Reese. He is the watch commander tonight, and the most senior
sergeant on P.M. watch. "Quiet down, this is a place of work!" he
barks, his voice gravelly from years of smoking cigars. A tightly built
Irishman with Popeye forearms and a bushy mustache, Sergeant
Reese eyes the occupants of the room. They all quiet down.

Two other sergeants follow, one a thick Samoan, the other, a
tall black female. Reese grabs a seat behind the desk while the two
sergeants stand. Unfortunately, our front-row status places us within
a few feet of all three sergeants, which seems to me to be perilously
too close.

"I'll be inside," says Reese. "Sergeant Fuela will be in the field
in L-twenty, and Sergeant Roberts will be L-forty."

I begin taking notes, as do the other probationers, writing in a
small pocket-size notebook. Reese reads the car assignments from a
large magnetic board he has carried in. "Johnson and Tanaka?" calls
Reese, reading off the last name of the senior man first in each two-
man car.

"Here, sir," says Al Johnson, A black P-III at the back of the
room.

"Here, sir," says Tanaka.

"You'll be A-fifteen. Catania,* Banderras?"

"Here, sir," says Catania from the back of the room.

"Here, sir," says Banderras from the seat next to me.

"You're A-twenty-seven," says Reese. "Beasley, Reid?"

"Here, sir," says Beasley, a P-III somewhere in the back.

"Here," says Reid, a probationer from two classes ahead of
mine.

Reese continues down the list, pairing me off on unit A-99 with
an officer named Don Murphy. I turn around to look for the source

of Murphy's voice, but am met by hard glances from the regular officers. Boots are supposed to keep their eyes forward. I turn back around.

Reese finishes off the list, then picks up a clipboard called the "rotator." It contains a myriad of information—from wanted suspects to police retirement parties. Anything's included that someone feels the watch should know about.

"From the rotator," bellows Sergeant Reese. "Rollin' Thirty Crips will be having a gang funeral today in A-thirty-one's area. Deavon Chalmers* will be memorialized at sixteen thirty hours. They also called him 'Cadillac Jim' and 'Payback.' Well, Mr. 'Payback,' some of you know well, was the recipient of a payback himself up on Sixth Avenue and Jefferson the other night, taking a lethal forty-four magnum round to the head. Blood P-Stones supposedly did this one. So be on the lookout for a retaliation by the Thirties over in the Jungle tonight."

Reese flips a page. "Here's a note from CRASH," he says. The Community Response Against Street Hoodlums is LAPD's gang task force, utilizing patrol officers with extensive knowledge of street gangs.

"Be careful if you make a traffic stop on any early-eighties white Ford Mustangs or Escorts. A gang member by the name of Grady* was involved in a narcotics dispute which ended up in the shooting deaths of two Swan Bloods down in Seventy-seventh Division the other night. He's driving said-type vehicle, and is a male black, six feet, one hundred and ninety pounds, age of twenty-five to thirty, short hair, no further description." Reese examines the page for a moment. "No real name is listed here. It does say he is a possible Fruit Town Brim, so that means he might be living in A-fifty-five's area. This gentleman has stated to other gang members that he will kill any police officer who stops him." Reese reads the death threat as if it were a weather report. No emotion—as if he's heard it all before. And there is no tension from the officers in the back of the room. They simply make a note of the car and wait for the next item. "Also, it says, any info on who this guy may be in real life, if you got a birth name for him, contact Detective Cutter* at South Bureau Homicide."

Reese turns a few pages on the clipboard, passing over information that he feels is useless. He settles on something that makes him smile.

"Death and funeral notice for Jimmy Economeides, lieutenant. Last post was DHD. Came on the job in 1940, pensioned off in 1960." Sergeant Reese stops, begins counting on his fingers. "So that means he got the city for over thirty years of pension. Not bad. Good job, Jimmy." There is a murmur of approval.

Sergeant Reese flips a page. "OK, we have some outstanding suspects here."

When other police departments read off their "Wanted" lists, they read off all types of criminals: burglars, drug dealers, petty thieves. In Southwest, there are so many wanted criminals that usually only the murderers are read off. It's all there is time for because roll call lasts only forty-five minutes. The other wanted bad guys, the nonkillers, are just too plentiful. At any given time there are an estimated fifteen hundred felony warrant suspects in Southwest Division.

Reese reads off a few of the murderers' names. There is one in particular that catches everyone's attention. It is a gangster named Kevin Smith who was seen dealing drugs on the corner of August Street and Nicolet Avenue in the Jungle the previous day.

"Ain't he the guy who was on *America's Most Wanted?*" asks a P-III.

"Yeah," says Sergeant Reese.

"He hangs out with P-Stones," says another P-III. "Been chasing his ass since he was a little pooh-butt wannabe."

Smith is wanted for a pair of murders in Louisiana. According to the account, an AK-47 assault rifle was used. Smith is also known to carry a .357 magnum revolver. He has recently been seen driving a lime-green Suzuki Samurai with personalized plates.

"Whoever gets him," says Reese, "your life story will be on TV."

"I can just see it now," says a balding P-III. "My name in lights."

"Have to put some makeup on that high forehead first," counters a P-II. "Gonna burn out the camera lens with that glow!"

Reese continues, "If you see the Samurai, arrest all occupants and impound the vehicle," then he flips a page. "There's a movie shoot up on Harvard and Adams," he says. "They'll be using blanks, so be mindful if you get any calls in the area."

Somebody in the back sings a few lines of "Hooray for Holly-wood." Reese looks through the rest of the clipboard. Nothing catches his attention. He puts it aside and scans the crowd. "Anybody got anything?"

A black P-III speaks up. Don Payne is built like a fireplug. He plays defensive back on the Los Angeles Centurion Football team, LAPD's barnstorming full-pads team.

"West Boulevard Crips stole a maroon Chevy Astro van two nights ago in Wilshire," he says. "CRASH found it parked at Adams and Hillcrest unoccupied, and were sitting on it. But they pulled off for a help call. It was gone when they returned. Right now, it's buried in some garage someplace. But it will be out tonight according to CRASH. Word is they're gonna do a drive-by on the Rolling Twenty Bloods."

"I want you to spend all your available time up around Adams and Hillcrest, Donnie," says Reese. He looks down at the lineup sheet. "Who'd I say was working A-fifteen? Johnson?" He scans the room for Johnson, the senior officer on the car, and finds him. "Al, that's your area. Shake it up a little and see if you can find the van."

"Roger," says Johnson dully, using LAPDese for "I understand."

"Keep it in mind, guys," says Sergeant Reese. "Oldsmobiles and Astro vans are the vehicles of choice for the drive-by shooter. Anything else?"

"Yeah," says a P-III in the back. A husky Italian, Hank Catania also plays for the Centurions. He has a sharp tongue and a wry smile. "It's my birthday next week," he says. "Be sure to get me a present."

"Yeah," coos a female P-III. "I got your present, Catania."

"But it's probably too small for me to accept," he shoots back. Catcalls and comments fill the room. Reese shakes his head. "Awright, knock it off," he barks, and order returns. Reese then looks at us boots in the front row. There is something wicked on his mind.

"We have some new officers here," he says. "They're fresh from our very own Los Angeles Police Academy." Hisses emit from the back of the room. "Easy, folks," says Reese. "We were all there one day." He looks at each of us, his eyes emphasizing what he has just said. He then seems to scan us, as if he were looking for something else. His eyes settle on Tanaka. "Officer Tanaka," he says. "One minute, one second."

"One minute, one second" is a tradition from the LAPD Academy. In one minute and one second, individually, new recruits have to tell their Academy class about themselves: where they were born, where they went to school, their hobbies and sports, their current marital status, why they decided to become police officers, and anything else they found pertinent.

Tanaka stands up, a big smile across his face. At five feet five, he was one of the shorter members of my Academy class. But he is absolutely fearless. When we had "boxing" matches (which were more like sixty-second brawls performed at the end of a quarter-mile foot race), he was like a Tasmanian devil, a whirlwind of arms constantly moving forward. His aggressiveness earned him the nickname *Sumite,* a combination of the words *sumo,* a chip on his Asian heritage, and *termite,* a chip on his size.

"Dale Tanaka, twenty-two, attended Oregon State University on a baseball and wrestling scholarship," he begins. Tanaka has a surfer accent. If you were to put him behind a screen, you would swear he had blond hair and wore baggies. "I was born and raised in Huntington Beach, and I still live there, uh, with my parents."

Oops. Wrong thing to say. He gets kisses and catcalls from the crowd. He blushes.

"Near the beach," he adds. This calms the crowd some. Beach houses are coveted by LAPD officers. "I like to ski and surf. I'm not married. I have a girlfriend, but I play around."

This last part brings cheers from the crowd. He has redeemed himself. He smiles broadly.

"And I became a police officer because I wanted to help people."

Tanaka gets wide hand clapping from the crowd. A very good one minute, one second. As Tanaka sits, Reese is already looking for another victim. He settles on Banderras, who has been looking at her hands.

"Banderras, you're on."

Banderras stands up and walks to the front. I can feel some of the male officers in the room shift in their seats.

"Daisy Banderras," she says. "I'm twenty-four years old, from

Upland," she adds, referring to a small city about halfway between Los Angeles and Palm Springs.

"Where the hell is Upland?" interrupts a P-II.

"It's above Downland," chimes in Catania, bringing laughter from the crowd.

"Knock it off," yells Reese. Acting like a concerned father, he turns to Banderras. "Officer Banderras, please continue."

"I was a waitress before I got on the job," she says. "I'm single. I have a four-year-old boy named Jeffrey, who is a handful." She pauses for a moment, the thought of her son bringing a smile to her lips. "I always wanted to be a police officer. So I applied, and luckily, I made it."

This last sentence gets Catania going.

"Hey," says Catania. "You didn't just luckily apply and make it, *girlfriend*," the word *girlfriend* grinding out of his mouth like a taunt. "This is a job for the fucking elite of society!" *Hear! Hear!* and *fuckin'-A* echo from the crowd. Catania sits up, pointing a thick finger at her, a jab that pushes her back even though she is standing twenty feet away. "Lotta fools applied for your job. Only one out of every hundred who fill out an application wear that uniform you have on. You worked your ass off to be in that front row. Remember that."

Banderras stands nervously. Reese wiggles his finger, indicating she should sit down.

"Good job, Officer Banderras," he says, and she sits down. His eyes run over me, landing on my other side. "Dozier, you're on," he says.

Dozier stands up.

"All right, a brother," says a black P-III.

"And a fine-looking one," says a female voice. This brings an instant response from Catania.

"Watch that sexual harassment," yells Catania.

"Ain't no harassment," she says. "It's a black thing." More laughing.

"Ain't no black thing," says Catania. In a feminine voice he sings, "It's a love thing."

"Quiet down," interrupts Sergeant Reese. "Go on, Dozier."

"Daryn Dozier," he says. "I'm twenty-nine years old. Played

football at Sonoma State University. Quarterback. (*Ooohs* and *aaahs*.) I was selling real estate in Inglewood before I came on the job." He is smiling, confident. "I joined the department because it seemed like an easy job for the money. . . ."

The second the words fall out, I can tell he wishes he could suck them back in. They were definitely the wrong thing to say.

"*Easy money!*" growls Catania. "Who's his fuckin' T.O.? He'll show you how easy the fuckin' money is!"

Dozier twitches nervously. I know he didn't mean to say it, but it's out there. Along with the boos and hisses from the crowd, and more than a few choice words.

"Sit down, 'Easy Money,' " says Sergeant Reese, his eyes narrowed. Dozier grabs his seat.

"I meant to say *good*," he whispers under his breath. "It's a *good* job for the money."

A ball of paper smacks him in the back of the head. Dozier doesn't acknowledge it. He looks straight ahead like a statue. Then I feel Reese looking at me.

"You're on, son," he says.

I get up and turn, and am standing facing the entire roll call, which is unnerving. Speaking in front of a group of cops is not easy; especially since I know that these little speeches we give are done not only as an introduction, but to see how well we can handle public attention. I take it as a personal challenge, especially since Catania is desperately trying to think of something funny to say. Then I remember what a guy named Viramontes did in the Academy during his one minute, one second. I decide to go for broke.

"My name is Bill Dunn," I say, my voice somber. Then I look at Catania as if in a confessional. "And I am an alcoholic."

There is a silence in the room, an uncomfortable silence. A chill runs through me. When Viramontes goofed on Alcoholics Anonymous in the Academy, we nearly peed in our pants. Even our drill instructor, Todd Rheingold, laughed, and *he* seemed to smile only when we had to run five miles in ninety-degree weather. But this group is just sitting there. Maybe they don't get it.

A flash of sweat hits my entire body, then I see a smile on Catania's face. He begins to laugh, and with him, so do the rest of the P-IIIs. I breathe again, because for a moment there, I felt I was dead.

"All right, all right, quiet down," says Reese. He looks at me. "Get out the rest with a little less tongue-in-cheek, son."

"Yes, sir," I reply. "I'm a Los Angeles native, lived here all of my life. I grew up in the Valley, went to Birmingham High, then to college at UCLA. I was doing sales for a company in the Valley before I became a police officer. I live in Hollywood, am single, but I've been with the same girlfriend for close to a year. I'm a snow-ski fanatic, I like to hit the slopes whenever I can, and I'll play anyone who wants to play racquetball. I joined LAPD for two reasons: a steady paycheck, and because I'm tired of the crime I see in my city. But mainly for a steady paycheck."

Reese nods his head a few times in approval.

"All right," says Sergeant Reese. I sit down. Reese then looks at the crowd, shrugs, a way of saying "Anything else?" No one answers.

"It's showtime!"

DOUGHNUTS AND COFFEE

I feel like I am living a cliché. Right out of roll call, Don Murphy takes me straight to Winchell's Donuts. I cannot believe it. I thought cops standing around doughnut shops eating pastries and holding steaming plastic cups of coffee were seen only in the movies. But here I am, standing under an enormous ceramic doughnut, sipping java.

Although it's still daylight, it's a cold and cloudy day, and my partner is wearing a heavy jacket. Winter is just beginning to bite at the Southland, having weeks ago pushed out tanning weather in preparation for the torrential rains that plague Los Angeles every January. Although winter is short here, it can bring with it temperatures that hover around freezing, and although short sleeves are the uniform during most Los Angeles nights, there does come a time when even the stoutest of officers has to cover up his arms. I can tell this is going to be one of those nights. That works out fine for me, because the only street uniforms we were allowed to purchase while in the Academy were long-sleeved, which I now wear with the requisite black tie and silver tie bar.

"So, you feel like a real cop?" he asks.

Murphy, a P-III, has worked with the LAPD on and off for eighteen of his twenty-five years in law enforcement. "Murph" to the other officers on the watch, he has a slight paunch, a balding head, and now a devilish grin on his face. He leans against the front fender of our black-and-white, stirring his coffee without looking at me.

"Uh, yeah, I guess so," I reply.

"Well, doughnuts are real cop food." He smiles.

"Oh" is all I reply.

It was in Murph's first year with LAPD that the Watts riots broke out in Los Angeles during the scorching summer of 1965. But four years later, a wild romance-turned-marriage made him leave the LAPD and California. He soon found himself living in his new wife's home state of Colorado, where he joined the Boulder Police Department.

Because Murph had "big-city" police experience from his time with the LAPD, and was an unknown face to local law enforcement, he was immediately assigned to a specialized state task force looking into police corruption. He spent the next two winters as a bartender in a high-class Boulder sports bar frequented by organized crime figures and, unfortunately, a number of high-ranking local police officials. By the time he was through testifying at grand jury indictments and federal trials, Murph was a very unpopular member of the Colorado law enforcement community. He was a real-life Rocky Mountain–style Serpico, putting some very bad coppers behind bars. But after numerous death threats from fellow officers (and from his new wife, due to Murph's attraction to some of the barmaids he had worked with while undercover), he hit the road, eventually landing back with the LAPD. He is now happily married to an LAPD sergeant who works North Hollywood Division.

I look at the doughnut that he's purchased, standard circular-type, half-dipped in chocolate. A very American doughnut. When we exited the shop a minute ago, he walked straight to our patrol car and promptly laid it on the hood, which is where it stays. This strikes me as a little odd. It's a very brisk afternoon, and the only reason I can imagine that he'd do this is to let the doughnut chill— but I always thought doughnuts were to be served at room temperature. But there it sits, still uneaten, I might add. And I've already finished mine. It's the first doughnut I have had since entering the Academy, and it's gone down like an expensive shot of smooth tequila.

"I'm not your regular training officer," he says in a serious tone. "That's Kyle Jackson.* He's off tonight, so you'll begin working with him tomorrow. He's the one who will be rating you and instructing you during your first two deployment periods. He'll let you know when you do well, and when you mess up. Then each deployment period after that, you'll switch training officers with the other P-Ones. It will give you a chance to see how different officers resolve different situations. Or screw them up." He takes a long sip from his coffee. "Tonight, you'll get to see how I screw things up," he says, that devilish grin back on his face. "We'll go out, handle some radio calls, try to catch a few bad guys. Maybe see if we can get a G-ride," he says, G-ride being LAPDese for a stolen car. "We're gonna have fun," he adds.

I finish my doughnut and throw the paper wrapping in the trash.

"Want another?" he asks.

"No, I'm fine," I reply.

He nods, then takes his doughnut and tosses it in the trash. Uneaten.

"Aren't you hungry?" I ask.

"Yeah," he says. "But I hate doughnuts. I just brought you here 'cause all boots think cops eat doughnuts."

He opens the driver's door, stops, and then that smile emerges on his face again. "You know what's the most important thing you have to learn about this job?" he asks.

"No," I reply.

"It's nothing like what you see on television."

According to Murph, each of the radio calls we've handled so far has been "routine," although none of them seemed routine to me. First, there was a robbery phoned in by an elderly Hispanic man. We find him on a street corner nearby, where he states that two black juveniles, both about fifteen, ran up behind him, hit him on the head with some type of club, then took his wallet and ran off. Problem is, he knows they are gang members, so all he wants us to do is to go find them and get his money back. He does not want them arrested. He does not want to press charges. He does not want to go to court. He just wants his money back and then to forget about it. When Murph tells him that if we find them we have to make an arrest, he declines to cooperate.

"I don't want no trouble with the gang-bangers," he says, then walks away.

After that, we go to check out an argument between a black husband and wife. He called her a "bitch," so she called us. Murph told him not to do that again. The husband agreed, saying next time, he would call her a *whore* instead, of course causing a further deepening in the rift between the couple. But when we tried to make plans for the husband to spend the night at his friend's house, the wife became angry. "I ain't lettin' that dog outta my sight!" she huffed, adding that a night away would just lead to his having another extramarital affair. She told us we could leave, that she was no longer angry with him. So we did.

Next, there was a rowdy group of Hispanics who were drinking beer and playing loud mariachi music. We ordered them to take it into their homes, because the neighbors were complaining, which they did, but only after one of them threw up in the gutter.

Then we came upon a new Toyota MR2 wrapped around a telephone pole. Luckily, neither of the occupants, a grandfather and his young grandson, was injured. Unless you count the grandfather's ego. When leaving his home not fifteen minutes earlier, the last thing he had said to his wife was "Damn it, Juanita, he's twelve years old. What harm will it do if I let him drive me to the store?"

All this in the first two hours!

Answering radio calls is like playing *Let's Make a Deal;* you never know what's behind door number one. Sometimes you get the brand-new, fully loaded luxury car. Other times you get the burro pulling the wooden cart, and no shovel to pick up the excrement. It is the ultimate in the unexpected.

The best part of the night is watching Murphy work. There is nothing like seeing a veteran LAPD street cop ply his trade. He is the ultimate deal maker. When he walks into a situation, he does it with his head up and his eyes open; and most important, his mouth closed. He grabs people with his eyes, then listens to what they have to say. On domestic violence calls, he lets both parties spit out a little venom for half a minute or so, then he grabs control of them using his voice, which is calm and overshadowed with authority. He tries to give realistic advice, at the same time letting both parties know that a continuance of the conflict will not be tolerated. He doesn't coddle people the way you see it done on television. That kind of psychology rarely works. Murphy gets the facts about a situation, then tells the parties what they need to do, based on what our laws dictate. We are not there for family counseling. We are there to dispense information (such as phone numbers for counseling centers), and to enforce the law by stopping unlawful behavior. Period.

Each call seems potentially dangerous. Human beings in need of police assistance are generally either angry, scared, sad, or just plain crazy. Rarely are they calm and fully rational. At each call, I make a conscious effort to scan our location for a possible ambush. I look hard at our victims for signs that they may be there only to set us up. Murph notices this.

"Good," he says. "It shows you're thinking."

During Academy training, students are shown numerous video-tapes of ambush scenarios encountered by officers. It's amazing to see some of the horrifying situations which officers have survived—and others in which they've died.

While I was in the Academy, two Rampart Division patrol officers issuing a traffic citation to a bicyclist were stopped on the edge of MacArthur Park near downtown. An eighty-year-old Hispanic man walking down the sidewalk approached them. Neither officer was paying much attention to an elderly citizen who just seemed to be out for a stroll. But suddenly, the man pulled a knife and stabbed one of the officers in the shoulder. Both officers then pulled their weapons and shot the still-attacking man dead. The man had not known the bicyclist, had no criminal record, and according to his family, had not had any previous negative contacts with the police. The dead man took to his grave whatever his reason was for his mysterious and unprovoked attack.

So we are taught that you have to be prepared for anything, a readiness that borders on paranoia. A mild case of paranoia actually is healthy for the on-duty police officer, because one moment you might be in the calmest of situations, and all hell might break loose the next. You must be wary of everyone, even eighty-year-old men. Alertness can keep you alive.

THE BLOCK PARTY

We are backing A-55 on a loud-party call. Night has fallen, and the myriad lights inside our vehicle make me think I'm inside an airplane cockpit. Light glows from the dashboard, from the computer, from our lightbar indicators. They are so bright that Murphy's face has a pale yellow hue even though we are driving down a completely darkened residential street.

I hit a button on the mobile digital terminal (MDT), the computer device in our patrol car from which we can read fine lines of text regarding a call. The alert is pretty vague. It just says, LOUD PARTY WITH THE NUMEROUS GANG MEMBERS CONGREGATING AT THE LOCATION, which is on Gramercy Place. That is all we're told.

As we turn the corner onto Gramercy, I am shocked. Before us is a sea of African-American gang members. They are on the sidewalks, in the streets, in the front yards, a true mass of humanity all centering around the residential intersection of Thirty-ninth and Gramercy. There must be more than two hundred gangsters here, the majority young men in their late teens or early twenties, although some are as young as thirteen years. Women in the crowd are sparse, but many are visible.

The participants move in and out of the available light on the street like shadows around a campfire. Many in the crowd wear blue. This is to show their allegiance to the Crip "Nation."

Murph immediately stops, then backs up, and keeps backing up until we are out of pistol range, which is about a half-block away. Murph gets on the radio and advises the RTO (radio transmission operator—the person who dispatchs our calls and answers our requests) of what we have. They dispatch additional units.

We watch the group, waiting for other units to arrive. There is no loud music playing, no evidence of the "loud party" spoken of by the citizen who placed the call. The group is just milling about. Like a gathering for the dead.

"A lot of them, huh?" says Murph. I can feel him grinning at me in the darkness. I just nod. I am shocked. I knew gangs were big. But not this big. It's the kind of crowd size I would associate with a concert in the park. They arrive in groups of three, four, and five, either walking down the sidewalk from the darkness of the side streets, or pulling up in vehicles favored by gang members, which are mainly brightly painted older-model, full-size cars from the 1970s. Another unit now pulls up beside us.

"This is the wake for that Rollin' Thirty they buried today," says the passenger officer in the other unit. I only see her silhouette; neither of our units is running with any lights on.

"Yeah, a little send-off for the homie," says Murph, using the slang word for "close friend." "Let's wait for another unit and then do a drive-through to let them know we're here."

Numerous calls are now coming in from other residents in the area frightened by this large group of gang members. And I don't blame them. Imagine being in your living room watching television, having just finished dinner, and looking outside your front window at a legion of gang members before you, in the darkness, on the sidewalk, on your front lawn. There are no fences dividing these front yards—just connecting lawns, and the horde walks freely from yard to yard. They walk between residents' cars in their driveways, around their mailboxes, just about anywhere they want.

Two of the new calls by residents advise of a MAN WITH A GUN. I bring "further comments" on these calls, the actual comments made by the caller to the police, up on the MDT. (The operator types them into a downtown information center as the citizen speaks.) Unfortunately, the physical descriptions given by the callers are too generic. Both describe a male black in dark clothing. But each caller describes a different car, which could mean we have two different suspects, or one suspect who has been spotted with his gun at two separate times. We take note of the cars, a green four-door Cadillac and a gold Buick Riviera. I scan the vehicles visible near the throng of gang members. None matches the description. But from where we are, we can barely see more then a few yards, the crowd too dense for further viewing.

Unit A-27 now arrives with Catania and Banderras. Catania gets out of his car and walks between us and the other unit.

"Can you believe this shit?" he says. "It looks like a county jail reunion party. Anybody tell CRASH about this?"

"They were supposed to be working the funeral," says the female officer from the other unit. "But that was a daytime thing. They may not have stayed for the wake."

"I requested them, but didn't get a response," says Murph.

"Then they're probably end of watch," says the female officer.

"We thought we'd do a drive-through," says Murph, serious. "Let them know we're here."

"Well, let's go through," says Catania. "If anything happens, we put out a help call. And under no circumstance does anyone get out of their vehicle."

Catania gets back in his car, and Murph motions to the others that we are going to lead. Slowly, we pull forward, a caravan of three police cars. Murph removes his handgun from its holster and places it in his lap.

"Hold your gun in your lap," says Murph. "If they're gonna shoot us, they'll walk up on us quick."

"OK," I reply, and remove my gun, holding it in my lap.

"Put it in your left hand, 'cause you're the passenger and are responsible for your side of the car," says Murph. "And keep it down low, out of sight. If you have to shoot, fire through the car door. They're paper thin, and your round will fly pretty straight." Murph then notices something. "When did you put your window up?" he asks.

It's a chilly night, and I've had it up ever since sunset. "A couple hours ago."

"Put it down," he replies. "This is the LAPD. We always drive with our windows down. Even if it's freezing out. You have got to be able to hear what's happening around you. Some citizen could be yelling at you for help and you wouldn't be able to hear it. You also wouldn't hear someone coming at you from the side. Then they'll bust out that glass, and you'll get glass in your eye, and you'll be blinded. You won't be able to fire your weapon effectively. So keep that window down. It's a tactical concern. We can always turn up the heater if it gets cold."

"OK," I reply and roll it down.

As we reach the crowd, they grudgingly make way for us. Off to one side is a cluster of hard-core, older gang members, in their thirties and forties, shoulders prison buffed. They give us stern eyes, arms crossed in a rigid stance. I exchange looks with a few of them, but I don't try to stare anyone down. It's pointless and immature. I'm more concerned with waistbands and hands anyway, just in case one of them is crazy enough to show a gun in front of us.

Even though we are vastly outnumbered, the Crips give us a wide berth. At this time (before Rodney King), six LAPD officers commanded a fair amount of respect, even from two hundred Crips. Not that we could handle them as we are. We have no illusion that we are not greatly outnumbered. But we can request help, and within a short period of time have a force on scene that could resolve any situation in favor of the police. And there would be a response afterward—though not what you might think. If we were attacked, the stations' jails would be full of Crips for months to come—their arrests being for the most minor, but legal, offenses imaginable, such as driving without a driver's license. Impound lots would also be full of improperly registered Crip cars, and our ticket books full of valid Crip citations.

So we are given a wide berth out of forced respect.

Not respect for us, the badge, or the citizens we represent. But respect for what would happen if they showed disrespect.

A large, jovial female in her thirties comes up on my side. She wears a blue sweatshirt with the name of the murdered Crip printed in script on the front. The sweatshirt and its script signify her dedication to her gang. It's like wearing a bull's-eye on her chest, especially should she have to go through a Blood neighborhood to get home.

"Hello, Officer," she says. "There ain't no trouble here tonight. We're just sending off the brother."

"We understand that, ma'am," replies Murph. "We're just here makin' sure it stays peaceful. You know what's up. I'm sure the Bloods know about this."

"Ain't no thing," she says. "Fuck the Bloods. We're too deep. Ain't no Blood gonna try some shit here and now. But let me say, ain't no one here wants any trouble."

"OK," says Murph. "Just tell whoever needs to be told you gotta break it up inside of twenty minutes. It's getting too late, and people are clogging the streets."

"I hear that, Officer," she says. "We'll take care of it."

Gang members flash in and out of our running lights. Some of the street lights are out, possibly shot out prior to our arrival, and macabre figures move in and out of the shadows. I feel tense beyond belief. All I can see, seated down in the police car, are gang members wearing blue. They are so thick that I cannot see the houses behind them. We are in the crowd for what seems an eternity, although it's only the time it takes to drive slowly the distance of a city block. But we do not see any problems. No drinking in public. No fighting or loud partying. No gangsters with guns. I do not even see a green Cadillac or a gold Riviera. Soon, the crowd thins, and I can see landscape again. Murph speeds up and pulls over a block away.

"This is the quietest one of these that I've ever seen," says Murph.

"You've seen *this* before?" I ask him, incredulous. I cannot fathom seeing this many gang members together being a common occurrence.

"Yeah," says Murph. "They have funerals like this all the time. Big, lavish funerals followed by gigantic block parties." I crane my neck to look back into the shadows of the mob. The other two black-and-whites have safely followed us out. "Some of the richest businesses in the South End are the funeral homes. They make the big bucks, especially since you ain't a real homie until you're seen laying out some cash for your fallen comrades. I've seen sixteen-year-old gangsters laid to rest in sixteen-thousand-dollar bronze coffins."

The other two units pull parallel to us.

"They're going to do a payback," says the female officer. "I can feel it in the air."

"Yeah, and you know it's going to be tonight," says Catania. "I just hope the radio's quiet so we can jam a few of these fools."

"I don't think we'll have time to do any jamming," says the female. "Last night was real busy. We were running from one end of the division to the next. And tonight we're down a car."

"Then my boot's gonna get some experience in homicide scenes," replies Murph, glancing at me.

She nods. She swivels her head back, one last look at the gang. Confident that nothing is happening with them right now, she turns back to us.

"We're outta here," she says.

"So are we," says Catania.

Soon all I see are two pairs of taillights disappearing down the street. Having made our presence known, Murph follows them, and we move on to our next call.

CODE SEVEN

Finally, we get to eat dinner. The first time we asked for Code Seven (a break request), they denied us, sending us to another family dispute, which we handled. They also denied us this time, wanting us to handle yet another domestic problem, but A-63 bought the call from us so we could eat, bless their hearts. Because I was fading fast from hunger. The stress from the adrenaline rush each call generates sucks the energy out of my body. The average off-duty LAPD officer has an at-rest heart rate of about sixty-eight beats per minute. But when an LAPD officer is on duty, in the car, his *average* heart rate is about ninety beats per minute.[2] That means your body is sucking up a lot of fuel. Because I am a boot on his first night, my heart rate is probably at some number normally associated with either a severe heart attack or a severe orgasm. I am not sure which.

So Murph and I stop at a Chinese restaurant on Western Boulevard. Inside we find the two officers we'd spoken with at the gang party, whom I now recognize to be working 3-A-55. The female is a tall, slender P-II named Teri Bennyworth, whose husband works South Bureau CRASH. Her partner is a boot from three classes ahead of me named Brian Johnson. Murph and I grab a seat with them, a corner table in the back, an "easy-to-defend" position should "some asshole want to try you," points out Murph.

---

[2] In one study done by a local television crew, sensors were taped over the hearts of officers working Rampart Division, by far the most dangerous division to work in the LAPD (and the country). In the officers tested, the average heart rate was found to be over *one hundred* beats per minute.

Murph and the two officers talk about the night's events. I don't add to the conversation, still being keyed-up over my first watch. I simply listen.

A smiling waiter briskly glides up to our table, welcoming us with a short bow. The other three have eaten here before; they order using numbers without even looking at the menu.

"I'll have a six," says Murph.

"A two," says Bennyworth.

"A two also," says Johnson.

Their quick responses leave me glancing over the menu quickly, ordering the first thing I see, which is kung pao chicken. In moments, the waiter appears with our dinners, and I discover that I should have just thrown out a number like the others had, because their numbered dinners bring a lot more food than the named meals, and I am starving. I wolf down half my meal before even taking a breath.

"You really like Chinese food," says Bennyworth.

"I think I'm just hungry," I reply.

"He had a doughnut at beginning of watch," adds Murph.

"Well, I think you're going to have to get him another doughnut after this, because that plate doesn't have enough food for him," says Bennyworth. "You should be partners with Catania. He pigs down his food, too. We could get a trough for you two and put it in the backseat of your patrol car."

My normal eating habits are generally more civilized, but I am incredibly hungry from all of the nervous energy I've burned. I down water by the glassful. The thick, bulletproof Kevlar vest I wear under my shirt holds in the heat, causing me to perspire constantly. My T-shirt is damp and it clings to my skin like an added layer.

Murph has his rover on the table. We've been hearing normal chatter most of the night. Units calmly converse with the RTO, or each other, in normal radio traffic. Then—

"Three-Z-forty-six," puffs an officer. *"My partner is in foot pursuit, man with a shotgun, eastbound through the houses, Gramercy Place and Thirty-ninth Street. We need help!"*

The two T.O.'s have already thrown their money on the table and are halfway to the door. Johnson and I are still chewing.

"Come on, Dunn, now!" says Murphy. I fumble to get to my wallet. I still have to pay for the food, right? The dinner is only five dollars, but all I have is a ten. I hold it out to the waiter. He refuses it.

"You pay later," he says, smiling, pushing me out the door with a wave of his hand. I run outside, fumbling to put my wallet back in my pants. As I reach for the car door I hear, *"Z-forty-six, suspect is a male black, six feet, two hundred pounds, twenty years, white T-shirt. He's got a sawed-off pump. My partner is not accounted for!"*

"Not accounted for" is bad. It means the broadcasting officer has lost sight of his partner.

As I sit in the car, Murph burns away from the curb. The lightbar is activated, and we storm into traffic. I look back and see a herd of cars behind us calmly braking.

"I want you to clear these intersections for me," commands Murph. We get to the intersection at Exposition Boulevard. I see no cars coming.

"Clear," I say.

Murph guns it. As we cross Exposition, a Volkswagen in front of us is oblivious to our presence. And we are hard to miss—siren wailing, lights spinning. But this driver is in his own world. He tries to pull the Volkswagen into our lane, but quits halfway, straddling the line. Murph has to hit the brakes, waiting for traffic coming the other way to clear.

"Dummy!" he snaps to no one in particular.

Finally, there is a break in traffic. We round the Volkswagen. As we pass, I see a troll-like figure wearing glasses seated on the driver's side, hunched forward, peering for images ahead of him. He drives as though he were literally in a fog. He never even acknowledges our presence.

"I've found my partner, but I've lost sight of the suspect. I need a perimeter,[3] *Thirty-ninth Street, Thirty-ninth Place, St. Andrews, and Gramercy,"* says the officer, giving out four points of enclosure.

---

[3] A perimeter is where police close off an area, usually only one or two city blocks, then systematically search it for a suspect.

"Dunn, tell them we're taking Thirty-ninth Street and St. Andrews," says Murph. I quickly radio this information.

When we hit Thirty-ninth Street, we take our position, other black-and-whites whizzing past us, taking other points in the area. The perimeter is set up quickly, and the initial officers are certain the suspect is still somewhere within its confines. In both directions, across Thirty-ninth Street and down St. Andrews Place, I can see patrol cars with their ambers flashing. Units are like this completely around the block, every unit in sight of two others, forcing the suspect to run between two cars if he wishes to make a break for it.

An air unit now arrives and begins hovering overhead with deep, rhythmic thumps. I find out via rover that a canine unit is also en route. Although I've been studying maps of the division, I'm still not sure where I am in relation to the station. I pull out my map, examine it, and realize we are just around the corner from the gang funeral.

A chilly breeze is blowing in from the Pacific Ocean; the temperature is in the fifties. I still have not bought a black field jacket, and even though I have a bulletproof vest on under my long sleeves, I feel cold. It's considered poor tactics to sit in your black-and-white on a perimeter, especially with an armed suspect nearby. So I'm standing behind the passenger door of my patrol car as I was taught in the Academy.

Murph is standing next to the front of the car, the engine purring gently. I don't know why he is standing there. It would be safer if he had a door to protect him, but he hasn't moved from that spot.

"Boot, come here," he says.

I do, standing next to him.

"Do you know why I'm standing next to a wheel well instead of a door?" he asks.

I stand there for a moment. There must be some tactical reason. I think, *Hmmm. We're next to the engine. If there is any shooting, the engine block is the only part of the car thick enough to stop a high-velocity rifle round. So that must be why.*

Then . . . I feel it. Warmth! Blessed warmth—rising up from the engine through the wheel well like a trash-can fire in a railroad yard. It feels good.

"I know they teach that door shit in the Academy," he says.

"And it's fine on a hot summer night. But I don't want to literally freeze up. Your limbs can go numb from the cold, and screw up your reflexes. Hurt your shooting. Door won't be of much help if you can't shoot back. So we'll take the wheel well."

A canine unit now arrives, and soon I see a dog coming around the corner at the end of the block. Behind him is his handler, an officer the size of a pro lineman, wearing blue police overalls. He holds his 9mm loosely at his side. Three patrol officers, one with a shotgun, the other two holding handguns, follow him closely. The dog, a German shepherd, methodically searches the area, its nose sweeping back and forth like a demolition expert looking for land mines. Murph knows the handler and nods to him. The handler flashes back a smile as he passes by.

When they reach a yellow house not far away, the dog gets excited. The search team disappears down the driveway. Suddenly, there is yelling, and I begin to run that way.

"Dunn, come back here!" Murph yells, and I stop. "They'll call us if they need us."

I walk back to the car and wait.

"Code Four, suspect in custody," I hear one of the search team broadcast over the radio, signaling the end of the ordeal. Soon the dog comes back up the driveway, followed by his handler. The three uniformed officers are right behind them, escorting a shirtless male black who is handcuffed. The suspect is upset. He is not bitten or injured, but he's vocal about being caught.

"Muthafuckin' dogs" are the only words I can make out as he passes by.

The handler stops and talks to Murph.

"Where's your hair?" asks the handler, as if he were greeting an old friend on the street. Murph runs his hand over his bare scalp.

"It grows inside now," he replies. "Stimulates the brain."

"Is that what happens?" says the handler. "If only you had a brain to stimulate."

"At least the calluses on my hands aren't from walking on all fours," replies Murph. As they shake hands, Murph sniffs the air. "You been eatin' your partner's food again?"

They exchange a few more childish pleasantries, then get back to business.

"The suspect didn't have the shotgun on him," says the handler. "We found him between the garage and the fence of that yellow house. You guys may want to search the backyard there."

Murph and I do, but we don't find the shotgun. Which is bad. If we don't find the weapon, the bad guy can always say it was just a toy. Or a stick. Or some other lie. And worse, what is truly every parent's nightmare, some six-year-old may find it and decide to play "stick 'em up" with a playmate. Which has happened in the South End and lots of other places. So finding the weapon is a real concern.

We do find his white T-shirt, which he has stuffed into a bush. This will help to ID the bad guy. But we need the gun. There is an open crawl space under the yellow house, and I am about to get dirty entering it, when a CRASH officer broadcasts that he has found the shotgun in some bushes two houses away. The suspect had dumped it right after the officer broke off his foot pursuit. It's loaded with live twelve-gauge double-ought buck shells.

We drive around the corner to give Z-46 the white T-shirt. Unit Z-46 is part of a specialized Southwest unit made up of patrol officers called the Crime Task Force (CTF). They drive unmarked Chevys with no outside police paraphernalia, their assignment being to patrol the area incognito. Contrary to popular belief, plain cars are not easily picked out by gang members. So they make numerous observational arrests. One of the Z-car officers is Kevin Riley. He must be doing exceptionally well while on probation to be put into CTF. He sees me and walks over to my window.

"Man, Dunn," he begins in his drawl. "We stop to jam this one Crip fool, and this other homeboy comes running up out of nowhere to dump his ass with a shotgun! Didn't even see us. All I hear is *click-clack*! I turn, see homeboy with the gauge not twenty feet from me. Then he sees me and *bam*! He turns and runs. I coulda shot his ass!"

"Why didn't you?" I ask.

"It happened so fast, man," he says. "So damn fast. By the time I got my finger up on the trigger, all I saw was his backside."

I see Z-46's plain car pointing at an angle, high beams on, into a brick wall. The "fool" they were going to stop and talk to must have been on the sidewalk. The homeboy with the gauge stopped less then twenty feet from the plain-car's passenger door. Although the officers prevented an almost sure homicide by their presence, they came dangerously close to becoming victims themselves.

As we drive back to the station, Murph goes over the situation for me. "Everybody here had tunnel vision," he says. "The Crip walking down the street must have just been thinking of going home. The officers must have just been thinking of the Crip they were gonna jam. And the Blood must have been thinking about killing the Crip walking on the sidewalk. Imagine what would have happened if that Blood had stood his ground with that shotgun already in his hands."

Murph lets it set in for a beat.

"It's tunnel vision that'll kill you," he says.

PCP

I hear him the moment I enter the rear doors of the station. He sounds like a wounded animal, emitting a long, low howl that comes from deep within. He's in the holding tank, and through thick, bulletproof glass I can see he's been chained to the bench inside. He is a small Hispanic man with an Elvis haircut and a pained expression on his face. He wears only a pair of black, skin-tight disco pants, no shirt, no shoes. He sweats profusely. He looks back through the glass with squinted eyes, eyes that do not seem to focus or comprehend. A big P-III named Jeff Wilson is talking with Sergeant Pam Roberts, a trim female with a tight, short hairstyle.

"He's gotta be on PCP, Jeff," says Sergeant Roberts. "He displays all of the symptoms. I'll call over to South Traffic Division, see if they have a DRE working tonight who can come by and look at him."

A *DRE* is LAPDese for Drug Recognition Expert, an officer who's been trained to pinpoint the type of drug a person under the influence has used by recognizing symptoms displayed. The training is lengthy and rigorous, as well as expensive. Mainly because of the latter factor, DREs are few in number on the LAPD. Generally, traffic divisions have the most assigned there because of the amount of driving-under-the-influence arrests they make.

"Okey-dokey," replies Wilson. "He's gotta be on something more than tequila to be acting the fool he is."

As Sergeant Roberts walks into the watch commander's office, Murphy looks into the tank.

"What'd you get him for?" asks Murphy.

"Four fifteen," replies Wilson, referring to the California Penal Code section for disturbing the peace. "We were driving past Leonardo's, you know, that Mexican disco on Vermont?" He pronounces it *Mescan,* leaving out the middle syllable. "This fool runs out into traffic in front of my police car, then he just stops. Starts doin' some *la cucaracha* dance, like we wasn't even there. Made me brake real sharply, too. So I get out of my car, and I say, 'Hey, little Mescan fella, come here.' Big mistake." Wilson rolls a smile over his lips. He likes this story. "He turns, looks at me, lets out this banshee scream, like *aaarrrggghhh.*" He makes a sound like the Cookie Monster from *Sesame Street.* "Then he comes flying at me, a Mescan torpedo, all arms and legs, and he tries to tackle me. Strong little sonuvabitch. Was all my partner and I could do to cuff his ass."

Wilson looks into the tank. I see the suspect nod at him and smile, a gold front tooth peering out from between his lips.

"He is one crazy little man," adds Wilson.

I look at Wilson. A former Cal State Long Beach football player, he must weigh a solid two hundred forty pounds. I then look at his probationer, a tall male black who's about a hundred eighty pounds. Then I gauge the man in the tank. He must weigh a hundred forty, dripping wet. And he took on these two policemen. But that's PCP.

Sergeant Roberts calls to Wilson, asking him a question pertaining to the arrest. Everyone turns their attention away from the tank, except me. I watch the little man through the heavy glass. He's stopped screaming, sits motionless on the single stainless-steel bench, his hands restrained behind his back. He has a gold earring in his left ear, a cross hanging below his lobe. He wears another cross suspended from a thin gold chain around his neck. While crosses are traditionally a sign of religious reverence, in Los Angeles, they seem to be more of a fashion statement.

My focus moves from his jewelry to his eyes. He is staring at me, his lids pulled far back, his gaze intense and expressionless. He suddenly smiles and inhales so deeply, it's as if he's going to hold his breath forever. Then he does something I cannot believe. *BAM!* He slams his head against the concrete wall. Not just a tap, but as hard as he can. His eyes roll back as he shakes his head. I am shocked, not sure of what I have just seen. *BAM!* He does it again. Now I see blood trickle down the side of his face. He shakes his head again, focuses on me. He wants to make sure that I'm watching him. He smiles when he sees that I am.

I turn to the officers standing near me, checking to see if I'm the only one watching this. I am. I look back into the cell. *Bam!* More blood.

"Murph!" It belts out of me like an untethered balloon losing its air.

Murph turns, looks at me, then follows my eyes toward the tank. He doesn't catch what I'm looking at. Then the guy is again shaking his head, blood splattering on the glass.

"Jeff," says Murph slowly, "your guy's having a problem."

Murph's voice is calm, but serious enough to make everyone in the watch commander's office take notice. Then, as if on cue, *bam*, the suspect does it again.

"Hog-tie him, now!" commands Sergeant Roberts, referring to a restraint procedure whereby a strap is tied around the legs and then attached to the handcuffs, effectively immobilizing a suspect. She turns to me. "Get an RA," she says, ordering me to radio for an ambulance.

The door to the tank is opened, and officers are immediately on the suspect. He's about to hit his head on the concrete again, but is pulled away from the wall just as he tries to ram it. Taken to the ground, he is recuffed with a cord run around his legs to secure his feet to his hands. Some of the officers get blood on them. Murph is next to me, watching me.

"Did you get the RA?" asks Roberts. She has been calmly overseeing the entire incident, and already knows the answer. I haven't. I am too amazed by the little Hispanic man. I remove my rover.

"Three-Adam-ninety-nine," I say. "I need an RA at Southwest Station, in the holding cell."

The operator comes back.

"Three-Adam-ninety-nine, what do you have?"

"I have a male Hispanic with a head wound," I reply.

"What is his age, and is he conscious and breathing?"

"Early twenties, and he is conscious and breathing."

I wait for the operator to ask more questions, but none come. I look at Murph.

"That's all she needs to know," he says, then looks in the tank, and I follow his eyes. The suspect is hidden under Wilson, who sits on him, holding him with sheer body weight so that he can't bang his head on the concrete floor, which he's trying to do, bucking the big P-III like an angry bull.

I turn to find Murph. The excitement over, he's already walking down the hallway.

"Let's go clear out the car," he says. "Time to go home."

THE TRAINING OFFICER

Our second destination out of roll call is Mikoshi, a Japanese restaurant on Figueroa Street. My training officer, Kyle Jackson, is a fitness guru, and insists on eating as healthfully as possible. Mikoshi makes a vegetable and rice dish that Jackson advises me is high in protein and low in fat. This pilgrimage is made only after we visit a Korean-owned grocery store on Vernon Avenue called the Blue Star Market, where Jackson purchases two apples and a half pound of trail mix.

"You gotta take care of your body, man," he says, driving up Figueroa Street. "More police officers die from heart disease on this job than from gunshot wounds."

As we pass by a McDonald's, he points to it.

"You want anything?" he asks, his eyes looking me over with contempt. Just out of the Academy, I am in the best shape of my life. The Academy has a strict fitness regimen, and recruits are worked mercilessly by LAPD physical training instructors. An unending number of hills must be run; an excruciating number of push-ups and sit-ups must be grunted. Classes giving dietary recommendations are taught by fear-inducing instructors who reveal facts about cheeseburgers that make you want to hold up a cross every time you see a side of beef. So I feel lean and I feel hard. One hundred and eighty-five pounds of concentrated muscle. But as I sit here in the car next to Jackson, I feel like the Pillsbury Doughboy. He is in incredible shape. At six feet one, he is only an inch taller than I am, but he outweighs me by almost forty-five pounds. And he is solid, completely. A very dark black man in his forties with a shaved head, he looks as if he were chiseled out of a single piece of obsidian by an ancient Greek sculptor.

I reply that I do not need anything from McDonald's.

"You sure, man?" he asks. "I can tell by your eyes you have cholesterol on your mind." He says it hard, pushing sharply on the K sound in *cho-lesterol*.

"No, really," I reply. "Rice will be fine."

He looks at me contemptuously, which makes me a little nervous. Training officers are supposed to stress out their boots in any way they can, and he is trying this by staring me down. He is succeeding somewhat, as he is one physically imposing human being.

"I'm just the probationer, man," I say. I try to sound humble. "I'll just follow you wherever you go."

He lightens up a little.

"That's right," he replies. "You're just the probationer, and I'm the training officer. You follow me wherever I go."

He smiles, turning back to driving.

"And I'm going to get some rice."

"I also went to college," says Jackson.

Jackson is talking to me between spoonfuls of rice as we stand next to our patrol car in Mikoshi's parking lot. There are palm trees at the lot's entrance, and the afternoon sun allows them to cast long, barlike shadows.

"Really," I say. "Where?"

"Sacramento City College," he replies. "Went there two years to play football. I was going to transfer to Utah State on a scholarship, but I hurt my knee midway through my second year."

"What position did you play?" I ask. I look at his size and take a guess. "Defensive line?"

"Nah, man," he says. "Quarterback. The thinking man's position." He sounds a little offended that I would not guess him for playing at the one position that requires some brains. "I'm pretty good at reading defenses," he says. "I like the strategy of the game. Defensive line is just slamming heads. Which I don't mind. But I want to have to think a little, too. I like being the one making the decisions, the one who controls the play going down the field."

I could picture him doing it. Jackson carries himself with loads of confidence. He's a man who can make a decision, and then stick with it.

"You married?" I ask. We're both still trying to figure each other out, and I want to keep the conversation going.

"Yeah," he replies. "Two kids. And two girlfriends."

"Two girlfriends?" I ask. "You have a wife and two girlfriends?" Let me rephrase my previous thought: Jackson is the kind of man who can make a decision and *kind* of stick to it.

"Uh-huh," he replies. "I got my wife to take care of my house, and my girlfriends to take care of me."

Interesting arrangement.

"How about you?" he asks. "You got a girl?"

"Yeah," I reply. "I've been with her for a long while. But she's having a hard time with my being a police officer. I have a feeling I may be back out there sniffing around again soon."

He laughs at this.

"Well, you be careful where you sniff," he says. "Especially in South Central. We got a thing down here called 'War Brides.' They're ghetto girls who would love to get pregnant by you just so they can have a piece of your pension. Lotta cops down here paying nine hundred dollars a month for eighteen years because they 'sniffed around' the wrong one."

"What about you and your two girlfriends?" I ask. "Aren't you taking a chance at losing a piece of *your* pension?"

"I could be," he says. "Both of my girlfriends want me to leave my wife, and I know they've been trying to have my baby. But they don't know I've been fixed."

"You had a vasectomy?" I ask.

"Uh-huh," he replies. "No more babies for me. All I am now is a starter pistol."

A starter pistol who I get the feeling fires a lot of blanks. Jackson finishes his rice. He wipes his hands on a napkin. This seems to be a signal.

"Time to talk some police work," says Jackson. He takes a quick sip of Diet Pepsi. "During these first two weeks, you'll have a free ride," he says. "You will not be rated, so if you screw up, it won't be on paper. Unless you get me killed. Then I will write a shitload of paper on you." He smiles and takes another sip of his soda.

"I will handle all of the calls and I will drive. You only have to handle the log and try to learn the MDT," he continues. "Did you have MDT training in the Academy?"

"Yes," I reply.

"Can you use it quickly?" he asks.

"I wrote for my high-school newspaper for three years," I reply. "We had to type all of our own stories. So I'm a fairly good typist."

"So I expect you to be fast with the machine," he says.

Maybe I should have kept my mouth shut. Almost on cue, the machine beeps, signifying we have just received a call. I enter the car and hit the receive button. The screen fills with information.

"What does it say?" Jackson asks.

I look at the screen. It reads:

```
0003226      DIS   4100 LEIMERT      620F
```

The first seven numbers are the incident number of this call, this being the 3,226th call for service that the LAPD has received this day—and it's only four o'clock in the afternoon. On average, the LAPD will handle over 5,500 service requests each day. When you take into account that on a good day, the department can put 350 patrol black-and-whites out on the streets of LA, you realize that each pair of officers is handling about 15 incidents each day!

If I need more information, such as a suspect description, I can run the incident number by itself and find out what the caller told our dispatcher about the problem. The *DIS* means the call has been dispatched to me, and when I hit another button, it will read *ENR*, which means I am en route to the call. After that comes the address, which in this case is on Leimert Boulevard.

Last is *620F*, indicating the type of call made. The numbers are usually a penal-code section, with the letter being a specific type of that crime. Trying to remember what type of call a *620F* is, I know the *620* means dispute, but the *F* has me lost. It could be a business dispute, a family dispute, or a neighbor dispute. I take a guess.

"We have a family dispute on Leimert," I say.

"Good," he replies. "Show us en route."

I pat myself on the back for guessing right, then press a different button on the monitor to signal that we are en route to the call.

Family disputes are the most common call for a police officer in Los Angeles. Depending on the night of the week, they can account for as much as 10 percent of the radio-call load. Sundays are the worst. After a weekend of drinking beer and watching glitzy television shows, both husband and wife suddenly realize that their lifestyles are not those of the rich and shameless. Each decides that the other is to blame for their marital shortcomings, and they proceed to take it out on each other, either verbally or physically. When neighbors hear the ensuing battle, the police are called. For some families, it's a weekly occurrence.

Under California law, if either the husband or wife has struck the other, causing visible injuries, the police must take the inflicter to jail for felony battery. Because there is usually some level of intoxication involved, the courage to fight arrest is easily mustered. Many times the victim will try to come to his or her "loved" one's aid, even after just having been battered by this person. So domestic violence calls can get very messy, resulting in both husband *and* wife being carted off to jail.

"Remember, even though the comments say this is a 'dispute,' be careful," says Jackson. "Family disputes have a way of turning to shit."

As we arrive at the location, an older Spanish-style duplex, Jackson says, "I'll take the man, get *his* story. You take the woman, get *her* story. If the woman has visible marks, we're gonna handcuff the man immediately. Don't give the man a chance to size us up or get cocky enough to fight us. We'll just get him under control, and sit him on the couch."

Jackson is saying *man* and *him* when referring to the aggressor, which is understandable. In the Academy, we were advised that 95 percent of those arrested for spousal battery are male; women do batter men at times, but it is rare.

"Always keep me in sight," he adds. "And don't let the woman get near anything she can throw at the man. When we show up, some women feel safe enough to seek a little revenge. If you see any weapons laying around, knives, hammers, screwdrivers, put them out of reach. You can even put them under a couch if you want. And if you see a gun layin' around, man, you let me know."

Standing on the porch, we can hear low voices talking inside. They don't sound too hostile. Jackson knocks, and soon a short, thin, black man in his early twenties answers. He wears horn-rimmed glasses, a white T-shirt, and very tight blue jeans. He lets out a sigh when he sees us.

"Thank goodness you're here!" he says, as he opens the door wide. He points into the living room where another black man, also in his twenties, sits on the couch. He wears a muscle shirt that says BIG BOY on it.

"There he is, he's the one!" he says, pointing to the guy on the couch, who just shakes his head. He doesn't speak.

"What's going on here?" asks Jackson as I am wondering the same thing myself.

"My name is Wayne Price,"* he says. "He's a whore, and I want him out, now!"

Like they tell us in the Academy, there is no way that you can plan for everything that will happen on a radio call. The one plan we made, me taking the female disputant, is out the window, because both of our two disputants are male, gay males. Not that their sexuality is an issue here. They're citizens and they need a hand with a problem. It's just that I had been planning to talk to a woman, and now I don't know which guy to talk to. I look to Jackson for some indication, but he's concentrated on sizing up our participants.

"*I* pay the rent here," says Wayne. "My name is on the lease. I want him gone, like, yesterday."

"Dunn," says Jackson. I look over at him, and he nods toward the guy on the couch, signaling me to go get his side of the story. I comply. I walk past Price into the apartment.

"What's your name, sir?" I ask him. He moves as if to rise, but I hold out a palm. "That's OK, man, rest your feet." I would rather he remain sitting, giving me a physical advantage.

"Bradley Johnson,"* he replies.

"So, Mr. Johnson," I ask, "what's going on here?"

"I met another man," he replies. "And I'm moving in with him.

It's just that I can't move in until tomorrow. Wayne's very upset. We've been together for three years."

I must admit that I'm uneasy talking with this citizen, though I honestly cannot pinpoint why. Some of it has to do with his being gay, but I cannot pinpoint why that unnerves me. Maybe it's that I haven't really known any homosexuals, and their mannerisms and lifestyle are foreign to me. But I will just have to push my discomfort out of my head. My days of stereotyping and bias, at least as far as these eight hours are concerned, are behind me.

"How long have you lived here?" I ask.

"Two years," he says. "Wayne's name is on the lease, but I do pay one third of the rent. I have the canceled checks if you would like to see them."

"Maybe in a minute," I reply. "Has he hit you?"

"Wayne?" he smirks. "Nah, man. Wayne is not a hitter. He gets real excited, but he's actually a very peaceful person."

"You guys gonna be able to make it until tomorrow?" I ask.

"Yes," he replies.

"Without killing each other?" I add.

"Yes," says Bradley. "We've never been violent with each other. I wouldn't hurt Wayne. And I still care for him. I just can't stay here anymore."

Then I get stuck. I know there are other questions I need to ask, but I cannot think of any. His being homosexual has nothing to do with this lack of brainpower. I'm just a stumped boot who is not used to doing field interviews with real citizens. It's one thing to do interviews in the classroom, and a completely other thing to do them in the field.

What is worse is Jackson is still talking with Wayne. Their tone is low, so I cannot quite hear, but it seems like Jackson is getting to the heart of the problem. Bradley sits uneasily. I know he feels cheated by not having as lengthy an interview as Jackson is having with Wayne. But as I said, I'm a stumped boot. Finally, Jackson and Wayne finish. Jackson takes me aside.

"What have we got?" he asks. *Great. He's gonna test me,* I say to myself.

"Basically, a landlord-tenant dispute," I reply. "Price wants

Johnson out, because Price's name is on the lease. But Johnson has established residency, so he really can stay until he's evicted."

By law, in the state of California, paying just one dollar of rent means you have established residency, even if your name is not on a lease. That house or apartment is now yours until you have been evicted.

"Do we have any crime?" he asks.

"No," I say. "Not from Mr. Johnson's side."

"Price alleges that Johnson pushed him while arguing," says Jackson.

"Well, then we have a misdemeanor battery," I say. "Is Price willing to make a citizen's arrest?"

"Yes," says Jackson, rolling his eyes. "But, you'll see this on family disputes, a petty allegation of a battery, especially if one spouse wants to punish the other by putting them in jail. Usually, it's the woman. She'll say, 'He pushed me,' and then demand to sign a citizen's arrest. Even if we don't see an injury, it's off to jail for the night. The complaining spouse then refuses prosecution, and the case is dropped. It's a waste of our time and the taxpayers' money. So we'll try and mediate a little more. Will Johnson go get a motel room?"

"I didn't ask," I reply. That's one of the questions I forgot: Always ask the participants if one of them will get out of Dodge for a while. Jackson looks at Bradley.

"Hey, man, you got a place to go tonight?" asks Jackson.

"Yes," he replies. "I have a friend I can call."

"A friend?" says Wayne. "More like a piece of ass, you whore."

"Knock it off," says Jackson firmly. "Words like that don't do any good." Wayne calms down.

"Just let me make a phone call," says Bradley to Jackson. "I should be able to get someone to come by and pick me up."

"Have them meet you down at the corner," says Jackson. Bradley nods, then uses the phone on the living room table. After he hangs up, we stand by while he gets his belongings. They fit into two suitcases. As we head out the front door Bradley pauses on the steps.

"I love you, Wayne," he yells.

"I love you, too, Bradley," calls Wayne from inside. Which sounds very odd to me. Like I said, I have not been around too many homosexuals in my life, and I find I have to repress a grin of embarrassment. I throw a glance at Jackson, who's watching me with an admonishing look. I immediately lose my need to smile. Then Wayne is running out the door, pausing to throw a big hug around Bradley.

"Good-bye," says Wayne.

"Good-bye," replies Bradley.

Then they kiss, which is really a unique sight to me. The muscles in my face are fighting to turn upward again, so I run my left hand up to cover, my thumb and forefinger pressing the corners of my mouth into a frown. I don't even look at Jackson, but I can feel his cold, hard eyes on me. Soon Bradley is down at the corner and Jackson and I are back in the car. He does *not* seem too pleased.

"You are going to have to control your emotions better," he says sternly. "We run into many situations out here that we may not understand because of our cultural rearing. But you have to treat all situations with respect. When that badge is on your chest, you do not have an opinion. The only opinions you will express are those put forth in the California Penal Code, or the Department Manual. Otherwise, you will treat people unfairly as you will show bias. And that is not what this job is about. Understand?"

"Yes, sir," I reply.

"Good," he says. He looks over at the MDT and sees a red light on, indicating another call. "What is our next call?"

"Another family dispute," I say after hitting a button.

"Show us en route," he says.

JAMMING

Later, Jackson and I are on a traffic stop, this one on Figueroa Street, just off the eastern edge of the Los Angeles Memorial Coliseum complex. It's late at night, but the streets are full of traffic. The Reverend Louis Farrakhan has just finished speaking at the Sports Arena a block away, and the crowd is slowly moving from the complex to the freeway.

The Crips and the Bloods both identify strongly with Minister

Farrakhan. Many of the Muslims at the temple in South Central Los Angeles are current or former street-gang members, so Jackson and I are cruising the area to spot rival gang members looking for trouble.

At this time, before the Rodney King uproar, the LAPD was a "proactive" department. This meant police would go out and look for situations that could lead to crime. Our mission was to find criminals on the prowl: men walking down alleys late at night wearing all dark clothing; gang members driving four deep slowly along streets of gang-heavy areas; people standing on the same street corner for three hours for no particular reason; Crips wearing blue clothing in Blood areas; Bloods showing red in Crip areas. We would stop and talk to them all. In LAPDese, these stop-and-talks were called jamming.

The Los Angeles Police has never been a department where officers would get into patrol cars, roll up their windows, turn on the air conditioners, and then sit and wait for radio calls. We jammed. We would get in our black-and-white and go out looking for trouble. We would scour high-crime areas for suspicious persons and then stop them. Jamming was an effective tool to deter crime.

Before one screams *lawsuit,* the mechanics of a jam are within the law. First, you stop and *ask* suspects if they want to talk. In legal terminology, this is called a consensual encounter. If they don't want to talk, and there is no legal reason to detain them, they're free to go. Most bad guys, even the most bold, will stop and talk for at least a minute. And even if they don't, it still lets them know that the police are around. Then, if they will talk, we would *ask* for their identification. Find out who they are. We would then make out a Field Identification (FI) card on them to document the encounter. This card will have the person's name, description, date, and time spoken to, plus the names of other persons who may be there. A large component of police work is field intelligence. Knowing who the bad guys were in the area before a crime happened gives officers a place to start, especially if the crime is gang related. If officers were interviewing groups of Rollin' 40s intruding into Five Deuce Hoover Crip territory around ten at night, and we then find a Hoover dead at midnight, we know there is a good chance a Rollin' 40 was responsible. We would then go into the 40s hood and start talking to their members to see if one of them knows who did the killing.

So we were proactive with a capital *P*. We aggressively patrolled the streets of Los Angeles, trying to stop crime before it happened. We had to. For the number of officers we had, and the area size and population we had to patrol, we were (and still are) an incredibly small force. The city of Chicago has roughly the same population as Los Angeles but almost four thousand more police officers. The city of New York has four officers for every thousand residents, while we have only two, *and* we patrol an area almost ten times as large.

Yet our crime rate for violent crimes *was* almost half that of either city. So jamming worked. Too bad we still don't do it.

Anyway, Jackson and I are doing a jam. The vehicle we stop contains three Five Deuce Hoover Crip youths. We observe them "sweating" two rival gang members. *Sweating* is the gang equivalent of a jam; it's where gang members stop people and ask them their gang affiliation. It's a good thing we drove up when we did: Jackson recognized one of the youths they were talking to as a Fruit Town Brim, a bitter rival of the Hoovers. Blood definitely would have been spilled.

We get the gang members out of the car and up on the sidewalk. They're dressed almost identically: black Raiders jackets, baggie black pants, and Air Jordan tennis shoes. I am finding this fashion ensemble to be common among African-American gang members when they're out looking for trouble. The dark clothing blends into the shadows, and the loose fit allows colorful clothing to be worn underneath so they can make a quick change after committing a crime.[4] The suspect description of "male black, black Raiders jacket and black pants" is so common that recently a Seventy-seventh Street Division officer broadcast at the beginning of a foot chase of like-dressed suspects: "I'm in foot pursuit of two male *usuals*!"[5]

---

[4] I have arrested many gang members wearing *two* pairs of *pants;* the outer a dark pair of baggy khakis, the inner a lighter, tighter, distinctly different-colored pair of jeans or sweats. I have seen this even among young kids, all the way down to thirteen- and fourteen-year-olds, who are not only putting a lot of thought into their crimes but also *their escape,* should they be seen. Tell me that somebody isn't teaching our children how to be criminals.

[5] This broadcast caused said officer to get a personnel complaint filed against him for his "insensitive" wording, as well as time off without pay.

Because of their actions before we stopped them and the fear we saw in their potential "victims'" faces, we won't let these three walk away from us. I search each one of our suspects, running my hands completely over their bodies, trying to feel for anything that can be used as a weapon. Jackson stands guard, ready to react to any sudden movements from them, as well as any trouble from the vehicular and pedestrian traffic passing us. Other officers have had drive-bys done on them while on traffic stops, and the Rampart incident with the old man is still fresh in everyone's mind.

I complete my search and find that two of them have screwdrivers—a real pair of handymen, looking for something to "fix." Problem is, these screwdrivers will not screw anything. They have been sharpened to an ice-pick fine point. So I guess if they were to "fix" anything, it would probably be some Blood gangster's lung.

"We've been working on our car," says one of them, nodding to the weapons.

"Your car must be made of granite," says Jackson, " 'cause the only thing these are good for is chiseling stone."

Jackson takes the driver's license of the one behind the wheel, then nods up the street at where our two sweatees had been. I notice they are now gone.

"What were you talking with them about?" asks Jackson.

"Hey, man, they're my homies," says the driver. "We just be talkin'."

"What are their names?" asks Jackson.

"I don't know," he replies with a shrug. "I just be knowin' them."

Yeah, right, I say to myself.

Another unit now pulls up behind us. Two large traffic cops exit. Although traffic cops are basically patrol officers whose specialty is handling car crashes, they have identifying patches on their shoulders, a uniform addition over the slick sleeves we sport that gives them the appearance of being from some elite police unit. Our guys are not sure what to make of them, and they shift a little uneasily.

"I'm gonna check the car," says Jackson, meaning he's going to search it for weapons. I nod in agreement.

Suddenly, we hear five shots—*Bam! Bam! Bam! Bam! Bam!*

They ring out from somewhere in the distance, across the dark expanse of Exposition Park, about a half mile to the west.

"Someone's shooting!" says one of the youths enthusiastically.

"Sounded like a Uzi," says another, also smelling blood.

"Shit, man," says the driver. "That weren't no Uzi. Was a nine."

Our three youths forget their predicament. They are excited at the possibility of a nearby gun battle and try to categorize the weaponry, spouting out the two most common weapons used by gang members (outside of the small .22-caliber Saturday Night Special): the Israeli Uzi machine pistol and the 9mm semiautomatic handgun. I ignore them and turn to look at Jackson, who looks at the traffic cops and shrugs.

"Too hard to get there," he says.

He's right. The traffic is bumper-to-bumper.

"I'm sure we'll hear something on the radio if we're needed," says Jackson, his voice a little unsure. He wants to go to investigate it, but we're surrounded by a sea of traffic. Then the radio blares to life.

"*Officer needs assistance!*" The voice is loud and tense. An *assistance* call is our second-highest request for more officers, second only to a *help* call. This officer is saying he needs more officers *now*! "*I'm following two drive-by shooting vehicles northbound on Vermont at Thirty-ninth.*"

I look at Jackson, who is already at his driver's door.

"Let's go!" he says.

I race over, crashing into the ragged seat of the patrol car. A loose spring pricks my thigh, but I ignore it. I'm getting used to the LAPD's ancient patrol cars.

I still have the two screwdrivers and a gang member's school ID in my hand. I throw the ID out the window at the kids. I hold up the screwdrivers.

"You want these, you can get them at the station later," I say to them.

"I don't want them," says the driver.

Jackson checks traffic. There is nowhere to go. He jumps the curb onto the sidewalk as the radio voice continues.

"*Three-Edward-one, I'm following two vehicles still northbound Vermont crossing Exposition. One vehicle is a black Mustang five*

*point oh; the second is a blue Nissan two-eighty-Z with custom rims.
No plates on the vehicles, unknown number of male black occupants. Both vehicles are involved in the shooting."*

Jackson begins to glide carefully down the sidewalk. There are only a few pedestrians, as most of the Farrakhan rally-goers are already in their cars.

"Put up your window," says Jackson. "I want to hear the radio."

"You want me to turn on the lights and siren?" I ask.

"Why? Are we in pursuit?" He gives me a "Relax, pal" look, but I can't. The adrenaline rush has gotten the best of me.

"We're passing Jefferson," says the Edward unit. *"We need an airship."*

We are southeast of the chase; no way we can catch up. Jackson then reaches Exposition, where he jumps out into the street. He turns east, the way with the least traffic, but this is also going away from the pursuit!

"You're going the wrong way!" I say. "They're going away from us—"

"You want to drive?" he asks, then points at an approaching street sign. "I'm taking the freeway, man," he adds as we pass the green entrance sign.

I think I need to shut up and listen.

"We're getting on the Santa Monica Freeway westbound at Vermont. . . ."

I realize we're not that far away from them. We're on the Harbor Freeway northbound picking through traffic, but I can already see the interchange between the Harbor and Santa Monica freeways ahead of us. In a moment, we're on a freeway transition road westbound, headed for the chase. We're not that far behind them.

"Air Twelve, we're over the following . . ." radios the air unit.

And they are. I can see the helicopter a half-mile before us. Jackson is weaving quickly in and out of traffic. As we pass the Vermont on-ramp, another unit is entering the freeway. Even though I don't know them, the passenger, an old, grizzled P-III, smiles and calmly nods *hello*. He's definitely not stressed by what to me is quite a pressure situation. But I guess that calm comes with time. I do not respond.

"Now," says Jackson, "what do we have here?"

"What?" I ask, not ready for the conversation.

"What do we have here?" he asks again. He's quizzing me while his shoulders steer the wheel from side to side.

"Uh, we have a drive-by shooting with two vehicles involved," I reply.

"Any suspect information?"

"No," I say. It's hard to think, my adrenaline pumping. "I don't know . . ."

"Yes, we do," he says. He looks at me. "We know the suspects are an unknown number of male blacks."

I look forward. We are in the fast lane, which is clear, most traffic already having pulled to the left two lanes when the chase passed before us. A full-size, dual-cab pickup truck then pulls into our lane without signaling, unaware of our rapid approach. Jackson calmly veers into the emergency lane. We quickly pass it in a cloud of freeway dust.

"Gets the heart going, huh?" he says.

"Yeah," I reply. I can feel a little sweat on my palms, but I ignore it.

Then something unusual happens.

"The Mustang is exiting at La Brea," says the air unit. *"The Nissan is continuing westbound on the freeway."*

Great. The bad guys are splitting up. Now we have two separate followings.

"Three-Adam-twenty-seven," says Catania over the radio. *"We'll take the Mustang, and we'll be following northbound La Brea from the Santa Monica Freeway."*

"Three-Adam-fifty-seven," says Payne. *"We'll be their secondary."*

Jackson picks up the microphone.

"Three-Adam-sixty-three," says Jackson. "We'll be with the Edward unit on the blue Nissan if there's no one else available."

The RTO acknowledges us as the second unit in the chase of the blue Nissan. The operator then has the second following switched to another radio frequency to avoid confusion.

The air unit has stayed with our following, and I can now see 3-E-1 up ahead of us, a solid-looking beam of light shining down from the helicopter's night sun onto the car ahead of it. The Edward unit has only its rear-facing ambers lit, and is driving just a little faster than the flow of traffic. It does not have its full rack lit, as the Nissan is not driving in an overly reckless manner. He is simply picking his way through traffic, even signaling some of his lane changes. So there is no need to warn the public of an approaching hazard, a lit rack on the freeway at this point being a greater hazard as it might spook some citizen into a stupid move.

I now see the blue Nissan. It is a bright, metallic-flaked sky-blue with wide tires that extend almost a half-foot from the fenders. Its body shimmers in the night sun of the air unit. It has darkly tinted windows that make the passenger compartment look like a cavern. We fall in behind 3-E-1

A hand now stabs out from the passenger window of the Nissan, and a metal object is catapulted across the lanes of traffic, skittering over the asphalt with tiny, sharp sparks; disappearing in a pitched tumble into the bushes on the side of the roadway.

"Three-E-one, suspects just threw a handgun westbound Santa Monica Freeway about fifty yards west of the Fairfax off-ramp," the radio reports.

"Did you see exactly where it went?" asks Jackson.

"Yeah, I think so," I reply. "But it hit the bushes pretty fast."

"Make a mental picture so we can get it later," he says.

And I do. I look back real quick to make sure I can spot where I last saw it go. I look at the mile marker and the buildings along the freeway, filing them for future reference points. Then I notice there are other coppers behind us. A California Highway Patrol (CHP) cruiser, as well as another LAPD unit from another division. We're deep. We cross over the San Diego Freeway heading into the city of Santa Monica.

For a moment, it appears that we are in for a long ride. But just as suddenly as the incident began, the Nissan pulls sharply to the shoulder, slowing, but not stopping.

"Keep an eye on them," says Jackson. "They may try and run on foot. Or shoot it out with us." Jackson unlocks the shotgun. "You've got the tube," he says, using slang for *shotgun*.

I look down at it. The shotgun rests passively in a rack on the floor. Although I have fired it numerous times in the Academy, I

have never actually had to take one out while seated in a car. I pull
it from its rack and immediately bump the barrel into the roof. I
feel clumsy with it, which is not a good feeling. Especially when
there are twelve-gauge, double-zero buckshot rounds in it. I twist it
one way, then another, trying to get a comfortable hold on it while
still seated.

"Hey, don't you blow a hole in my roof!" says Jackson.

"It's hard to hold," I reply, momentarily forgetting the car in
front of us. Maneuvering this gauge is not easy.

"Crack your window about six inches, and put the barrel outside," he says. "Then rest the butt in your crouch." I do it and find
it's easy to hold.

The Edward unit activates its overhead lights. The Nissan stops
almost immediately, its brake lights blazing brightly. Jackson is in-
stantly out of our car. I'm out a beat behind him, and I rack the
gauge. *Click-clack!*

It is a powerful sound, one that gives confidence, especially in a
possible shooting situation. I level the weapon at the Nissan with
the knowledge that I can devastate anything I hit by a simple flick
of the trigger. The shotgun gives an officer the same firepower as
firing six .38-caliber rounds at a target at the same time. It's a fear-
some weapon, one that by simple reputation has caused many an
armed suspect to surrender. It is not uncommon for a suspect to
survive four or five rounds fired from the Beretta 9mm. But rarely
does a suspect survive one blast from the shotgun, and never two.
Even if the bad guy has a bulletproof vest on, the shock of the blast
will simply kill him.

The CHP unit has stopped traffic a hundred yards back. Other
police units pull up, and there are quickly a dozen guns aimed at
the Nissan. The driver of 3-E-1 begins to shout commands.

"Driver, turn off the engine!" he yells, but the freeway noise
from the opposing side is hard to overcome. He has to shout many
of his commands twice, even three times, before the suspects fully
understand him. I stand there, shotgun aimed at the suspects, half
expecting them to make a mad dash, which could be a problem for
me, because running with a loaded shotgun is not recommended.
But there is no mad dash, and soon there are two gangsters handcuffed on the cold freeway concrete. Jackson does a quick search of

the Nissan but finds no weapons. Then we talk to the two officers from 3-E-1.

"We were just cruising down the street, watching the crowd when we *see* muzzle flashes coming from the Nissan," says one of the officers, a white guy named Long, who not too long ago was underage to drink. "Right into a crowd of people on the sidewalk. Then right behind him, *bam!* Someone from the Mustang also fires into the crowd. They must have hit somebody! I mean, it was crowded."

"Yeah, but whoever they hit is GOA," says the other, meaning the suspects were *gone on arrival*. "A-fifty-seven went to the shooting scene while we were following, but couldn't turn up a victim."

Then we find out via rover that the other vehicle, the Mustang, was stopped shortly after it exited the freeway. Three suspects were pulled out, but no handgun was found. They probably threw their weapon while in traffic, but concealed their action from any officer's view.

We head back to the spot where we last saw the gun. As we drive I look at the car next to us. Don Murphy (my first-night partner) is driving the suspects' Nissan back to the station, followed by his partner in their black-and-white. Because the suspect who was driving has a narcotics warrant and there is the possibility the shooting was a dope deal gone bad, they want the car sniffed by a dog for drugs. Murph's balding head is barely visible in the lowered passenger compartment of the brightly colored vehicle.

"Lookin' good, old man," yells Jackson above the freeway noise.

"I'm gonna have this done to my truck," he yells back, his head bouncing up and down in rhythm to the roadway, the shocks of the vehicle bottomed out. "Feels real good on my hemorrhoids."

Jackson lets out a chirp of a laugh. Murph then cranks up the stereo, gangster rap spilling out. Murph bobs his head to the music. "I think I'll go pick up some chicks," yells Murph.

We peel off at the next exit and soon are standing at the side of the freeway, flashing light into the brush, hoping to find the weapon we both saw sailing through the air. It takes us fifteen minutes before we find it—or actually, what's left of it. It was a fairly new stainless-steel .357 revolver. But after hitting the pavement at sixty miles per hour, the metal tortured into what looks like an artistic interpretation for a combined abortion/gun-control ad. There are two spent casings in the revolver, with four still live. It's a miracle that one of the rounds in the cylinder did not discharge into the crowded freeway from the impact.

"The officers don't have much," says Jackson once we're back in the car. "Just reckless driving on the two drivers. They might get the two in the Nissan for having the gun. But a sharp lawyer will just have each suspect say the gun was the other's—have each one deny possession or knowledge. *We* didn't see either one holding it. We just saw a hand come out the window and the gun fly."

Which is true. I cannot really say whose hand went out the passenger window. The tinted rear window obscured any motion inside the vehicle. It just as easily could have been the driver.

He turns back to me, finishing his previous thought.

"Anyway, without victims, the district attorney may just drop the whole case," says Jackson.

"So these guys will probably skate?" I ask.

"Except for their driving," says Jackson. "You can't just run from the police. But nothing near what they should get."

"You think they had hits?" I ask.

"Could have," he says. "If they have serious wounds, we may find them at some hospital. Or we may not, especially if the one hit is a wanted person. I've seen gangsters with some hellacious scars because of homespun surgery. They do a Rambo, just dig the bullet out with a sharp knife, and then cauterize the wound with a red-hot butter knife. Even if they die, their homies may just dump them out on the street, let it look like a drive-by or a robbery. A lot of these fools take this gangster code of silence seriously. They won't rat on each other, even if they're in rival gangs, *even* if someone gets killed." He thinks for a moment. "They'll just take care of it on their own."

DRAGNETITIS

Today marks the first day of my third week. Jackson and I are in the report-writing room, a small, windowless space in the center of the station. And I mean *small*. It appears to have been designed with an eye to maximizing the amount of furniture while minimizing walking paths. Not much elbowroom in here.

There is an L-shape countertop running along two of the walls. Officers sit on stools, writing elbow-to-elbow. The other two walls consist of the doorway, a heavy wooden cabinet filled with thin shelves packed with report forms, and a short bench for arrestees equipped with two sets of handcuffs attached to a steel cleat. This is where juvenile arrestees are detained, their custody necessitating constant supervision by at least one officer. It is currently occupied by a lone male, all of fifteen years old, with dirty-blond hair.

"Has somebody called my mother?" he whines for the umpteenth time.

"Yes," I reply for the umpteenth time. Most juveniles are quiet and respectful when they're in handcuffs. But some, like this one, turn into blubbering babies.

In the middle of this boxlike room is an antique, wooden government-issue desk, at the moment full of booty from a jam that Jackson and I did on this juvenile. We saw him looking into car windows, and when we stopped him, we found he had some burglar tools and two freshly stolen car stereos in a schoolbag.

Jackson sits next to me, his legs crossed, rocking back on a metal chair as he checks the report I have just written. During the first two weeks of the deployment period, Jackson wrote all the reports, letting me read them afterward so that I could review and evaluate situations I had observed and then see which elements Jackson determined were necessary to record. Among the numerous robberies, burglaries, and other calls for service we had handled during those two weeks, Jackson deemed about two of them *each day* worthy of written record for possible future prosecution. So he would complete a two-page Preliminary Investigation Report (PIR). We also had made five felony arrests, which means five felony-arrest reports, each of which runs about four pages.

That is a lot of writing.

At times, it seems Jackson is more secretary than police officer. But it has given me a chance to review police reports, an almost blinding number of them to read, and because I'm now in my third week, my new set of responsibilities includes writing them. I have just written my first report, a PIR in connection with our juvenile arrest.

I have been watching Jackson closely as he examines my work.

His forehead has wrinkled no less then four times while digesting its contents. This is not a good sign.

"You went to college, right?" asks Jackson.

"Uh, yup," I reply. *Why is he asking a question he already knows the answer to?* I ask myself. I feel the proximity of sarcasm.

"They ever mention a word there called *the?*" he asks.

I was right: sarcasm.

"Yes, I believe so," I reply.

"Huh," he replies. "Then you must be part Chinese."

Jeff Wilson is also in the room, which is not good, because he is truly a member of the Royal Order of the Sarcastic. The conversation catches his attention. Jackson hands him the report.

"How does this look to you?" asks Jackson.

I look over Wilson's shoulder, trying to figure out what the problem is. The first two sentences, written using official LAPD departmentally approved word abbreviations, read: "Vict stated he sec'd veh at 1800 hrs. Upon ret'g one hr later, vict obs'd front pass door of veh open."

Translated in plain English: "*Victim* stated he *secured vehicle* at 1800 *hours*. Upon *returning* one *hour* later, *victim observed* front *passenger* door of *vehicle* open."

"You watched *Dragnet* as a kid, right?" asks Jackson.

"Why?" I ask.

"Because you're suffering from *Dragnet*itis," he replies. "You're writing like you're a damn Joe Friday robot. There is not one *the* in the whole paragraph."

I should probably keep my mouth shut. But of course, I have to try to justify myself.

"I'm just trying to be economic with my word usage," I say.

"*Economic,* huh?" says Wilson. "You can use a big word like *economic,* but you can't use a small word like *the?*"

"I just figured that with all the abbreviations we use, we were trying to keep our reports as short as possible," I say.

"We do," says Jackson. "But we need the *the*s in it to give it some flow. The word *the* gives a sentence an even rhythm. Taking the *the*s out breaks up that rhythm, giving us an unnatural irregularity."

A what? I say to myself.

"It's like potholes in the road," says Wilson. "Your sentences bump along like you drivin' on a Mescan highway."

Or a Los Angeles street. Wilson gives the report back to Jackson, who grimaces.

"Victim stated he secured vehicle," Jackson reads sourly. "It doesn't have any natural flow without those definite articles. But if you say, '*The* victim stated he secured *the* vehicle . . . ' " Jackson looks at me for approval as if he had just quoted Shakespeare. "Need I say more?"

"No, no," I say. "Obviously I have made a mistake. The way you say it sounds so much better."

"If you don't use the *the*s, it sounds like you're constipated," says Wilson, adding in his P-III wisdom. "What's that psychological term they use?"

He looks at me as though I should know. I am not sure what he is talking about.

"It's where you hold in all your shit," he says.

"You mean *anal retentive*?" I ask.

"That's it," says Jeff. "It's like being constipated, right?"

"Yeah, something like that," I reply.

"You're being anal retentive with the way you use *the*."

"That's right, you are," agrees Jackson. "And you better be careful. That's why Joe Friday always had a frown on his face. He was anal retentive. He held back those *the*s in his reports."

"Damn right," says Wilson. "Joe Friday couldn't squeeze a *the* out if he'd have sat on the pot all day."

Their combined wisdom is too great for me to fight. I quickly promise I will no longer forget my *the*s in the future. Then I correct my mistakes on the report. Jackson looks them over and nods his approval.

"I like it," he says. Then, in his best Tarzan, he adds, "Take report to sergeant."

DEPLOYMENT PERIOD TWO

Detective Cutter from South Bureau Homicide is in today for his biweekly briefing on the homicide situation in Southwest. He begins by informing us that there were "only" eighty-three homicides during the last twelve months in Southwest Division.

"We're down some from previous years," he says. "For a while there, it looked like we were going to break a hundred. But the bad guys didn't do much killing after Halloween. Probably because they knew Santa Claus was watching them."

This brings a few smirks. Cutter is a well-liked man. In his late fifties with fully grayed hair, he was once a pretty fair bantamweight, although he has a deeply furrowed brow that looks like a battle scar. In a worn and cracked leather shoulder holster under his left arm, he still carries an old .38 revolver. He puffs on a cigarette, despite the NO SMOKING signs on the walls of the roll-call room.

"We're still looking for Albert Mason,"* says Cutter. "He's a Ninety-ninth-Street Mafia Crip, descriptors being a male black, five-nine, one sixty. Probably driving a gray eighty-one Caddy with traffic accident damage to the front right headlight. He did a homicide five days ago down on Twenty-seventh Street. His mom lives up on Abourne Avenue, and he is known to associate with the Rollin' Forties Crips. As far as we can tell, he doesn't know he's hot."

"Keep an eye out for Andrew Lewis,"* Cutter continues. "He's a Rollin' Thirty they call *Devil Pup*. Male black, six feet, one ninety-five, twenty-two years old. There's a one-eighty-seven warrant in the system from a homicide in Denver, Colorado. From what I understand, it was a narco hit. He was seen in the division up on Jefferson

56

around the dope spots, driving a brown, late-model Cadillac, last three on the plate being two six eight. We also want to question him about the one-eighty-seven on Marlton Avenue a few months back. Be careful. I'm sure he knows he's hot."

Cutter looks through some of his notes. He then takes a long draw on his cigarette, his eyes squinting in the smoke that floats about his face.

"How many of you know Branson Stewart?"* asks Cutter. There are no answers. "Deals narco up on Rolland Curtiss with his brother Wilfred.* Male black, twenty-five years, about six feet." Cutter motions toward his own hairline. "He wears those Rastafarian kind of braids." Still no one admits to knowing Stewart. There is a feeling in the room that knowing him may have meant you made an error, such as letting a homicide suspect walk away from you after a contact.

"Someone in here should know him," he says. "He's been FI'd five times in the last six months," meaning officers have stopped him five times in six months and made a record of their contact. A few hands now reluctantly go up.

"Well, if you see him, pick him up," says Cutter. "It turns out he did a triple homicide in the country of Belize last year, and Belizean authorities would like to get hold of him. We know he's somewhere in the division. We can't arrest him for the Belizean homicides, but we can do him on some traffic warrants he has. So grab him if you can, and notify us or your watch commander immediately. We'll work it out with the Belizean consul. And don't tell him about the one-eighty-sevens. It may take us some time to do the paperwork to deliver him into their hands, and we'd hate for him to bail out."

The briefing continues, Cutter giving us the rundown on a few other recent murders. All are either narco hits or gang-related killings. The names change and the situations vary, but in most instances, the victims could just as easily have been the suspects.

"Cancel the *want* for Don Rogers,"* Cutter says, trying to finish up as the sergeant points to his watch. "He's the contract hit man we had a *want* on last week for killing two drug dealers up on Jefferson and Victoria. Mr. Rogers himself was shot and killed last night down in Seventy-seventh in an apparently related homicide.

As far as we can tell, it was a dispute over payment for the contract on the two dead drug dealers." He looks through some papers in his hand. Not finding what he wants he adds, "I guess I forgot to bring Rogers's killer's info but I think the suspect's name is William Aurn.* Anyway, I'll try to get you Mr. Aurn's information before he gets knocked off himself."

HEAD SHOTS

The ambulance does not seem to be going fast enough. The guy on the gurney in the back has lost a lot of blood, and we are still five minutes away from the University of Southern California Medical Center (USCMC). He has two head wounds, both caused by gunshots. From a small hole in his forehead, crimson fluid wells up in a quiet, throbbing trickle. The other wound, on the left side of his head, has been sealed by bandages. But the paramedics seem to be having a problem with the forehead wound, and they are discussing the situation with a doctor by radiophone.

I have been at Southwest five weeks now, and shootings have been a daily occurrence. I have yet to work a P.M. watch where we have *not* responded to some sort of call involving shots fired. I have also been at a number of homicide scenes where we were the second team to respond, generally arriving after paramedics had draped a clean white sheet over the decedent. But this is the first time Jackson and I have handled a shooting where the victim may actually die—before my eyes.

I have found that the average shooting on the streets of Los Angeles, although a real attempt at murder, is a poor attempt at marksmanship. It's a simple fact that bad guys know very little about the proper use or care of a firearm. They just point the gun and pull the trigger, generally causing a lot of smoke and noise, but very little destruction. Even when they get close and really want to kill, they just can't hit a damn thing. There is an old saying: "Sometimes even the best of intentions go unrewarded." Fortunately, that saying is generally true among criminals in South Central. But this victim has *two* head shots.

It came out as a "Shots fired—victim down" call. By the time we arrived, our victim was lying face to the pavement in a black-asphalt parking lot across the street from the Latino nightclub where he worked as a security guard; the suspects were only moments gone. At first, Jackson was contemplating CPR, but then he turned the man over and found his face to be covered in thick, oil-like blood. We could then hear the ambulance, which had been alerted from the same phone-in, so we backed off, looking for witnesses.

A slender Hispanic man had told me that he had seen the entire incident from start to finish. He was not fifty feet away when the shooting happened, having just walked his wife to the market for some milk and bread. The security guard had been standing outside of the club when he saw two young Hispanic men in the act of trying to steal the purse of an older Hispanic woman as she entered her car. When the guard tried to intervene, both men pulled handguns and each shot the guard once in the head. The guard had put up no fight, simply shoving the men away from the woman, and had time only to shout "No!" before the shots rang out.

Looking at the security guard closely, I see he is a male Hispanic, not more than thirty, with the weather-worn skin of someone from a desert land. He is wearing the blue work shirt of a "rent-a-cop," with a gray metal badge over his heart. He has on blue jeans and a black leather utility belt with holders for a straight stick, Mace, and handcuffs. There is no holster for a handgun. He is unarmed.

The ambulance gently bumps over the patchwork of surface streets that ring USCMC. The area is old, the streets are ancient; the potholes seem to cave into each other. The medical center itself looks Gothic, jutting up out of a landscape of low-lying industrial buildings and a nearby Southern Pacific railroad yard. It could easily pass for a castle on the Rhine. It is fifteen floors of soot-stained concrete with spires on top. I half-expect to see armored knights on the roof, waiting to pour boiling oil down on us. I look back again at the victim. The paramedics are no longer talking to him. I want to ask them how he is, but I resist, fearful that a negative response from them may affect the victim's will to live, even though he is unconscious.

We enter the emergency-room parking lot. If this were television, you would see a team of white-gowned doctors and nurses racing toward us with a sterile white gurney and all manner of life-support machinery pushed before them. But this is not television. Gunshot-wound victims arrive in a constant flow here, and if doctors and nurses performed in the frantic response mode common on film, they would pass out from exhaustion before they got halfway through their shifts. Instead, I see two other ambulances parked quietly, having already delivered their cargo. I also see police cars from three other agencies, all here on criminal investigations. But I do not see any medical personnel. The closest we get to seeing hospital personnel are two hospital janitors sitting on a table having a quick smoke.

The paramedics exit the vehicle, take the victim out of the back, and gently wheel the gurney into the evaluation area, a partitioned and curtained space in the center of USCMC's large, busy emergency room. In this floor space, three patients can be examined, X-rayed, and worked on at the same time, a sort of triage section where doctors evaluate what next to do with a patient: either send him off for stitches and then home, or upstairs for major surgery. I'm sure our victim will be in the latter category—unless he is sent downstairs to the morgue.

Some orderlies come over and transfer the patient to a hospital gurney. The paramedics talk briefly to a husky, war-weary nurse who nods a few times as they speak, then she begins to examine the victim's wounds.

"This a drug thing?" she asks without looking at me.

"No," I reply. "He's a security guard who was shot during a robbery. Apparently, he was trying to help a lady who was getting her purse stolen. They had guns—he didn't."

"No shit," she says. "An actual good person. I ain't worked on one of these in a while."

Another nurse, much younger than the other, brushes past me, and I notice that I'm in the way, as space is limited here. I back over to a white curtain that acts as a doorway. I watch the nurses work, their moves seeming almost mechanical. I get the feeling they must do this ten times a day.

"The one bullet exited *here*," says the older nurse to the younger, straining to look deep into the wounds. "I can't tell with the other."

Jackson is still back at the crime scene. Because we were the primary unit to respond, he is in charge there. For what it's worth, I'm in charge here at the hospital, but am confused as to what I should be doing. *There must be something I can do besides watch,* I tell myself, trying to remember what I was taught in the Academy about homicide scenes. I do remember that there are three areas of police responsibility.

One is already moot, that being to get a dying declaration—any statements made by a victim prior to death, implicating a suspect in the murder. Such statements are admissible in court and are powerful evidence for a jury, as few would conclude a victim is lying when facing his own imminent death. But there won't be a dying declaration here. Even if our victim could talk, the nurses are now medicating him heavily, so if he does die, it will be silently.

Another police responsibility is to get a diagnosis on the victim. It may seem odd, but the diagnosis will determine who does the investigation of the crime. If the doctor feels there is a good chance the victim will die, the crime scene will be handled by divisional homicide detectives and their scientific staff. If it appears he will live, patrol officers will handle the investigation, with no scientific backup. Unfortunately, intent means very little anymore in police investigations. The key word here is *death,* which in police work is synonymous with the word *budget.* If you have a death, you can spend just about as much money as needed. If you don't have a death, the purse strings are very tight, simply because murders make the newspaper and woundings don't. Police departments want to look good, so they spend their money on the murders, even though you may have a more dangerous criminal loose with the lesser crime. So if some gangster with blood in his eye and an AK-47 cranks off thirty rounds at a party but hits no one because he's a bad shot, he will generally not get as much investigation as the neighborhood drunk who shoots out a streetlight and kills his neighbor with the ricochet. Therefore, the doctor's prognosis this first hour, life or death, is very important in determining how much investigation will be budgeted.

As for the third police responsibility—I cannot remember it.

"X ray is here," says the younger nurse, looking in my direction. An X-ray technician, one with thick glasses on her nose, brushes past me.

"You may want to stand outside for a moment, Officer," she says to me. "I'm going to be making some exposures."

"Of course," I say as I move out of the area.

The mobile X-ray machine is then rolled in, and everyone scatters, leaving the area while the technician takes three quick pictures. When she is finished, the doctors and nurses return, hovering about the victim.

I watch the staff as they work on him. The victim is now naked, except for a washcloth-size linen that has been laid over his penis. I guess even the unconscious are thought to be modest. Tubes are jabbed into him. I am amazed when a doctor sticks his finger into one of the bullet holes, which oozes thick blood and yellowish fluid. A nurse reaches around him, dabbing at the fluid as it runs down the side of the victim's face, her hand moving in quick, jabbing motions like a bird pecking seed.

Moments later, the technician returns with the X-ray photographs. She clamps them to a light box next to me. I look at them, front and side views of a boney skull. Even though I'm no medical expert, I can see a distinct oblong shape near the victim's right ear. One bullet is still inside his head.

A doctor separates from the crowd, holding out bloody hands as he views the X rays. I give him a moment, then ask him for a prognosis.

"How's he look?" I whisper, my voice low to avoid the appearance of being a vulture hovering overhead.

"I can't tell yet" is all he says—which is not good for us, because back at the crime scene, they want to know if they should roll out the detectives or not.

"Get a prognosis as soon as you can," says Sergeant Roberts when I phone her. She is the acting watch commander today. "I'm going to roll everyone out anyway. If it turns out his wounds are survivable, let me know immediately so I can inform the detectives." When I ask the doctor the same question fifteen minutes later, his reply does not change.

Another gunshot victim is now brought in. A grossly fat male in his thirties, he has taken a shotgun blast to his hip. Huge chunks of flesh dangle from a gaping wound. Although weak, he manages to yell, "Watch out, bitch!" when a nurse touches the wound. My third responsibility now surfaces in my mind with the arrival of this new patient: protection of the victim. Suspects have been known to follow victims to hospitals in order to finish off unsuccessful murder attempts. There have even been shootings inside this very hospital, inside this very emergency room. Although the chances of suspects following my victim to the hospital are low, this new victim next to him could have been wounded in a bad drug deal, or have been the victim of a gang hit that went bad. I keep half an eye on the entrance to the emergency room.

They work on "my" victim nonstop for quite some time. I look at my watch and find that I have been here over an hour and a half when he is pushed out of the room toward the elevators. I pin down the doctor as he passes me.

"Doc, what's up with my guy?" I ask.

"We're still not sure," he replies. He is busy and tries to walk away from me.

"Doc, give me some kind of indication," I plead. "I have to tell my supervisor something."

He lets out a deep sigh. He does not like to make statements. "We have to do surgery right now," he says. "He's in extremely critical condition. If he lives through the next twenty-four hours, he has a chance of making it." He turns and walks from me, then stops. "About this much of a chance," he adds, holding his thumb and index finger together as if he were measuring the head of a pin. He then walks off to the elevators and surgery.

I call Sergeant Roberts and report the doctor's prognosis, carefully telling her of the close proximity of the doctor's thumb and index finger. She advises me that the homicide detectives are at the scene with a member of Scientific Investigation Unit, who will be doing a full-blown investigation even though the victim is still alive.

Jackson comes and gets me about thirty minutes later. As we are walking out, another victim of a gunshot wound arrives. A large kid in his early teens, he took a bullet in the jaw. His teeth chatter as if he were in a winter freeze, the nerves in his face exploding as his body tries to control such an unnatural wound. He is pushed past us on a gurney, disappearing into the emergency room.

"It goes like this all night," says Jackson. "As if it were a battlefield hospital during a war."

*   *   *

Two months later, the security guard died from his wounds, having never regained consciousness. He left a wife and family in Mexico. Sometime later, Cutter came into roll call and told us he had identified both suspects, but thought they had fled to the state of Guerrero in Mexico. As of this writing, the suspects are still at large.

Midway through the next night, Jackson and I respond to another shooting. It turns out to be my first stone-cold homicide in which we are the primary unit, where *we* find the body. No ambulance needed. No rush to save his life. The victim is obviously dead and has been for some time.

It is dispatched to us over the MDT as a POSSIBLE 187—"187" being the California Penal Code section for murder. The comments on the screen read, ANONYMOUS MALE CALLER STATES SOMEBODY IS DEAD IN THE ALLEY, near the intersection of Nicolet Avenue and Pinafore Street, in "the Jungle."

The Jungle was built in the 1950s to provide housing for airline pilots and stewardesses working out of the recently completed Los Angeles International Airport, which is less than five miles to the south. When new, it was Los Angeles apartment living at its finest. A planned community, the Jungle was a sea of two-story structures with bright bay windows mostly facing a large, crystal-blue swimming pool. Each apartment building, ringed with palm trees, had its own name scrawled in big white letters above the entrance: PALM TERRACE, OCEAN BREEZE, COCONUT GROVE, and similar names added to the atmosphere. The area was dubbed "the Jungle" by developers who hoped to cash in on a connection with a spate of tropical-theme motion pictures that were popular at that time.

But that all changed in the mid-1970s. Many airlines moved their home bases from Los Angeles (American to Dallas, United to Chicago), and with them went the pilots and flight attendants. With a rising rate of vacancy, the Jungle soon began to accept federally assisted housing recipients. The buildings quickly fell into disrepair, and then despair.

Now, the palm trees have tree rot, many of the bay windows are broken and boarded up, and the crystal-blue swimming pools have long ago been filled in with brown, weeded dirt. The building names are either gone or missing many of their letters, sometimes due to target practice by P-Stone gangsters, the Blood gang that claims these streets.

Nicolet and Pinafore meet in the heart of the Jungle. Because there are a few different alleys near that intersection, we just pick one to start—the right one.

I am on one side of the alley, flashing my light, scanning the area, while Jackson examines the other. Heavy steel gates twelve to fourteen feet high guard the carports and apartment entrances from this alley. Some are topped with razor wire, others with sharp, gothic spikes. Torn pieces of clothing hang like streamers from the tops of the fences, evidence that the area crackheads will brave any peril just to steal a car radio that may bring at most ten dollars.

It is a night with no moon. The slender alley is canyonlike, the sides of the apartment buildings jutting straight up. It is dark here visually, but it "feels" even darker. It "feels" like a bad place.

"Partner," says Jackson, "come here. And watch your step."

In that instant, I know he has found the body. His voice is even and flat, very businesslike. He stands next to an open Dumpster, a large commercial unit with deep dents. I shine my light on the ground, making sure not to step on any evidence, and walk over to him. Jackson is already on his rover requesting some additional units for a crime scene.

I do not look in right away. I hesitate. I have not seen many dead people in my life at this point. My total personal exposure to death until a month ago was limited to two open-casket funerals for family members. But my experience is rapidly growing. Since last month, I have added three corpses covered by white sheets. Nothing really graphic. Yes, there were red splotches of blood staining the sheets, and two had a flow of red liquid on the pavement surrounding the body. But before today, nothing this up-close and personal. Yes, there was the security guard, but he was alive when I left him. So death is not a familiar concept to me at this point in my career. My adult life has been college and a few years in the business world, and there is very little death and murder done over exam scores or sales contracts. So I don't even know how I am going to react.

This uncertainty is discomforting to me. In the Academy, we

were told stories of officers having thrown up or passed out when shown a body. There are even those who quit on the spot. Although the third alternative is a definite *no* for me, the possibility of the first two is there even though I feel fine at the moment.

Jackson holds his light into the Dumpster, asking me to appraise what's in its glow. He watches me closely. I know he will evaluate my reaction to see if I can handle this part of police work.

I then remember that I have a cigar in the car, and I think of going back to get it before I get too close. In the Academy we were told that dead bodies can get rancid-smelling rather quickly, but the odor can be overpowered by cigar smoke. I choose to forsake the cigar to show fortitude, feeling that getting it would show weakness.

So I look in, focusing on that which is lit, and I am not shocked. To be honest, I am more saddened, because what I see *is* sad. There is almost no trash in the Dumpster. Just a thin layer of papers and vegetable peels accumulated since the trash was collected earlier in the day. On top of the trash, on his back, lies a male black teenager. His eyes stare beyond me to the stars. His head is a mixed swirl of dark colors, his blood having ebbed from his face to settle nearer gravity at the back of his head. He has bullet holes in his chest, in his leg, and in his right cheek. None of the wounds seems to have bled very much, and his white T-shirt and blue jeans still look very clean and tidy. The T-shirt actually looks new, or at least freshly bleached and ironed. Just a small amount of bright-red blood speckles it here and there. Then I notice something odd. His shoes are gone. And the first thought other than sadness burns through my mind. *Did someone kill him for his sneakers?*

"Probably a drug hit," says Jackson, dispelling my thought. "Execution style. See, his hands are tied behind his back." Yes, I see that they are tied with steel wire. "And they took his shoes, probably so he wouldn't be able to run well."

I push all this through my mind, trying to calculate a reason for this murder. No good one comes out.

"Don't try and think it through," says Jackson, as if reading my mind. He clicks off his light. "I'll go get some crime-scene tape. You start a crime-scene log. There's gonna be a lot of people here soon for this investigation. I want you to be sure to get all of their serial numbers and work assignments."

I'm glad for the chores Jackson gives me. They take my mind off the murder. I am soon involved in the investigation, and it's almost an hour before I think of the dead boy again.

NATURAL-BORN KILLER, PART ONE

Jackson and I are walking out of the station. I've just given a sample of my urine to the "stream team," a group of police detectives who run a random drug-testing program of officers to insure a drug-free workplace for the LAPD.

"Probationers gotta pee," says Jackson, glaring at me suspiciously. "You're all probably just a bunch of drug-crazed hippies, the way they're hiring now. Probably do drugs they don't even test for. You're probably high right now, we don't even know it."

"I could be," I reply, glaring back at Jackson, which surprises him. Then I cross my eyes.

"You must be messed up on something," he says, shaking his head as we hear three beeps advising that a "Hot Shot" is about to be broadcast. We get serious.

"Any available Southwest unit, shooting in progress, the corner of West Boulevard and Adams Boulevard. Any available Southwest unit come in."

I advise the dispatcher that we will take the call, and she tells us to respond Code Three (lights and siren), which we do. The comments of the call are pretty thin, just a citizen stating that he and his friend are being shot at. By the time we arrive, a fire department rescue ambulance is already at the scene, and a small crowd has formed.

Our two victims are both West Boulevard Crips. According to them, they were standing on the corner drinking beer when a yellow two-door Chevy drove by, the driver firing two shots from a revolver before fleeing the scene. One of the Crips, a skinny teenager named Freddy, has been struck once in the leg.

West Boulevard is an anomaly among Crip and Blood gangs. Its members are comprised of both blacks and Hispanics, a result of recent formation, and having been started in a residential area populated evenly by the two cultures. Most Crip and Blood gangs exhibit the same degree of racism as southern hillbillies (especially in the way they deal with our Korean population), but there are a few exceptions, which is what we have here. Freddy is a second-generation Los Angeles Hispanic. His homie, a barrel-chested parolee in his twenties named Hub, is a dark-complexioned black.

Jackson talks to Freddy while I interview Hub. Hub has a baby face that is in a constant sneer. He tells me right off that he is on parole for assault with a gun.

"I want you to call my P.O. and tell him I didn't do shit," he says evenly, referring to his parole officer. "I was just standin' here on the corner when some muthafuckin' fool starts bustin' caps at me."

After giving me his parole information, Hub is short with me when I question him about the shooting. Twice while I stand there he does a thing called "sucking teeth." Simply put, this is making a sucking sound with your teeth, and is a sign used by prison inmates to nonverbally say "Fuck you" to prison guards. I ignore it.

"So why are people shooting at you?" I ask.

"'Cause niggers just be shootin'," he replies.

"You know who these guys are?" I ask.

"I don't gang-bang no more," he says, using the street term for hanging out with other gang members and not referring to the sexual act. "I got a kid." The reference to his having a child, and the fact that this should exclude him from being involved in criminal activity, is something I constantly hear from gang members. They know that most police officers are family men, and they use it as a play for sympathy. But if he were a real family man, what is he doing on parole, on a street corner drinking beer, hanging out with another gang member? He should be home with his kid.

Hub looks at my hair, which is still pretty short from the Academy. He also takes in that I'm wearing long sleeves and a tie, LAPD's dress uniform, which is the only uniform combination issued in the Academy. Short sleeves with an open collar, the usual dress for a street cop, is a post-Academy purchase for LAPD officers, one I have yet to make because I'm working nights and it's winter, and I don't need the short sleeves yet. So Hub is analyzing my appearance. He is deeply in tune with the world of cops and robbers, and by his eyes I can tell that he concludes that I am a boot. He doesn't say anything, seeming to just file it away for reference, should he need it.

I ask him a few more questions, but I don't get any real information. He chooses his words carefully, almost like a politician. He tries to direct the line of questioning back to information about how his homie is doing, while not seeming to care whether the Hispanic youth lives or dies. He just wants to know how much of a payback he has to inflict upon the perpetrators.

Gangstering is a game to him, like a deadly game of tag.

Because he is not being cooperative in discussing the shooting, I decide to ask him questions about the West Boulevard Crips. Being from the white part of the Valley, I do not understand gangs and gang shootings. Not that I feel gangsters themselves understand why they do what they do. But I still want to try to get a look into his mind.

"So who does West Boulevard fight with?" I ask.

"The world," he replies, looking over my shoulder at the paramedics who have cut off Freddy's pants.

"How many members do you have?" I ask.

"I don't know, man," he replies. "We don't pay no dues." I can tell he is getting a little annoyed with me. I don't really have "street" talk down yet and I know it. But I'll eventually pick it up. For now, I could not care less what this knucklehead thinks of me or how I ask him questions. Right now, I just want to learn what I can, so I ask him another question.

"He's Hispanic yet he's a Crip?" I ask. "You guys have blacks and Hispanics in your gang . . . why?"

He's tired of me. He takes a deep breath.

"Yeah, man, we got niggers and spics," he says. "We'd take white folk, too. Wanna join?"

Well, the look into his mind has shown me he is pretty much an asshole. We lock eyes for a moment. Then I catch and stop myself, as this is going nowhere. I smile. "Thank you for the information." I suck my teeth, then walk away. Back in the car, I tell Jackson about my chat with Hub.

"That's right," says Jackson. "Talk to these guys as much as you can. Don't be embarrassed because you're white. Listen to them. Even if they're lying to you. You can learn from their lies. And their anger. What do you think about that guy? You just talked to an *average* hard-core street gang member. Guys like him are the heart and soul of these gangs we see out here. Think he'd kill you if he knew he could get away with it?"

I had not thought about that one. I think about the conversation, or lack thereof. I remember how he was not concerned about his homie, but how his eyes seemed to be planning, constantly evaluating the situation he was in—like a strange dog you encounter on the street. Even though it wags its tail when it approaches, you're still a little hesitant to pet its head, not sure if you'll get your hand back in one piece.

"Yeah," I reply, "if he thought he could get away with it."

Jackson then tells me he knows Hub, who has been arrested numerous times, twice for attempted murder. Both cases involved rival gangsters and were dropped, as the victims refused to testify against Hub. Jackson feels the victims dropped the charges due to threats against their families by Hub or his gang.

"Both of the attempted murders should have been good homicides," says Jackson. A wry smile cracks across his face. "Mr. Hubbard just seems to have a problem with trigger control. Pulls to the right. With just a little more firearms training, he could be a very successful murderer."

Jackson does not know how close to the truth he really is. A month later, a series of brutally cold robbery/homicides would begin in West Covina. The suspects, two men and two women, would drive to local shopping malls, kidnap elderly customers out of the parking lot, drive them to a remote location, rob them, and then execute them with gunshots to the head. In total, five people were murdered over a two-month period. The normally sedate white suburb was thrown into a state of panic. The police had no leads until they received a tip from an arrestee who traded information about the murders for a reduced sentence. Police raided a one-bedroom apartment in a poorer section of West Covina where they apprehended all four suspects. The leader of these four was Vincent Hubbard, the above West Boulevard Crip nicknamed "Hub."[1]

---

[1] There is a great photo that was shown in one of our local papers of Hub sticking his tongue out at both the media and victims' families during the West Covina murder trial. It was Hub's last act of aggression toward the public at large. Hub is currently serving a life sentence in the California prison system for the West Covina murders.

ORIGINAL GANGSTERS

Jackson and I are standing just inside the front picture window of a burned-out two-story wood tract house on Raymond Avenue. A gentle breeze strokes my face, as most of the glass that once was a barrier here lays crushed on the floor at my feet. In days past, this place in which we stand was a comfortable middle-class family residence, complete with twin shaggy maple trees in the front yard and a rose-lined brick walkway leading to the entrance. But it has been a long time since this residence could be called comfortable. The trees are now rotting, the rosebushes have long since dried up, and the structure remaining has been reduced to an observation post for two policemen as they watch a group of ex-cons deal drugs.

The territory itself is ominous. It is the center of the Rollin' 30s Crip gang, one of the largest Crip gangs in Los Angeles. They are also known for violence toward police officers. Two weeks ago in roll call, we were advised to use caution when in their neighborhood because of threats made by gang members to "take out" an LAPD black-and-white. Threats against officers by gangsters are common, and generally given little notice. But a recent raid on gang members by LAPD detectives and CRASH officers netted a cache of dynamite, this coming only a few days after Alcohol, Tobacco, and Firearms (ATF) agents arrested a Rollin' 30 nicknamed Woody Woodpecker who was attempting to purchase a LAWS handheld rocket launcher.[2] He had told the agents, who he thought were fellow gang members, that his sole purpose for purchasing a rocket was to "smoke a blue suiter."

We have parked our patrol car in an alley two blocks away, taking the chance that it may not be there upon our return. But Jackson feels that this will be an important learning experience for me. He wants me to see some hard-core drug dealers in action. We have snuck from shadow to shadow to get here, a necessity to avoid detection from the lookouts who ring the area.

---

[2] LAWS is the acronym for Land Air Weapons System. It is a handheld unit, much like a bazooka, and fires a high-speed rocket that can chase down most helicopters.

Jackson has spoken to me only once since we left the car, that being when we reached the rear yard of the structure. After jumping an ancient whitewashed wood fence and landing in a forest of waist-high weeds and overgrown ivy, he whispers to me, "Be real quiet. Hypes use this place to shoot up, and there will probably be a couple of them sleeping on the second floor." The rear door was off its top hinge, forced over at an angle, and after gingerly stepping through the portal, we make a quick and quiet search to ensure we have the lower half to ourselves.

As we look out the window, glassless since an arson fire gutted the first floor years ago, Jackson taps me on my side and hands me a small pair of ten-power binoculars. I begin to raise them to my eyes to inspect the ex-cons at Raymond and Adams, but Jackson taps me again, pointing in the opposite direction down Raymond toward Twenty-seventh Street.

"Lookouts," he whispers, indicating with his hand the shadows off to the left of a house on the corner.

I put the field glasses to my nose and zoom in, picking them out immediately. A pair of juveniles, in their late teens, are on the front porch with no lights on. They are dressed all in black. One sits in a chair with a view east and south; the other leans against a pillar with a clear shot west. They are alert, their punishment for failed duty being a lot worse than a dockage of pay. But they are watching the streets below us, our position being out of the area of their responsibility.

I turn the glasses north, to the ex-cons, and focus in. There are about ten of them there, all black males, ranging in age from their mid-twenties to their late fifties. None of them wears anything related to "gang" attire. But they all have that distinctive "ex-con" air about them. They move slowly, deliberately, and their eyes are cold.

"All of those men there are OG, 'original gangster,' " says Jackson. "Prison tough and street rough. Ain't one of them has ever worked a day in his life. They are dedicated career criminals, to the man."

A few of the younger ones are dressed flashily, with thick ropes of gold chains around their necks. Others are dressed in low-key sportswear, the only appearance of wealth being a Rolex watch or a diamond earring. Two of them are especially hard-looking, with shaved heads and wearing Loc[3] sunglasses, designed, it seems, with the gangster in mind. Dark-chocolate lens with equally dark frames, they wrap around a gangster's face like a slash from a knife. Even in profile, the eyes cannot be seen. If the eye is the window to the soul, these guys don't want their souls seen. They look especially mean, since it is night.

Some of the men are gathered around two wire-wheeled 1978 Cadillac Sevilles, one green and one blue. The others sit on the steps of a fourplex under a sign that warns, in bold black handwritten and misspelled words: NO DRUGS! NO PROSTITUSHON! NO LOYTERING! NO ESCEPSHONS!

It is a sign not highly regarded.

The men all seem to be talking trash, having an old-fashioned bullshit session, like a bunch of buddies telling stories around a barbecue. But as I watch them, a beat-up, older-model Toyota Celica pulls around the corner. The driver, a rail-thin Hispanic, stops parallel to the men and leans over, speaking to them out of the passenger window. The men ignore him, except for one, who absentmindedly motions back toward the fourplex. Then I notice for the first time three women who have been leaning against a yellow Monte Carlo in the driveway. One woman, whose pregnant belly has stretched her printed maternity dress to its limits, walks down the driveway to the Celica and leans into the passenger window. After a few words, the Hispanic presses a roll of twenties into the woman's hand, and she stuffs it into her bra. Then she walks back up the driveway and disappears. The men do not acknowledge the activity, although their lack of notice seems purposeful. Their eyes are everywhere but on the Celica. Soon, a pair of juvenile males walk down the driveway. Both are no more than fourteen. One has a small paper bag, the kind a market gives you to hold a quart of milk. It's new and crisp, and the top of it has been carefully folded over about halfway down. The other boy wears a heavy coat, both hands tucked deep into his pockets. He wearily looks up and down Raymond Avenue, watching for signs of the police. The boy with the paper bag leans into the car and places it on the passenger seat

---

[3] Loc is short for loco, which is Spanish for "crazy."

without a word. Once it's in the car, both boys walk back up the driveway, and the Celica drives off.

"They're not doing nickle and dime stuff here," whispers Jackson. "They only sell to other dealers. Minimum price is two hundred dollars."

Soon another buyer comes. "Look at the cars, look at the suspects," says Jackson. "Get a feel for who they are and what they drive. Don't necessarily remember the faces or license plates, but get a feel for *them*. Build your instinct for spotting *them*."

I don't quite understand what he means. The suspect just looks like a normal guy, and his car, although a little dirty, looks like any other on the street. The something Jackson wants me to pick up here, the *feeling*, I'm not quite getting it.

Soon the suspect leaves, only to be replaced shortly by another. At most, it is five minutes between buyers, with sometimes two arriving at the same time.

"It goes like this all night," says Jackson. "They like it here because there's a freeway off-ramp just around the corner. Dealers from all over the county come here to buy rock cocaine."

We are there twenty minutes, and I can feel that Jackson is just as antsy as I am about our car.

"You want to go?" I ask.

"Yeah," says Jackson. "I don't want to have to walk back to the station. But let me show you something first."

Jackson pulls out his rover and keys the mike.

"Three-A-sixty-three," he says. "Show us doing a follow-up to a narcotics location, corner of Raymond and Adams."

The RTO replies, and we stand there and watch. It is not ten seconds before a heavyset woman comes waddling down the driveway, talking loudly. I can clearly make out the words she speaks, *muthafuckin' po-leece,* even from this distance.

"They have a scanner," says Jackson, "listen in to everything we do."

Some of the men get in one of the Cadillacs and drive south toward Twenty-seventh Street. Others quickly retreat with the woman up the driveway and out of sight. In all of thirty seconds the scene is reduced to just two of the cons leaning against the yellow Monte Carlo.

"These are some serious people," says Jackson. "These OG here are at the top of the gangster food chain."

A HISTORY LESSON

How the gangster "food chain" in the city of Los Angeles ever began is generally a point of confusion even to the gangsters. Gang members are generally not gang experts, knowing very little about the gang picture beyond the five or ten square blocks in which they roam.

Gangsters may not even know everyone in their gang, knowing only their homies; the small "cell" of ten to twenty gang members with whom they go to parties, or share malt liquor on a front porch, and that's it. This is easy to see in gangs like the Rollin' 60s, which have over seven hundred members. There are just too many fellow gang members to know. Of course, gangsters know the names of the gangs they are supposed to be at war with. But it's rare for them to know the individual names of their rivals, and even rarer for them to know them by sight. That's why gang members have to "sweat" people on the street to find their rivals; they usually have no idea who or where their enemy is. This of course can lead to some confusion on the streets, and there have been numerous homicides where one gang member has mistaken one of his own for the enemy.

Asking gang members why they do what they do, why this gang with which they associate themselves hates the rivals they have, is an effort in futility. They plainly just don't know. They know nothing of the history of the gang, nor do they care; their minds are locked simply into the here and now. If you ask ten Los Angeles associated gangsters the history of their gang, you will get ten different answers.

Detective Mark Hanes* is a true gang expert. He grew up on the streets of South Central Los Angeles, joined the LAPD shortly before the Watts riots in 1965, and was shipped straight to the South End. There Hanes stayed for nearly twenty years, working his way through the patrolman and detective ranks in the heart of South Central Los Angeles. Hanes is teaching the "L.A. Black Gangs" section of a class I am taking on southern California gangs.

The class is broken up into a series of blocks, where we receive training on each of the different types of gangs we will encounter in southern California. A full two days of training is needed, because there is such a multitude of gangs in this area: white biker gangs (for example, Hell's Angels and Vagos), Asian gangs (Korean Killers and Hellside), prison gangs (Mexican Mafia), Mexican street gangs (18th Street and White Fence), Central American street gangs (La Mara Salva Trucha), European gangs (Armenian Power and the Russian Mafiya), and, of course, black street gangs, many of which I've already named.

"The Los Angeles black community has a long tradition of street gangs," says Hanes, a thick man with gray streaks running through a thin Afro hairstyle. "The words *cuz* and *homeboy* have been in the language of South Central for generations, starting as slang used by gamblers and pimps as far back as the 1920s.

"Black gangs started slowly. During World War Two, you had a large contingent of blacks from the southern states, like Alabama and Georgia, move into South Central to work in the war effort. Big defense plants like Firestone Tires and Kaiser Steel employed nearly ten thousand people at their height. The black community was prospering here. There were plenty of jobs, neighborhoods were crime-free, and the schools were excellent. So many black families wrote happy reports back home to the South that soon their friends and families moved here.

"But after the war, things for blacks in South Central went downhill. Returning white GIs took most of the available jobs, while defense plants had layoffs. Some businesses relocated, some failed. Black unemployment skyrocketed. So we began to see more crime.

"In the 1940s," Detective Hanes continues, "some black youngsters began to copy the Hispanic gangs which had been roaming the streets of East Los Angeles since the turn of the century. Black kids saw the zoot-suiters tooling around in their lowered rides getting the women, looking cool. So they started up their own street gangs, using names like the Businessmen, the Gladiators, the Black Cobras, and the Ice Picks. These gangs were small, and were looked down upon by the black community as being hoodlums. They did small-time crime, mainly penny-ante stuff, and any disputes they had were for the most part settled with their fists. And they stayed within the black community. They kept their crimes local.

"Then in 1950, a Washington High School student named Raymond Washington, who just happened to be the leader of a small gang called the Crips,[4] stabbed to death a high school football star named Ballou after a dance at the Palladium. Raymond killed Ballou simply because he wanted Ballou's letterman's jacket. It was a senseless killing, as most gang murders are. But this was the 1950s, and this was the first gang kill before the media. At the time, the entire city of Los Angeles had maybe a hundred murders a year. Citizens were still shocked by murder. The local papers gave the story an incredible amount of coverage. Soon, all of Los Angeles was calling for an end to black street gangs. Which as always has the opposite effect when it comes to the criminal mind—it caused gangs to grow."

Hanes shifts his position in his chair and goes on. "If you were a rebellious black youngster, you immediately went out and joined a gang, especially the Crips. So the Crips grew in size almost overnight. And they took the South End by storm, gobbling up neighborhood youth in clumps, 'cause if one kid joined, all his running buddies soon followed suit. The Crips started out as one big gang. But soon they had splits, mainly due to geography. First you had what were called East Coast Crips, who were east of the Harbor Freeway, which had been a barrier since the 1950s. They split from the West Coast Crips, who were west of the freeway. Then the West Coast split into two factions, the Hoovers, who were nearer to the Harbor Freeway along Hoover Avenue, and the Rollin' sets, who were lined up along the numbered streets along Normandie Avenue to the west. At first they didn't fight each other. They still hung out together under the Crip name. But that would change later.

"To fight the Crips, other black youth gangs formed, the early 1970s bringing into existence the Compton Piru, the Van Ness Brims, and of course, the Bloods. The Bounty Hunters, the gang that rules the Knickerson Gardens housing project, was the first gang to call itself a 'Blood' gang, taking the nickname from black soldiers

---

[4] *Crips* is a shortened form of the original gang name, which was *Cripplers*.

returning from the Vietnam War who called each other *Blood*. The Bounty Hunters stood up to the Compton Crips, who were a break-off from East Coast. There were numerous shootings and gang fights. A lot of blood spilled. It was our first major Crip-Blood war.

"Soon citizens were calling for a gang crackdown, and the LAPD command staff responded. They formed specialized units to gather intelligence, allowing the LAPD to closely monitor every gang member. They gave the street cop tremendous leeway in dealing with any gang member. We put the gangster down hard. Real hard. Back then, only people who cried about the police being too tough were the criminals, not Joe Citizen. By the early 1970s, black gangs were actually decreasing.

"Then along came Stanley Williams, a Crip they called 'Tookie,' " says Detective Hanes. "He's currently serving a life sentence in Pelican Bay for murder. Tookie is a very strange dude. He used to walk around talking to himself. And strong. About five feet seven and two hundred fifty pounds, most of it muscle. Tookie could bench press near five hundred pounds. You did not mess with Tookie. For some reason, the Crips loved him. He became a leader of sorts for them. Tookie was a proponent of forming a 'Crip Nation'—one big family that moved as a unit, with Tookie at the helm. One night in the mid-seventies, he had over two hundred Crip gang leaders in Sportsmans Park. He was trying to unite the Crips in a crime wave, to take over the city right then and there in one big riot. And he was almost successful. Only thing that kept us from having riots like the Watts riots was Tookie and some of his homies went to jail for murder. The Crips then fell apart again—there was no one to unite them—so gang activity dropped."

Detective Hanes stands and paces about the room, hands in pockets. He is relaxed, presenting his history lesson in a continuous flow of thought. He does not need notes; he lived it.

"About the time Tookie went to jail, we saw the first fights within the Crips. That was between the Rollin' Crips, like the groups called the Thirties, Forties, and Sixties, and the Hoover Crip gangs, such as Five Deuce and Eight Trey. In 1978, a Rollin' Forty was sexing up a Five Deuce Hoovers' woman, and the teens went to blows one day right in the lunch area of Manual Arts High School. Soon, the Forty pulled a gun, shot the Five Deuce dead right on campus. It started a Crip-on-Crip war, a war that is going on to this day! Not that any of these gangsters out on the streets now know how it started. Soon Crip gangs were fighting all over the city. Some would form alliances to get one gang, then that gang would hook up with another Crip gang to get the other two. It made the gang wars even bigger. We had around two thousand murders between 1980 and 1981; they were both record-setting years. It was like Beirut in South Central.

"But the gangs had nothing to unite them other than the adventure of living a violent lifestyle. And most of the kids grew tired of the killing. Gang membership was actually on its way down again in 1982. It looked like the gangs were on the outs. But that's when it began to snow in Los Angeles. And I do not mean the kind of snow you can ski on. This weather front moved right in from Miami."

Detective Hanes pauses for a moment, sipping coffee from a blue mug with the words "LAPD CRASH" in white.

"In the 1970s, most of our cocaine came into Florida from Colombia by way of Cuba. The drug people in Cuba were charging big bucks to fly onto their island and then transfer the drugs to speedboats. And I mean *big bucks*. It costs a pharmaceutical company all of twenty dollars in materials and processing to make a kilo of cocaine. And it's probably half that cost when some farmer makes it in the jungles of Bolivia. So the cost of making the drug is nil."

Hanes leans on his desk and looks at us hard.

"By the time cocaine hit the streets in Miami in 1980, a pure kilo was running about thirty-five thousand dollars. *Thirty-five thousand dollars!* The most *gold* has ever cost was about eight hundred dollars an ounce. That's about twenty-eight thousand dollars a kilo, almost seven thousand dollars less than cocaine. And it costs a helluva lot more to mine gold than it does to brew up cocaine. I don't think I would be stepping too far out on a limb to say that cocaine is the most profit-filled commodity ever in the history of mankind."

Hanes lets this settle in for a moment. "At the end of the 1970s, Mexican drug runners began showing the Colombians how weak our California-Mexico land border was. It was easy to walk ten kilos of coke in a backpack over some desolate part of the border—much easier than boating or airlifting in a hundred under radar. And much less expensive. You need a pro to bring it in by boat or plane. Any yahoo can walk a backpack filled with drugs across the border. So the Colombians gave up trying to bring coke into Miami. They went to people in Panama and Mexico, and set up land smuggling routes. And with that, Los Angeles became the new cocaine capital of the United States."[5]

Hanes continues his teaching. "In 1982, Colombian cocaine came to our town. But the Colombians still needed locals to sell the stuff. And they chose the black gangster. They saw these large groups of disorganized youngsters doing street robberies, stealing cars, and most of all, killing, and figured they would be naturals at moving drugs. And they were. So the Crips and Bloods became street soldiers of the Colombian and Mexican cartels, whether they knew it or not.

"With the money from coke flowing in, black gangs began to grow at incredible rates. It's not hard to see why. Unemployment for young black men in South Central is something like fifty percent. Ain't many jobs down in the hood. We saw gangs nearly double in size when the Colombians made their move. Because now if you hung with the homies, you could make enough green in six weeks to buy a car.

"We had major coke wars in Los Angeles in the mid-eighties. All these different Crip and Blood gangs fighting for a bigger piece of the pie, trying to rule the city. It was much like the gang wars in Chicago in the 1920s between the Italians and the Irish.

"In an effort to fight the gangsters and their drugs, LAPD set up CRASH," says Hanes. "CRASH was successful at holding the gangs in check during the mid-1980s. They took care of business. The

---

[5] While doing research for this book, I discovered many aspects of the criminal world that disturbed me. But I was completely shocked when I researched the profitability of drug smuggling. There are five major Mexican drug smuggling cartels. According to a Justice Department investigation, the leaders of two of them, the Ciudad Juárez and Gulf cartels, each has an estimated net worth of $10 billion. And that is with a *b*. To put this number in perspective, that is currently the same net worth as Bill Gates, CEO of Microsoft, who was recently at the top of the *Fortune* 500 "Wealthiest People in America." Ten billion dollars is also the amount Wells Fargo recently offered to purchase First Interstate Bank. So in the Mexican drug smuggling world alone, there are two men as wealthy as, if not wealthier than, the richest man in legitimate America.

murder rate fell, and gangsters slowed down. Police pressure worked—somewhat.

"Because CRASH, as well as our narcotics units, were hitting the gangs hard, the Rollin' Sixties Crips, our gangster innovators, did two things. First, they set up fortified rock houses. This way, the transaction didn't take place on the street—so an arrest wasn't as easy. We would literally have to have SWAT blow a hole in a fortified house every time we wanted to get at some dope. And second, the Sixties took their cocaine on the road."

Detective Hanes shows by the slow emphasis in his voice that the next is a significant point.

"The cheapest coke in the United States is here in Los Angeles," he says. "Gangs like the Rollin' Sixties Crips discovered this, and soon, not only were they opening rock houses in South Central, they were also opening them in Lincoln, Nebraska, and Denver, Colorado. An ounce of cocaine that sold wholesale for two to four hundred dollars in Los Angeles, could be cut and sold for eight hundred to two thousand dollars in Middle America. Remember, sixty percent of cocaine abusers are categorized as being in the white middle and upper class. We've all seen the undercover videos of the dirty black cluckhead buying a ten-dollar rock on the ghetto street. What they do not show is the Rollin' Sixty selling a couple of grams to the white attorney in a polo shirt in some suburb of Seattle.

"The Los Angeles Crips and Bloods have made a fortune in cocaine. For example, there was this one kid I used to chase off street corners in Seventy-seventh Division called Li'l Tommy. He was a skinny little punk, but a *smart* skinny little punk. At fourteen years old, he was selling chips. By eighteen, he had a whole crew working a corner with him. When I went to the Major Narcotics Unit, we took him down—at his four-hundred-thousand-dollar home in San Dimas. He owned a Ferrari, had a gold chandelier in the entryway of his house, and his name, Li'l Tommy, was written in Italian brick at the bottom of his swimming pool. He was twenty-one years old! When we went through his home, we found photos of him butt naked with some of the most beautiful women I have ever laid my eyes on! You cannot get away from the fact that Li'l Tommy made one helluva lot of money sellin' crack. And he is not the exception.

A lot of these gangsters have good business minds. Rollin' Sixties Crips have rock houses in Portland, Oregon; Las Vegas, Nevada; Tulsa, Oklahoma; Minneapolis, Minnesota; Shreveport, Louisiana; and Albuquerque, New Mexico. They've diversified. Things get hot for them in one city, they just sell a little more in the others. And to help hide their money, they own record labels, car dealerships, and real-estate investment companies.[6]

"I can't tell you how many times I've seen some fool I used to chase out here slingin' dope, rappin' on MTV. So instead of having Tookie pushing for a gang army to rob and plunder the city, we have rappers advocating the gangster lifestyle, which means slingin' cocaine."

Hanes takes a deep breath.

"Our black youth see this. They idolize the gangsters on the street and the fools on video who say they 'used' to be one of them. Makes the young ones all want a piece of it. So the gangs are again growing.[7]

"Because they have a reason to grow, one that transcends protecting your hood and hangin' with your homeboys. Being in a gang is no longer about fightin' for turf," Hanes finishes. "It's about having employment to support yourself and your family."

---

[6] Eazy-E, the rapper who started NWA with Ice Cube and Dr. Dre, in a newspaper interview said he took to rap purely as a business venture after dealing crack in Los Angeles in the early 1980s. He started a recording company with the proceeds from his sales. Many of the lyrics in his songs are about incidents that occurred during his days of dealing on the streets of South Central.

[7] In 1980, there were an estimated 50,000 gang members on the streets of Los Angeles. In 1995, that figure had grown to an estimated 165,000 hard-core gang members out of a population of 2.9 million. This figure does not include all of the family members and associate gang members who support them.

DEPLOYMENT PERIOD THREE

I am sitting in the roll-call room. I am stunned. I neglected to watch the news or read a newspaper this morning (something I find myself forsaking with greater frequency due to the slanted and at times defamatory media reporting), so I have just heard for the first time that Tina Kerbrat, a North Hollywood patrol officer, was shot and killed yesterday on Lankershim Boulevard in the San Fernando Valley. It is my third month out of the Academy, and this is the first officer killed while I have been out in the street.

"It was some kind of ped stop," says Dozier. "The papers said she and her partner were going to write the suspect a ticket for having an open container of alcohol in public. They saw him walking down the street, beer in hand. When they pulled their car over to the curb, he just started shooting. She got hit in the head."

My first reaction is visceral. "Did they get the asshole?" is all I ask. Because if they didn't, I want to know who to look for.

"Yeah, he was KMA at the scene," says Dozier, using LAPDese for dead. "Her partner shot the suspect dead right there."

Banderras hands me a black, circular piece of elastic. She points to her badge, which is covered by a similar black elastic piece, and I realize she has handed me a mourning band. I do the same to my badge.

"I knew her," says Banderras quietly. "She was two classes ahead of us. She was still on probation."

"They said she and her partner were writing the citation to check off her probationer's book on RFCs," says Dozier. He is referring to a release-from-custody ticket, which is issued for nontraffic violations such as being drunk in public or playing loud music. "They

83

saw he had an open beer in his hand. And that's all they wanted from him. Just a ticket for the beer."

We sit quietly, each of us having our own thoughts. Mine go to another death, one only a little over four months prior. During my last deployment period in the Academy, Russ Kuster, a Hollywood Division detective, was killed in a shoot-out in a Burbank restaurant by an illegal immigrant who had only moments before been ejected from the establishment. Banderras's thoughts seem to be on something else.

"She's the first woman killed in the line of duty for the LAPD," says Banderras to me in a hushed tone. I can feel Banderras pull a deep breath. This last statement has hit home. "This is bad," says Banderras quietly, pressing her fingers into the desk before her. "I mean, I have a kid to think about," she says quietly. "If anything happens to me, he's got nobody to take care of him. His father ain't worth a shit. I don't even think he has a job now. And I wouldn't want my family to bring him up."

Banderras is confiding in us because she knows us from the Academy. But behind us, Jackson has been listening in on our conversation.

"Don't feel any less secure about your ability to perform your duties," says Jackson. "It happens, police officers get killed, and this won't be the last one, either. You just have to believe that *you* will always live."

"That's kidding yourself," says Banderras. "You're ignoring the fact that if officers die, you being an officer means it could someday be you."

"Hey, pedestrians die all the time," he says, flippantly. "Does that mean I ain't crossin' the street? No way, baby! You can't give in to the fear. Because if you do, if you give in to the fear on this one thing, you'll give in to the fear on others. And you'll go crazy."

"It's not the same thing," says Banderras.

"Sure it is," he says. "Fear is fear. And if you can't control it, quit."

Banderras sits quietly, reflectively.

"Don't tell me you're only *now* thinking about getting popped?" asks Jackson. His voice is calm. "What did you think, that because you're a woman, the bad guys won't shoot at you? You're wrong, 'cause this is the nineties. Bein' a woman means nothing to these assholes nowadays. They'll kill a woman just as soon as they'll kill a man. And the sooner you get that in your head, the better. 'Cause you got to know this ain't playtime. Tina Kerbrat is just the first. There's gonna be other women going down after her. And someday, *you* may have to kill somebody. I've shot two people so far on this job. Neither of them died, lucky bastards, 'cause I was sure trying to kill them. Because if I hadn't put them down, they may have killed me. And if you can't get that straight in your mind, there are plenty of other jobs out there."

Jackson looks at her hard.

"You have the ability to do this job," he says. "You just have to remind your head of that."

"You're right," says Banderras with a faint smile.

But I am not so sure she believes it.

THE P-II

This is my first day back from a stretch of three days off, and my scalp is itching. And it's not from dandruff, either. My girlfriend Kelly* and I spent those days at a beachside motel outside of Santa Barbara. We needed to get out of town together. She has a job as an engineer, basic nine-to-five work, which does not combine well schedule-wise with my night-shift patrolling. So in my two months on the job, we've seen little of each other, and Kelly has become rather cranky. She misses me.

Anyway, we spent a few hours lying on the beach, and the top of my head now itches, my scalp being sunburned to a deep-red glow. In the Academy, we were required to keep our hair cut no longer than one quarter of an inch from the scalp. That's very short hair. Combining this with the absence of sunshine I've endured lately due to my nocturnal shift, and it's easy to see why my sensitive scalp never stood a chance.

I am in a black-and-white, westbound on Martin Luther King Jr. Boulevard, working 3-A-63 with a tall, thin-bodied brunette named Julie Richards.* Richards is behind the wheel, twice giving me a curious glance while I scratch my head. My hair is slick with sunburn treatment, and the greasiness of the product gives my slowly returning hair a fifties-style look.

"You got lice or something?" she says to me flatly.

"No, no. I got sunburned at the beach with my girlfriend," I reply, glad for a chance to explain. "I went to Santa Barbara this—"

"I don't really care," she interrupts.

She looks at me dully and shakes her head, then looks forward into traffic. I'm a little startled by her rudeness, but this is not the first thing she's done that is, for lack of a better word, immature. The minute we met outside the roll-call room on this, our first day working together, Richards promptly told me, "Boots don't drive my car." That is against training policy, as the third deployment period is when probationers are supposed to go behind the wheel. But since she has rank on me, and an attitude, I don't say anything.

Although Richards is only a P-II, which is a non-training-officer grade, she has been assigned to train me this DP due to a shortage of P-III training-rank officers. LAPD is in the middle of a hiring frenzy in an attempt to offset a large number of officers who are retiring. The department had a corresponding hiring frenzy twenty years ago in the early seventies. Vietnam, although a horrible war, was a good training ground for police officers, and LAPD hired as many qualified returning vets as it could. At that time, one of the department's biggest carrots was a twenty-year retirement at 50 percent pension. That meant that an officer could join at twenty-one (LAPD's minimum age) and retire at forty-one with half of whatever salary he was making at his time of retirement, payable for the rest of his life. Many officers who joined under that program are now exercising their option.

So LAPD currently needs to hire replacements—to the tune of almost one hundred per month—for the next three years! Unfortunately, the department has been spending its money on new hires and not on teaching and promoting qualified training officers. So P-IIs, officers who at times lack tutorial qualifications or experience gleaned from time on the job, have been forced to instruct some of the new officers, even though they themselves have not been instructed in how to execute this task.

Most of the P-IIs do not mind working with probationers. To them, it's all in a day's pay. Others resent this assignment outside of their job description, and feel that the Los Angeles City Council is trying to cheat them out of the 5 percent pay increase given a P-III.

"I don't like to work with boots," Richards says, her eyes now hidden behind a pair of mirror sunglasses, which she has pulled from a shirt pocket. "They don't know shit about police work."

Richards obviously falls into the latter grouping.

"I'm a P-Two," she continues. "I like working with other P-Twos. I don't have time to train a boot."

I sit for a moment, trying to think of a reply. This is one of the bad things about being on probation in the LAPD. You do have to take a lot of guff from your fellow officers. Sometimes it's done to toughen up new cops. Other times, it's done simply because a veteran officer doesn't like you. Whatever the reason for her attitude, I am expected to bite the bullet and show respect. So I decide to go the brown-nosing route, in an effort to alleviate some of the tension.

"Yeah, I don't know why they do this," I say. "You should at least get temporary P-Three pay."

"What do you know about it?" she quickly replies. "You don't have enough time on the job to know anything." Her voice is somewhat menacing, and I feel I have transgressed into some forbidden zone, one where P-Is have no opinion and are not to use their powers of speech. "Let's get a few things straight," she adds. "This is my car. You are here to watch what I do and to do what I say. When we're on a call, you just stand back and observe. If you don't like the way I do something, you ask me about it afterward. Otherwise, keep your mouth shut."

I begin to imagine what she would look like with a Napoleon hat on her head and her right hand stuffed into her open coat.

"I look at it like I'm working an L-Car," she continues, using LAPD terminology for a one-man unit. "You're nothing but a ride-along. All I ask is that you keep your stupid mistakes to a minimum, and don't get me killed."

I look at her closely for the first time. She is a lanky five foot nine with a deeply tanned, leatherish face. She wears no makeup or jewelry. Off duty, I've seen her wearing only lipstick, a dull pink that looks more like Chap Stick. She has the look and demeanor of a cowgirl, and I mean a real one. She is hard and dusty. I get the feeling that even though I outweigh her by fifty pounds, she could drink me under the table if it were to come down to shots of tequila.

I think better of replying. Instead, I sit in the car silently with her for what seems like an eternity. We drive past a group of five gang members standing on a street corner, all dressed in black. One of them "mad dogs" me, forcing his face into what he thinks is an intimidating scowl. I almost laugh. Somehow I feel it is *more* hostile in my police car right now.

"Pull up the status of A-fifty-five," she says.

I punch in the appropriate numbers, bringing up the current whereabouts and call assignment of the other unit. When it returns, I turn the screen so she can see it.

"What are you doing?" she asks. She says it as if she has just witnessed an action of incredible stupidity.

"I'm showing you their status," I reply.

"I don't want to *see* their status," she says. "I want you to *tell* me what they're doing."

Ah, a test, I say to myself. I bring the screen back around and examine it. The other unit has three calls, which show up on the screen as follows:

0003022	ACK	3765 VAN NESS BLVD	390-M
0003041	ENR	3125 CRENSHAW BLVD	906-B
0003102	ACK	1142 ROLLAND CURTISS	415-W

"They're en route to a Nine-zero-six-B at Thirty-one twenty-five Crenshaw Boulevard, with two calls holding," I reply.

Not bad. I think I passed the test.

"Nine-zero-six-B, what the hell is a Nine-zero-six-B?" she replies.

Uh-oh. What is a Nine-zero-six-B? I do not remember. I really have to brush up on these things, I promise myself silently. I think for a moment. I know *390-M* is a drunk male; a *415-W* is a disturbance caused by a woman, but a *906-B?* I cannot come up with an answer.

"I, uh, don't know," I reply. A look of total disgust comes over her face.

"Boot, you have *got* to spend time on your codes," she says. "How am I supposed to prepare for calls if you can't even tell me what they are?"

I feel bad. Well, not really. But I act like it. I think she is getting bent over nothing, but I do not say so.

"Punch in the incident number of the call," she says, "and hit the transmit button."

This command brings up the comments of the call, which read: AUDIBLE ALARM SYSTEM COVERING THE EXTERIOR.

"It's a burglar alarm," I say, as though I have unraveled some hidden mystery.

"Brilliant," she says.

I then notice A-55's call is in our patrol area. We had not been "clear" (available for calls) when it had been dispatched, so it was sent to them as they were available.

"Should I buy it?" I ask. "Buying a call" is telling the RTO that we will handle the incident, canceling the other unit so that they can handle problems in their area.

"What do you think?" she replies, a little sarcasm in her voice.

She is starting to get on my nerves.

Ninety-eight percent of all burglar alarms set off in Los Angeles are false alarms. This includes alarms in citizens' personal residences, as well as businesses. Usually an electrical problem or act of nature (like a strong gust of wind) causes the alarm to go off, or occasionally someone bumps into a trip switch and activates an alarm by mistake. That's what we have here on Crenshaw. In a strip-mall a shop is being remodeled by some handymen and one of the workmen accidentally set off the alarm while working on the wiring, which angers Richards. When the workman apologizes, she doesn't want to hear it.

"You've wasted our time," she grunts, then shakes her head and walks out of the store in a huff, leaving me standing there. I look at the workmen, who are nervous and confused by my colleague's actions. They think they may be getting a ticket for this, or have interfered with our saving a life in some other part of the city. But I know that it is no big deal.

"Don't sweat it, guys," I say. "Just try to be a little more careful."

When I get out to the car, Richards is still heated. "We got better things to do than this shit," she says.

Of course we do. Even while en route to the alarm call, we were sent two other calls. But things like false alarms happen; it's par for police work, and it's better to have alarms that occasionally send false messages than to have no alarms at all, because we do catch a lot of criminals with them.

As we pull out of the parking lot, there are two middle-aged "transients" lazily sitting against a block wall near the entrance sunning themselves. *Transient* is a word officers use to describe what most citizens roughly term bag people or street people, and is simply a reference from the LAPD booking computer, which assigns "1942 Transient" (the number stands for LAPD's police teletype address) whenever an arrestee does not give an address.

Officers generally leave transients alone unless there is a citizen complaint. Although one LAPD survey found that roughly 75 percent of transients have criminal warrants, the majority also have some extreme mental illness, one that requires medication and booking at a hospital downtown. That means *lots* of paperwork and a long drive downtown, so they are left to themselves unless they are bothering the citizenry. But Richards is in a mind-set most officers are not. She grabs the microphone and turns on the public address system.

"Get out of here," she says into the microphone. The two men are jolted into consciousness by the volume. They look straight at us. "Pick up your crap and move it."

Oh, brother. Now she is heated at the transients, I say to myself silently. Yes, they are loitering. And I'm sure their presence is not appreciated by businesses in the mall. But still, they are just sitting. We have no call on them. And yelling at them will *just* get them moving to someplace else; someplace that may require a call for police. I would prefer just to leave them alone.

"We're going, Officer," says one of them, rising on flamingolike legs. He is a thin Caucasian male, his skin a sickly yellow and his body malnourished. Typical drug user: too much heroin and not enough fiber.

"Don't come back," she answers through the P.A. "If I see you here again, you're going to jail." She stews for a moment, then turns to me. "Fuck those guys," she says. She waits while they slowly gather their few belongings. Too slow for Richards. She opens her door and steps out. She takes her baton out of its ring, a gesture meant to intimidate the two men.

"Move your asses, now!" she says.

"Yes, ma'am," replies one of them, and they quicken their pace. They move down the street as we drive off to see what other "good" we can do for our fair city.

I think Richards needs to lower her caffeine intake. But I'm not going to tell her.

THE RED BARON

It is near the end of our watch and I'm glad this night is almost over. Richards is annoying me. Although she works hard, she complains constantly about the amount of radio calls; the types of people we deal with; and the lack of respect we get from the public. She unleashes a nonstop torrent of negativity. And when we leave calls, she makes snide remarks about the people we deal with. After one family dispute involving a rather homely-looking couple, she advises me that "they're a two-bagger: Both have to put bags over their heads before they can fuck."

On the LAPD, we like to have what we call "positive citizen contacts." Lieutenant Ross, who seems to be our resident verbal judo expert, says a positive citizen contact is where we "interface with citizens in a manner that leaves them with an agreeable, satisfied feeling which will lead to future assistance from that citizen." It's an "I'll be nice to you today so you'll be nice to me tomorrow" kind of thing.

But Richards has a different thought on this. More of an "I'll be a jerk to you today and an even bigger one when I see you tomorrow" kind of thing. Richards is not what I would call a "positive citizen contact" type of officer.

In my three months out, I am beginning to see a pattern in the police officers I work with. I find that 95 percent of all cops are an easy bunch to get along with. They do their jobs and go home, usually enjoying their daily interaction with the public even though they may complain about it when among other coppers. But they definitely care about the public, and take deep pride in their work.

But there is this 5 percent who are just downright mean and egotistical; who do the little things like make snide remarks or write unnecessary tickets, as well as the big things, like ignore calls for service or slap handcuffed suspects. The badge weighs heavily on their chests and they like to drop it on citizens' toes whenever they get the chance. They give the other 95 percent a bad name. Richards is definitely a "5 percenter."

As we drive, I can see that she is obviously tired, too. We have handled fifteen radio calls in a little over seven hours, and our Code Seven was cut short by a backup call on a 415 man with a gun. But it has been like this since I arrived at Southwest. South End coppers spend the night trying to catch up to the radio. As soon as we clear from one call, the RTO sends us three others.

"Let's start heading for the station," she says. "Morning watch should be down soon."

I am in total agreement. We stop at the light eastbound on Adams at Western. I slowly roll my neck around in its socket, small pops from tired muscles echoing in my ears like gravel under a car tire. A motorcyclist pulls up next to us. Something is odd about him. A white male, he has a black leather football helmet on his head, black fighter goggles on his face, and a long, red scarf around his neck. He sits stiffly astride the bike as if he were on a polo pony. He looks out of place here in South Central. Hell, he would look out of place anywhere. His head swivels toward me as he examines our car.

"Look at this guy," I say.

"Real fashion plate," replies Richards with a smirk. "He looks like the Red Baron."

Suddenly, he guns the bike, wheels screeching, blasting through the intersection against the red light. Before I can say another word, Richards in one move slams on the lightbar, floors the gas, and grabs the radio mike.

"Three-A-sixty-three," she exclaims. "We're in pursuit north-bound Western from Adams."

Things are happening fast now. Richards flips me the mike as the RTO comes back over the radio.

"All units on all frequencies stand by," says the RTO. *"Three-A-sixty-three is in pursuit northbound Adams from Western. Three-A-sixty-three, is there a vehicle and suspect description?"*

My adrenaline has gone from zero to one hundred in nothing flat. I sit there dazed for a second, not sure what to do. We practiced being in pursuits in the Academy, and I did back up the following on the freeway with Jackson. But now I am *in* one!

"Dunn," says Richards. "Tell them it's a black motorcycle with a male white suspect, and we're approaching the Santa Monica Free-way. And get us an air unit!"

"Sixty-three," I say. "We're approaching the Santa Monica Free-way in pursuit of a black motorcycle, suspect is male white, and we need an air unit!"

"Any air unit, any air unit," says the RTO. *"Come in on South-west frequency. Three-A-sixty-three is in pursuit of a black motor-cycle, suspect is male white, northbound Western approaching the Santa Monica Freeway. Any air unit, come in on Southwest fre-quency."*

"Can you read the plate?" asks Richards. I strain my eyes, but he is pushing ahead into the darkness.

"No," I reply. "It's a California plate, but that's all I can make out."

The motorcycle now enters the on-ramp for the westbound side of the Santa Monica Freeway. In a cloud of smoke and dust, he opens it up, leaving us far behind.

"We're losing him," shouts Richards. And we are. He seems to be disappearing into the night lights ahead.

Suddenly . . .

BOOM! Like some heavenly moonbeam, a spotlight blasts down out of the sky onto the motorcycle.

"Air Three," says the helicopter observer. *"I'm over the pur-suit."*

And it is. A ghostly sphere of flashing aircraft-warning lights, the LAPD helicopter glides above the freeway, the motorcycle lit below it like a stage performer. LAPD, with its thirteen helicopters and two fixed-wing airplanes, has the largest police air force in the nation. And we need it, our sphere of influence being one of the largest municipal police districts in the nation.

I feel relieved, sure we will get him now. Only problem is, the air unit and its spotlight begin to fade in the distance up ahead. Although it's late, we are still on a freeway in Los Angeles, which is always as busy as rush-hour traffic. We cannot pick through the maze of cars as easily as the motorcycle can. Richards wheels us into the center emergency lane.

"Still westbound," I say into the mike. "Santa Monica Freeway approaching the La Brea off-ramp."

"Dunn," says Richards, "let the air unit take over the broadcast."

She is telling me to let the copilot in the airship call out the suspect's location. He will not do it unless requested to. And I better request him to, because I have already lost sight of them—the spotlight disappearing into the mix of overhanging freeway lights.

"Air Three," I say, "take over the pursuit."

I say this just as we are approaching La Brea Boulevard.

"Roger," replies the air unit. "Suspect vehicle has exited the freeway at La Brea, northbound on the surface street."

I look up just in time to see the La Brea Boulevard off-ramp sign whiz past. Damn! We missed the off-ramp. Richards puts on the brakes, gradually pulling over to the right shoulder. As you can guess, she is upset.

"Fuck!" she yells. She hits the steering wheel, shaking the car. She glares at me. "Why weren't you watching! You should have seen him exit!"

Probationer or not, I am only going to be pushed so far. I give her a long, hard look, which she returns.

"What?" she barks, her voice issuing a challenge. But a challenge for what I can only guess. I must have fifty pounds on her, and the only threat she holds over me is one with the pencil she uses to write my rating reports, which is a very big challenge. So I ignore her and look into my rearview mirror.

The mirror just shows black, my angle projecting back down the on-ramp to La Brea. The suspect is down there, somewhere, probably taking La Brea up into the Hollywood Hills to try to hide in a canyon. Then a strange thing happens. I see a flicker of light, then the glow of the air unit's searchlight comes back into view, coming up the on-ramp!

"Suspect is now reentering the freeway," says the air unit. *"Shop Four forty-two, suspect is coming up behind you!"*

The copilot is reading off the numbers on the roof of a black-and-white, I look at the shop number on my car keys.

"We're Shop Four forty-two!" I say.

"Thanks, Einstein," mutters Richards, flooring it.

As we hit sixty, the motorcycle passes us two lanes out. Richards had shut down the lightbar, so when we pull off the shoulder and light up, the biker looks over at us with complete surprise. He hadn't seen us!

Richards pulls us in behind him. We streak down the freeway past Fairfax and then, by La Cienega, right on his tail. Another unit enters the freeway at La Cienega, but their car is only doing the speed limit, so we pass it like it's standing still.

The suspect decides to exit the freeway at Robertson Boulevard. This is a mistake. The off-ramp has a real sharp turn at its bottom, and there is always water in the roadway. When he hits it, his tires slide on the wet road, his right knee skimming perilously close to the ground. He swerves wide into oncoming lanes, almost hitting the opposing curb, almost dumping the bike. Like a circus performer on a high wire, he canters back and forth, leaning from one side to the other, finding his balance and pushing the steering back to the right side of the road as he finally gains control.

We stay with him all the way. Robertson Boulevard is bare of significant traffic at this time of night, and once again, the biker opens it up as he screams down the cracked cement street on what is the eastern end of Cheviot Hills. Expensive homes whiz past, soon replaced by expensive shops as we enter Beverly Hills. In a little under five minutes, our roller-coaster ride has taken us from the grafitti-strewn hovels of South Central to the estates of Beverly Hills. Amazingly, our ancient Chevy police vehicle, with a hundred fifty thousand miles on the odometer, acts like an old stallion, rising from the dead to give its masters one last, hard ride. We are not losing this motorcycle. We are staying with it.

I am now completely focused on the pursuit, my senses taking in everything this suspect does. I know something has to happen soon; the suspect will either crash the bike or drop it and run. Trying to outspeed us is no longer an option. The near crash he experienced coming off the freeway has made him timid. His speed, although fast, is not what it could be, and not fast enough to outrun our Chevy, which he must know. So he moves into a residential area and begins taking every turn he can. The air-unit copilot seems to be having a hard time picking out the streets, calling them out with some delay. He must be looking at a map that has small print. He finally misses one.

"They're now southbound, unknown side street," says the air unit.

Fortunately, I have been watching the street signs as we pass. "We're southbound Preuss from Eighteenth Street," I cut in, happy for my contribution.

The bike now hits some dips in the roadway, almost throwing the rider, as if he were in a rodeo. He begins to squirm on the bike and is again about to lose it. He regains control, just in time to make a left at the T-intersection at Cadillac Avenue. Richards hits the turn perfectly at its apex, and we smoothly slide around the corner barely losing any speed.

After his second near spill, the motorcyclist has lost total confidence and is not driving fast now. Richards gets right up on his tail. I then look in the rearview mirror and see no other units behind us. We have been the only ones to keep up this mad ride!

Suddenly, he veers over to the curb, letting the bike go as he runs on foot. The bike travels forward, crashing into the rear of a parked Volvo. He takes off between two houses, knocking over some garbage cans in his frantic dash. He hits a chain-link fence as I run up behind him. I draw my gun.

"Don't *move!*" I shout. My gun is pointed center mass. He doesn't even look at me, though. He just keeps on climbing the fence, which surprises me. After all, I'm a police officer, pointing a gun at him. He should do what I say, right?

Wrong.

"Dunn!" yells Richards. "He's getting away!"

Richards is off somewhere behind me. I holster my gun, scaling the fence right on his heels. He runs through the backyard to another fence. Once again, I draw my gun.

"Stop," I shout, "or I'll shoot!"

He hits the fence. No hesitation. I holster my gun and hit the fence belly high, flipping over it. I do not hear Richards anymore, and assume she didn't make the fence. But I don't care. I am getting frustrated, which is the beginning of anger.

As I get over the fence, the suspect has already hit the next one. I have fallen too far behind by drawing my gun twice. I decide to cut him off. I run to the back of the yard, scaling the rear wall. I drop into an alley. I can hear him in a backyard two houses away. I run down the alley. With no more fences to climb, I am soon parallel to the yard he is in. Suddenly, his head pops up at the rear fence. He is out of breath. He looks over his shoulder, thinking I am still in the yards behind him. His hands grab the top of the fence, and he pulls himself up. Then he sees me advancing through the alley toward him, and freezes. I grab him with my left hand, trying to pull him over the fence to my side. But the majority of his weight is on the other side of the fence, so all I can do is hold him at the fence. He grabs my hand, and I see his mouth open. "Don't you bite me!" is all I can say, but he's trying to. I had no time to take my baton when I exited the car, but I now find I have put my flashlight, which is metal and sixteen inches long, in my rear sap pocket. I remove it. His goggled eyes become saucers. I draw back to belt him with it.

"No!" he screams.

Like a duck shot in a penny arcade, he flips sideways back over the wall, narrowly avoiding the blow. I hear a resounding thud as he lands squarely on his back. I again draw my gun. I point it at him through the fence.

"Stop!" I say, checking my hand for bite marks. There are none. But there is a slick of slobber. *Ugh!* And again, he ignores me. And now I am angry!

Quickly, he spider crawls backward away from me. No thought for the gun; no thought that I could have an accidental discharge

even. There was a time in the state of California that I could have
shot him as a fleeing felon. But that was decades ago. As it stands
now, I am the one who would do time for the felony. For all I know,
this guy could be running from us because he is wanted for homicide. But I can only act on what I know: that being that he blew a
traffic light and has failed to yield to us.

The suspect now gets up. I watch him as he runs between the
houses, but I don't try to follow. I am tired, and I now realize we
have been in the air unit's spotlight. I let *them* follow him. I turn
up my rover and hear the air unit directing other officers to my bad
guy. Their spotlight stops moving in the front yard of the house I
am behind. They soon broadcast that he is in custody.

A police vehicle now pulls into the alley with me, screeching to
a halt. "You OK?" asks a burly white P-III from the unit. He has a
rail-thin P-II with him.

"Yeah," I reply. "Can you give me a ride?" I'm too tired to
climb any more fences.

"Hop in," he says.

I get in. I know I'll soon get to tell my first war story, and I wait
for the questions: What happened? What did he do? But these two
guys do not ask. They just sit there like nothing has happened. They
don't even speak. Then I feel a breeze between my legs, and look
down to see a tremendous rip in my pants. *Great.* Not only do I
not get to tell a war story, but I am looking down at a ten-dollar
sewing job. Oh, well.

They drop me off where the chase ended, where I see the suspect
already being driven off to the station in another unit. He no longer
wears his helmet, goggles, and scarf, which rest on the trunk of a
patrol car like a trophy. There is a tangle of units, our scurry across
three divisions bringing an army of black-and-whites. There is even
a news crew already on the scene taking pictures. I walk through
the crowd of officers and neighborhood residents as they talk about
my pursuit. I begin to strut a little, a triumphant warrior. Then I
spot Richards, who is talking with Sergeant Reese. I catch her eye
to let her know I am back, and am OK. She seems uninterested. I
look at her uniform, then at mine. I have dirt streaks and plant
shavings to go with my uniform tear; she has nice, clean, pressed
trousers. And she shows no signs of fatigue.

Hmmm. Aw, the heck with her, I tell myself. I look around for some other P-Is to whom I can brag, but there are none to be seen. Then I notice two citizens pointing at me, smiling. I realize my crotch rip is bigger than I first estimated, and my white Jockey shorts are saying hello to the world. Not too professional. I go and sit in the car.

The pursuit puts us into overtime—*six hours'* worth of overtime, the majority of which is spent writing. There is much paperwork to do when a suspect flees in a vehicle to evade capture. Richards writes a seven-page arrest report which includes five pages of handwritten narrative and two pages of blanks to be filled in. There is also a four-page Vehicle Pursuit Report that has to be written by a sergeant and then checked for accuracy and initialed by both Richards and me. Even before we write, we are required to redrive the entire pursuit route to determine its exact distance, which in this case, turns out to be 8.3 miles.

Our suspect is charged with evading, which carries a ten-thousand-dollar bail. When I run him on the computer for *wants,* I find that not only does he have four misdemeanor traffic warrants for failing to appear on four separate court dates, but he also has a felony warrant for assault with a deadly weapon, stemming from an incident with a neighbor during which our suspect pulled a handgun.

His total bail is over $31,200. This is par for the course with people who run from the police. More than 70 percent of those arrested after a police pursuit have some type of felony want out on them. This includes those pursuits begun over a matter as simple as an officer stopping a car for a traffic violation. Good people do not run from the police.

Our suspect is also mentally altered by a recent infusion of an alien substance into his system. Coupled with some bumps and bruises he incurred running through the dark backyards of residences on Cadillac Avenue, it is decided it would be best if he were housed at the hospital jail ward downtown. So even before we complete our reports, we put him in the car for a ride downtown. The drive gives us a chance to talk with him.

"What's going on tonight?" asks Richards. "Why the high-performance driving?"

"Oh, man," he says. His voice is slow, peaceful, as if he's been smoking too much ganja. "I could tell you were reading my brain. You knew I was wanted for that bogus gun thing I did. So I had to run."

"You risked your life because of a warrant?" I ask.

"Yeah," he says. "That, and I had just scored some shit. But I threw it and you'll never find it." He smiles about this. It's a small victory for him that we did not find the dope he threw during the chase.

"Was it a lot of shit?" I ask, using his vernacular.

"I don't know," he replies. A serious look comes over his face. "How much money do I have left?"

"Two dollars and forty-six cents," I reply, reading the amount from his money receipt.

"Oh, man," he says. A depressed look comes over his face. "It was *a lot* of shit."

It's almost midnight by the time we get the suspect to the jail ward downtown, located at the back of Parker Center, LAPD's nine-story headquarters. The outside of the ward looks like a loading dock. There is a concrete walkway elevated five feet aboveground which runs below a row of thick windows covered by steel bars. A short ramp leads from the ground to the walkway. When you walk your prisoner up the ramp, you enter through a thick, steel door after hitting a buzzer to announce your arrival.

On entering the ward, we are overwhelmed by noise. Rampart Division Vice has done a sweep of its male prostitution area. Thin men in brightly colored dresses and hot pants, about a half-dozen in all, scream and cackle in Spanish. They are not upset about their arrests. They are happy to have a chance to strut their stuff in front of their peers.

I do not understand this scene before me. Why would a man want to put on women's clothing? It's a concept that is completely foreign to me, one which seems to play both to sexual desires and the need to shock others. They are men who act out aberrant thoughts to an extreme, especially since many of them have surgically altered bodies that sport full, round breasts and flattened Adam's apples. They have created for themselves some space not between men and women, but off to the side of both. This is another group with which I will have to get used to dealing.

Not only do the Rampart Division suspects need medical examinations for AIDS-related symptoms (something that is alarmingly common among both male and female prostitutes throughout Los Angeles), but one of the prostitutes scratched one of the plainclothes officers, a burly Swede, on his arm.

"Can I get AIDS from this?" the Swede asks his partner, an older white officer with a thick beard, a round belly, and wire-rimmed glasses. The Swede is dressed in blue jeans and a white T-shirt; his partner looks like a beatnik, with a black turtleneck and a long silver neck chain.

"I don't know, man," replies the bearded partner. "Have the nurse clean it before it infects."

"I better not get AIDS," he says, shaking his head. The Swede then glares at his attacker, a thin, red-haired Latino boy who wears a tube top over protruding breasts. The boy has an effeminate figure, except his hands are too large. They throw a curve into the rest of his illusion. The officer then walks into the doctor's office, a bright room with white walls and stainless-steel tables surrounded by thick, bullet-proof glass. Almost immediately, a nurse is pouring a solution on his arm and scrubbing his scratches, giving them the same attention she would a laceration needing stitches.

It takes over an hour for all of the Rampart suspects to be seen by the doctor. When we finally get our suspect in to see the doctor, it is only a five-minute examination. First the nurse takes his temperature, his blood pressure, and then wipes off his scratches.

"You know he's under the influence of something," says Dr. Rye,* a thin, aged black man with a Nigerian accent.

"Yeah, we know," says Richards. Her reply comes with a note of finality. She does not want to talk anymore about the subject, because that might mean we would have to enter an additional charge of driving under the influence of drugs. That would be a problem for us, since Richards and I are not drug experts. Alcohol is no problem; we can both do alcohol recognition. The signs are easily recognized and take no expertise. But for a driving under the influence of drugs arrest, you need more training than either Richards or I have.

At this time, the Los Angeles district attorney's office will not file "driving under the influence of drugs" unless the suspect has been examined by a Drug Recognition Expert. As described earlier, this is an officer who has been specially trained to recognize the type of illegal potion one has consumed. There are no experts working tonight—Richards has already checked. While Richards and I could do a four-page report on driving under the influence of drugs, it would go nowhere, because even though we know he is zonked—we're not "experts."

By the time we get finished with the suspect, it is nearly three in the morning. Richards is not pleased because she hates working overtime. Back at the station, she vents some of her frustration on me. We are sitting in the report-writing room with some other officers. She asks me to number the pages of the arrest report, which I do. When I hand them back to her, she notices I missed one. This sets her off.

"You can't even number the fucking pages?" she says. "Why do I have to fucking work with boots!" She looks at the other officers. "These fucking boots," she huffs. "They're worthless, totally worthless!"

I feel like I am dealing with a spoiled child, one whose emotions ride on how many sugar cookies she's recently eaten. I begin to steam. Boot or no boot, I'm not putting up with this shit.

"Let me talk to you for a second in the hallway," I say calmly.

"Why?" she blares.

"In the hallway," I say.

She follows me out of earshot of the other officers. When I turn around to face her, her fists are balled, like she's ready to duke it out with me. I don't even acknowledge the display.

"Don't talk to me like that again," I say firmly. "If you cannot talk to me normal, let's go into the WC's office right now and change partners. Because I won't put up with that kind of bullshit."

"Oh, what? Are your feelings hurt?" she replies. "You can't take a little harsh language? You fuckin' college boys are worthless."

"Worthless," I say. "You want to talk *worthless*? *Worthless* is not following your partner over a fence when he's in foot pursuit."

This hits her like a ton of bricks. Whatever it means to her, it hurts her deeply. To me, her not making the fence wasn't a big deal. She did an outstanding job driving, especially so in light of our chasing a motorcycle, which is next to impossible for any car, even a police car, to stay with. Her driving skills were her contribution. But I have her beat by miles in the physical arena, so I stayed with him in the foot pursuit.

I am prepared now for more argument. But she simply turns around and walks off down the hallway, without saying a word. I stand there for a beat, waiting for her to return. But she disappears out the back door of the station, so I go back into the report-writing room, and finish numbering the pages.

Catania is in there with another P-III. I guess we were not totally out of earshot, because I can tell by their eyes they have heard it all.

"Don't worry, man," says Catania. "Everybody had an asshole training officer at one time or another. You just do what you did. Stand up without being insubordinate."

"Thanks" is all I say.

It is two weeks since the motorcycle pursuit, and Richards and I have had quiet nights—and I mean quiet. Not that crime rates have dropped or our workload has lessened. It's just that our patrol car has become "civil." Richards has not raised her voice to me once since that night, and she has even been rather subdued in the way she handles citizens around me. The snide remarks have all but ceased. She still dings me for mistakes I make, and they are still plentiful for me, especially since I'm completing only my third month out. But she has become more professional in the way she does it, and the rating she has written for me, that life-blood piece of paper that is the key to my continued employment and which I now hold in my hands, is not only a passing evaluation, but a fair assessment of my abilities.

Six of my classmates have left the LAPD so far, generally due to pressure from their training officers. One of my classmates here at

Southwest has received two unsatisfactory reports. I've heard that he will have to make a big improvement if he wants to keep his job. I feel sorry for him, but he does have some real problems, such as not knowing when to draw his gun. Just the other day, I heard that he and his partner stopped a vehicle possibly used in an armed robbery, and prior to exiting their car, he asked his partner if he should draw his gun. To an outsider, this might appear to be a trivial point. But in police work, where we are paid to make decisions, not knowing when to pull your gun presents a major problem.

I take the rating report Richards has signed for me in to Sergeant Fuela, who is my "Den Mother," the supervisor in charge of ensuring I am being properly trained. I hand the report to him. Sergeant Fuela is full-blooded Samoan, a bear of a man with a gentle nature. He has been aware of the rift between Richards and me but has not taken sides. Which he shouldn't, because if I can't handle a little stress from Richards, I'm going to have serious problems with other areas of this job.

"I see she passed you," he says. "I wasn't really sure she would. What did you do to piss her off so much?"

"I don't know," I reply. "We just never clicked."

"Richards is really OK," he says. "You'll find out there are some cops on this job you will just not click with. There are eight thousand four hundred of us. You could be the most easygoing guy, and *somebody* in this department will think you're a jerk."

"I guess then *I* am somebody Richards thinks is a jerk," I say.

"Maybe," he says. "But she passed you. That's all that counts. The most important thing is that you have satisfactory remarks for this period. Which means that you are now one DP closer to making probation."

DEPLOYMENT PERIOD FOUR

The first time I met Katherine* was when Jackson and I arrested her and four other girls for grand theft, auto (GTA). They had stolen a 1976 Cadillac Seville, and were cruising Adams Boulevard trying to pick up boys when they became involved in a minor traffic collision. Jackson and I stopped to render aid, and immediately noticed an absence of keys in the Cadillac ignition. Our suspicions were confirmed when one of the girls advised us: "We stole it—but we weren't gonna keep it!"

Only sixteen, Katherine is a walking paradox. On the one hand, she is an honors student at Venice High School, and twice a week attends evening classes at USC for advanced placement credit. On the other hand, she is a dedicated Rolling 20s Blood gangsterette, going so far as to change her name from *Catherine* to *Katherine* so that she would not have a letter C, or a "Crip" letter, in her name.

I am standing against a strand of yellow crime-scene tape, talking to people in the crowd that has gathered, trying to find witnesses to the shooting of a kid already at a nearby hospital. His blood stains the asphalt about forty feet behind me.

Katherine walks through the crowd with one of the other girls I had arrested her with a few weeks earlier, a large girl named Keisha.* She is also sixteen. I give them a friendly smile.

"Hi, Officer Dunn," says Katherine. She says it in that melodic voice that young girls use when they're flirting.

"Hi back at you," I reply. "What are you doing here?" This is as much a police question as it is friendly. She is a Rolling 20 Blood gang member, and we are in Rollin' 40 Crip hood.

"I'm just using the phone to call my friend," says Katherine. "What happened?"

"Some guy got shot," I say. "I think he's a Forty. You been here long?"

"No," she says. "We just got here. What happened?"

"Two guys got shot," I reply. "Beyond that, I don't really know," and I add in a loud voice, "but anyone who saw what happened should call Southwest Station front desk—please."

I smile when I say it, and get a few smiles back, along with a few men in the crowd who say, "Damn, right!" or "People should call the muthafuckin' po-leece."

"Where are they?" asks Katherine. She sees the blood. "Are they dead?"

When I first arrived, the paramedics were working on the victims. One of them had a minor wound, but the other took one in the chest. He still had some life in him; some—but I don't think very much, because they were using an artificial breathing device on him, a mask with a squeeze ball attached to it. I have found it to be a kiss of death. Not one victim that I've seen that device used on has lived. That's not because of its ineffectiveness, but because it appears to be a last resort. The paramedics had been using it on him when they quickly loaded him into the ambulance and sped off.

"He doesn't look good," I say.

A few feet from me, an elderly male Hispanic lifts up the police tape and begins to walk through in an attempt to go to the market.

"Hey, yo," I yell at him. He stops, an electric jolt running through his body as he sees me. "What are you doing?"

But he hardly speaks a word of English, and just stands there like a deer frozen by a pair of car headlights.

"Dumb fucking Mescans," yells a black man, a hype, in the crowd.

"No es good," I say. *"Muevese para atras,"* I pidgin Spanish him, telling him to move back. He seems to understand.

"Am sorry," he says as he goes back under the line.

"People can be dumb muthafuckas," says Keisha.

"Watch your mouth," says Katherine, embarrassed that Keisha would swear in front of me. I smile at this.

"So, you staying out of trouble?" I ask. I'm tired of asking people about this almost sure kill, and am glad that I have someone here with whom to talk about something other than murder.

"Yes," replies Katherine. "I've been real good. No more G-rides for me," she says. "I've been staying home at night watching television. My mom won't let me out past six."

"And school?" I add.

"She been gettin' good grades," chimes in Keisha.

"All A's and B's," says Katherine. "Even in my AP [advanced placement] courses. Especially in history. I had a one hundred percent on my last test. Didn't miss one."

"Great," I say.

"And she don't hardly study or nothin'," chimes in Keisha proudly.

"What about you, Keisha?" I ask.

"I been gettin' C's," she says. "I don't like to study like Katherine does. But I'm pretty good at track. I may be able to go to college."

"You should," I say. "It's hard to make it in this world without that sheepskin."

"Just as long as I stay out of trouble," she adds.

"You're not still hanging with the gangsters?" I do not say who she hangs with, the crowd probably having more than a few Crips in it.

"Well, yeah," Keisha replies. "There really isn't anybody else to hang out with in my neighborhood."

"You think that's best?" I ask.

"They don't do any crimes when we're around," says Katherine defensively. And with her defensive voice, her grammar begins to slip into gangsterspeak. "We just kick it with 'em. We don't steal cars, or sell no dope with 'em. We don't get in no trouble with 'em. We peacin'," she says, meaning they're not looking for trouble. "They know what I'm about, they know what Keisha is about, and they respect that. If they wanta go to jail, that's on them. But not when I'm around."

"If we didn't hang with 'em, we wouldn't have no friends," adds Keisha. "We've been knowin' 'em since we were all babies."

I think for a moment. In the neighborhood where she lives, there probably are few kids who are not in gangs. They may be right: If they did not hang with the gangsters, they would not have any friends. And these are sixteen-year-old girls. They need friends, lots of them, even if they're bad ones.

"Well, just remember, you both got a future," I say. "You're your own people, and you have to make your own way. Don't let somebody else drag you down. Know what I'm saying?"

"I'm always careful," says Katherine. "Only way to stay alive in this world is to be careful."

I now notice Keisha is holding something. It's a small, sniffling bundle of short, brown fur that will someday be a large pit bull. Katherine runs her fingers along its back.

"Who is this?" I ask.

"This is my dog," says Katherine. "His name is Li'l Peaches."

I recognize the name, as it's used by a member of the Rolling 20s. Peaches* is a pumped-up ex-con who sells drugs on Jefferson Boulevard. He has an extremely violent record, and is as close to a ghetto star as anybody who claims membership as a Rolling 20 Blood.

"You didn't name it after who I think you named it after?" I ask.

Katherine studies my face. I then realize she did. Naming dogs after your favorite gang member is common in the South End. I'm sure there are more than a few pit bulls named Tookie running the streets.

"He ain't so bad once you get to know him," she says. "He really is a cute man."

"He's her boyfriend," says Keisha.

"He ain't really my boyfriend," she says, embarrassed. "We just friends."

I get the feeling Katherine may be close to Peaches. Real close. The thought sickens me. She is young and bright, with a definite future. Peaches is a cold-blooded ghetto star, not to mention she is just sixteen years old and he must be near thirty. But I don't say anything, more because I can't think of anything other than *Are you stupid, or what?* But I don't think that would be constructive, especially since my relationship with Katherine has been limited to two chance encounters. So I just scratch the puppy's ears.

"He's a purebred," says Katherine. "He cost my mom a hundred dollars. My friend let me pick first from the litter, and he was the biggest."

"He gonna be a killa," adds Keisha.

"No doubt," I reply.

My partner on this crime scene is a female P-III named Debbie Cole,* a veteran officer who wears pearl-rimmed glasses and two hash marks on her sleeve. She still carries the four-inch .38 revolver that was standard issue when she was a recruit in the Academy, refusing to spend the four hundred dollars it would cost to upgrade to the now acceptable, and far superior, 9mm semiautomatic handgun current Academy classes are issued. Prior to 1989, officers were issued .38 revolvers. When the LAPD switched to 9mm handguns, it did not offer officers with revolvers new guns. Those officers have to buy their own weapon if they want a 9mm, even though the LAPD has decided that the 9mm is a superior weapon. Cole calls to me from the other end of the crime scene, motioning for me to respond to her location.

"I gotta go," I say to the girls.

"Bye, Officer Dunn," they chime, making me smile.

I walk over to Cole. She is a physical fitness guru like Jackson. I have worked with her for less than an hour and we have already been to Mikoshi's for a bowl of rice. It was not five minutes later that we received this call, a drive-by shooting in the parking lot of The Boys Market at Hoover and Vernon avenues.

"You get the scoop on what happened yet?" asks Cole.

"Some of it," I reply. Before Katherine and Keisha arrived, two women who were exiting the market when the shooting occurred gave me their names and told me what they saw.

"The wits I've talked to say they saw a male black in his teens shooting at our victims and some of their friends as they ran through the market parking lot. But my witnesses were too far away to identify the suspect, and they don't know where he came from, and they didn't hear any gangster talk."

"Well," says Cole, "I just spoke with a Rollin' Forty who was a nonhit victim. He says that he was sitting at the bus bench at the corner with his homies when a black Ford Mustang with two Five Deuce Hoover Crips in the front, and their girlfriends in the back, stops for the light. They all throw gang signs and *muthafucks* at each other, and the driver of the Mustang gets out of the car and opens fire with a revolver. He chased the Forties across the parking lot, shooting at them, all the way to the doors of the market, where he ran out of bullets. He then ran back to the Mustang. The car, which was now being driven by one of the females, took off south on Hoover."

I think about this. It's a miracle no citizens were hit, because the parking lot and store must have been filled with shoppers. But that's typical of gangsters; they don't care who gets in the way when they shoot.

"Homie knows the shooter by name," says Cole, referring to the 40. "They call him 'Teacher.' "

Moe Landrum and Don Williams now arrive. They are Southwest Division's drive-by shooting team, which means they are the busiest officers in the division. Both are in their early thirties. Although P-IIIs, they do not wear field uniforms. One of the luxuries of their assignment is that they get to pick their style of dress, which in this case means designer suits covered by long, black trenchcoats. They look like they just stepped out of an Italian fashion magazine. The Euro-cop look. Landrum walks up to Cole.

"Moe, you know a Five Deuce Hoover named Teacher?" she asks.

"Yeah," says Landrum. "He did this?"

"According to one of our victims," says Cole. "I believe he used a revolver."

"He's just out of CYA," says Landrum, referring to the California Youth Authority, a sort of state prison for youthful offenders. Landrum seems annoyed. "He's only been out but three months. And he was in for the same damn thing—one-eighty-seven drive-by."

Williams comes over and smiles a hello to Cole.

"Wits say Teacher did this," says Landrum.

"No shit," says Williams. He shakes his head somewhat in disbelief. "He's the guy on probation for murder."

"Probation for murder?" exclaims Cole.

"Yeah," says Landrum. "We just got the report to keep an eye on him. He's on probation for murder."

This is a rather startling development. For somebody to be

placed on probation for *murder,* this would mean that he not only committed a murder while a juvenile, but was also released from custody while still a juvenile—which means he spent very little time in custody for taking a life.

"That's right," says Landrum. "He was young, maybe twelve or thirteen, when he did the killing. A drive-by, just like this. Just a pooh-butt making a rep."

I watch as the two P-IIIs examine the scene, looking for clues and making notes. They talk with a group of witnesses, then decide that two of them need to go to the station for further interviewing. We transport them to Southwest.

At the station, Landrum runs Teacher. We find out something comforting: Teacher's eighteenth birthday was two weeks ago.

"Homie may not even know he's eighteen," says Williams. "They don't have birthday parties in lockup, so he may still think he's a juvenile."

"Hopefully, this time they'll keep his ass in prison," says Landrum.

CRUISERS

Cruise Night on Crenshaw Boulevard. A night when youths from all over the city congregate to show off their cars and find romance. How do I dread it? Let me count the ways.

One, there is the traffic, which runs bumper-to-bumper on Crenshaw Boulevard all the way from Vernon Avenue on the south to Adams Boulevard on the north. It is gridlock at its thickest, making Crenshaw impassable, greatly reducing our response time.

Two, there is the noise, lots of it; a cacophony of sounds, including the deep thud of blown-out stereo systems and the thick crackle of modified mufflers. But the mechanical sounds are overshadowed by those coming from the humans who flock to the area. Teenage boys shouting introductions, teenage girls squealing in reply; the prattle echoes up and down the boulevard like mating calls in an aviary. It can wear on one's nerves if one has been out of high school for any appreciable amount of time.

Three, the last reason (but also the worst) is that Cruise Night falls on a Sunday, which means we run a maximum deployment.

That means only the most senior officers get the day off for as long as Cruise Night lasts—which is all spring and summer. And I am far from being a senior officer. So I don't like Cruise Night.

"This looks like a good time," says Cole. "If I were still in school, I'd be here every night checkin' out the boys."

Cole is divorced, and thirty-six. With almond-colored skin and exotic dark eyes hidden behind thin glasses, she is one of those women who downplay their looks. She wears almost no makeup, not that she needs it. She looks as if she has just stepped off of the beach of a Caribbean island. But she has no Caribbean accent; hers is the sharp tongue of a South Central project girl.

"Look at those boys," she says, pointing at a carload of athletes in their lettermen's jackets. "They are too cute."

We are parked on a side street off Crenshaw, watching the slow parade of cars as if it were a lava flow. A mass of humanity, hormone-charged teenagers are everywhere. They drive past—four, five, and six deep. The boys desperately look from female to female, hoping to receive some sign of interest. And the girls alternate between flirtation and indifference.

I feel as if I am watching a contemporary *American Graffiti*.

But there is a twist: the Crip and Blood gangsters. They infest the crowd like bugs in a flour bin. They are noticeable. Their dress tends to be darker; their attitudes colder. They seem more interested in intimidating the other males than in flirting with the girls. As if on cue, I hear the deep growl of dual carbs, and I see the kangaroo hop of hydraulic lifts.

"There's someone looking for trouble," Cole says, nodding at the passing car, a low-slung blue Chevrolet Monte Carlo with two thin, dressed-down Crips in it.

"No doubt," I say. The passenger is wearing a blue bandanna, a proclamation of his gang affiliation.

"They are a one-eighty-seven looking to happen," she says.

"You want to stop them?" I ask. Cole is driving.

"No," she says. "They come here dressed like that, they probably ain't packin'. Probably got someone nearby watchin' their backs."

When I was growing up in the San Fernando Valley, we had "Drag Night" on Van Nuys Boulevard. Every Wednesday, high-schoolers from all over the valley would congregate on "The Boulevard" to flirt and flex. There were real hot rods back then: GTOs, Barricudas, Corvettes, Chevys with 427s, and Pontiacs with 455s—all tricked out and sparkling, racing from every stoplight. Carloads of girls and guys hanging out windows cooing with each other. It was fun, and the crowd was not so dangerous. I even recall some underage kids being dropped off by their parents!

But those days are long gone for Los Angeles.

Cruise Night in any part of town attracts gangsters. When they are around, you are taking your life in your hands. Cruise Night on Crenshaw has been the scene of numerous shootings and homicides. LAPD has been forced to form a ten-man "Cruise Night detail" assigned specifically to patrol the one-mile strip on Crenshaw Boulevard north of Leimert Park.

"Here we go," says Cole, nodding to a jet-black early 1960s Chevy Impala with bright Dayton rims and new, mirror-chromed bumpers. Inside are OG—"original gangsters"—four deep, angry-looking OG. Each one's whole persona conveys aggression and ego. They have on heavy black sunglasses that hide their eyes. Their heads are shaved, their upper bodies shirtless to reveal prison-pumped arms, and their faces are blank. No expression at all. They are here simply because they get off on intimidation.

The front passenger rests a beefy bicep, at least nineteen inches around, out the window. He gives it a quick flex as he passes us, then he reaches up and tips his sunglasses down as he turns to look at us. His eyes are intense, stone cold; mouth, in a sneer—what the gangsters call a "mad dog" look. It is a lion's roar of disrespect intended for me and my partner.

"You see that?" asks Cole quietly, putting the car into gear.

"That is one bold man," I say.

"I think you're right," says Cole. "You see the registration? That's our PC to stop," she says, referring to probable cause.

"Uh-huh," I reply.

I look at the license plate for the black Impala. The registration is three months overdue. I plug it into the MDT to check for warrants.

"Let's get another unit before we stop them," says Cole, implying I should call for one over the radio.

Cole signals to move in behind the Impala. There is a blue Seville in the lane behind them that at first will not let her in. There are two boys in the vehicle, both wearing baseball caps. I look hard at the driver, who is all of sixteen, or maybe even younger. It strikes me that he may be too young to drive, and I think for a moment that he may be the better traffic stop. I almost say something to Cole, but the driver lets us in behind the Impala, and I forget about the blue Seville.

The radio is jumping, and I wait for some clear air before I make my request. I watch the OG as we follow. Their bald heads look like four pieces of stone. They do not move. Even the driver just looks straight ahead, not even turning to check traffic.

Kids on the sidewalk notice as we slowly follow the Impala in thick traffic. We get a few *whoops* of harassment, a sound meant to imitate our siren. A young gangster from a rival set sees us behind the OG, and begins to laugh in a loud, exaggerated fashion. He is thin, wears a purple sweater, and stands on the sidewalk near a group of nervous youngsters.

"Get them muthafuckas!" he yells boldly. Then he flips his gang sign to the four cons, lips pursed in anger. He is showing off for everyone to see. The front passenger with the muscular arms slowly swivels his head toward his enemy. His face doesn't change. The youngster in the purple sweater then gives the OG a "mad dog."

"There are some crazy fools out tonight," laughs Cole. "Everybody has their dogs out tonight."

The youngster then defiantly flips his gang sign again. You know he wouldn't do it if we were not here. The front passenger points his index finger at the rival as if it were a gun. His thumb drops an imaginery hammer.

"Look closely at that boy on the sidewalk," says Cole. "He's another one-eighty-seven if these OG find him later."

I have the mike in my hand. I have not had a chance to request another unit. Officers are tying up the air with their requests.

"Damn, it's busy tonight," says Cole. "And damn, I need some food."

"You wanna eat, or you wanna jam these guys?" I ask. It doesn't matter to me. The boulevard is always busy. If we let these OG go, something of equal interest, or greater, will present itself. All we have so far is a mad dog, and an expired registration. I don't think either of us is really taking the mad dog to heart, and an expired registration is not high on either of our priority lists. But I think we're both curious as to what kind of person would mad dog us like that.

"Jam these guys," she says, "then we'll eat."

After the air clears, I make the request. Because of the number of units assigned to the boulevard, we have three extra units behind us before a minute can click away. This is good, because our OG in the Impala are big guys.

We get them out on the sidewalk. I'm glad we received the backing response that we did, because all of our gangsters outweigh me by thirty pounds, a very in-shape thirty pounds built by prison iron. They are old for gangsters, in their mid-twenties, which is unusual, because there is a noticeable lack of gangsters of their age in South Central. By that age, gangsters are usually dead, in jail, or doing rap videos.

We stand them in a line to search them. They calmly and quietly comply. They understand and accept the routine, having been jammed before, jams which may have led to some of their prison time. After asking them, we find out that they all claim Rollin' 60s Crip affiliation.

Cole is standing next to me when I finish searching the front passenger, who goes by the moniker "Dum-Dum,"* which sounds appropriate.

"What's with the look, my brother?" she asks.

"What are you talking about?" replies Dum-Dum, playing dumb.

"That's OK, if you don't want to stand up like a man, that's OK," she continues indifferently. This strikes a chord in him, especially since he's in front of three serious homeboys.

"I'll look at the muthafuckin' po-leece anyway I want," he says.

"That's cool," says Cole, looking at Dum-Dum sourly.

With Dum-Dum are Bopeep,* who is the driver, and Precious* and Cush.* Some real manly names here. I have noticed that the bigger the gangster, the more silly the nickname. Skinny little gangsters prefer nicknames like Capone or Scarface, tough names taken from gangster films. But the big gangsters get names like the ones above, as if they took their names from episodes of *Sesame Street*.

Cole turns to Bopeep. "Let me see your driver's license," she says.

Bopeep slowly removes his driver's license from his wallet and gives it to Cole.

"I still have to get a smog certificate for the car before they'll let me register it," he says in a quiet tone. "And I ain't got the money now. I been out of work three months, and I got two babies at home."

"If you got two babies at home, how come you're not there now takin' care of them with your woman?"

" 'Cause my homie just out of jail, and he wanted to check out the boulevard," he replies, nodding toward Dum-Dum. Cole looks at Dum-Dum, who is no longer giving any attitude. But then we do have eight police officers here, and others keep cruising by after hearing our request.

"You know what capital improvements are?" Cole asks. Bopeep looks at her oddly.

"No," he replies.

"When you cherry out your car the way you have, putting those thousand-dollar-apiece rims on it, and the expensive paint job, and chroming out the bumpers the way you have, it adds a lot to your car's value," she says. "This car would probably appraise at over fifteen grand now, don't you think?"

"Maybe," he replies suspiciously.

"You know you can get a ticket for not informing the DMV of the added value to your car," she says. "Which means your car will have to be reappraised, and your registration fees adjusted to the higher value of your car."

"What do you mean?" he asks.

"It means you will have to pay registration fees on a fifteen-thousand-dollar luxury car as opposed to the fees you pay on a beat-up old Chevy," she says.

It finally hits Bopeep. Cole is talking about a rise in registration fees to almost ten times what he is paying now.

"Oh, fuck, man," he says. "That's so fucked up!"

He starts cursing under his breath, looking at her hard.

"You can thank your friend over there with the arm twitch," she says, nodding to Dum-Dum, who looks at me dumbly, not comprehending, but seeing that Bopeep is visibly upset.

I turn away from Bopeep, who is now pleading with my partner to get out of the ticket. In the background I hear him say, "But I bought the rims cheap off some Mexican, and I painted the car myself . . ." But I am looking across the street. The blue Seville with the two youngsters in it is parked in a driveway. They are watching us intently. When the driver sees that I'm giving them a long look, he abruptly starts the Seville and pulls out into traffic away from us. I think for a moment of sending one of the extra units we have with us after them, but I am more comfortable with keeping these guys here, especially with the driver being as agitated as he is. So I watch the Seville turn at the next corner and disappear.

Cole finishes writing the ticket, then calls Bopeep over. He is fuming, but he does not curse her or show disrespect. He simply walks over.

"I've cited you for the expired registration," she says, referring to what amounts to a "fix-it" ticket. And that's all. He looks at the ticket for a moment.

"You didn't cite me for that improvements thing?" he asks.

"No," she replies. "I never intended to. Too expensive. I just wanted to give you and your man there some stress for the disrespect."

Bopeep lets out a deep breath as he puts his hand to his chest, a smile on his face.

"Thanks," he says quietly, then signs the ticket. Moments later, the gangsters drive off.

"I could have written him a fuck-y'all ticket," says Cole when we get back in the car. "I could have done him for a moving violation, too, cause with all this traffic, he was following too closely, which is one hell of a mover. But that's not what it's about. Yeah, sometimes you might write one when someone needs their attitude adjusted. Like when they just don't understand how badly they've messed up, or they're just being a stone asshole. But some of these tickets are too damn expensive. And people here don't have no damn money. Even though I gave him a fix-it ticket, it's still gonna cost him ten dollars to have DMV inspect it. And that's after he gets his car in shape to pass a smog, which will cost him who knows how much. And he probably ain't got a job. So even though his homie is being a fool, you have to be fair. You have to use your common sense. And there ain't nothing wrong with letting somebody think they're gonna get fucked up. Mess with their minds a little. Just as long as you're fair in the end."

Cole leans on the steering wheel and continues. "That's why I did what I did. You know they're up to no good. And they're messin' with us. But we still got to be fair. Even when *they* aren't." She turns and looks at me.

"I have a friend who works for an insurance company. I wanted to check rates, see how South Central rated with the rest of the county. So I asked him for some different quotes. To insure my car in Pasadena," she says, referring to a city about twenty miles north of Los Angeles, "his company would quote a price of about eight hundred and fifty bucks a year.

"To insure it in Hollywood," she continues, Hollywood being within the city limits of Los Angeles and a moderate crime area, "it would run about twelve hundred a year. But once you get south of the Santa Monica Freeway in Los Angeles, most of the quotes run two thousand to twenty-five hundred per year! There are even zip codes around the Imperial Courts housing projects which would run near four thousand per year! Once I heard that, I almost completely quit writing tickets. A ticket in the South End can have a dramatic impact on your life. I hope you'll be wise in what you write. 'Cause you can completely mess somebody up with a ticket down here— much more than you can in other parts of town."

Later, Cole and I are grabbing a quick burger in the parking lot of a fast-food joint, using our black-and-white for a picnic table. We have a big pile of fries sitting in a broken paper bag, which Cole has smeared with ketchup. Because of Cruise Night, our conversation has turned to high school days. Cole tells me that she was raised in South Central, having graduated from a high school not far from the Imperial Courts housing projects.

"We're gonna have our twenty-year reunion soon," she says. "I don't think it's gonna be all that much fun. So many of my classmates are dead."

"Really?" I reply. "Just how many are we talking?"

"Probably a hundred between the gangs, drugs, and normal stuff," she says.

"A hundred?" I ask.

"A hundred," she confirms matter-of-factly. "Out of a graduating class of about eight hundred. But a lot of people are in prison, so it's hard to tell who died and who got locked up."

"A hundred dead from your high school," I say. "I can maybe count on both hands all of the people I have known my *entire life* who have died!"

"Yeah, but where you grew up people were not killing each other the way they do here," says Cole. "Half the people in my community are at war. The other half are in the way."

Although I work in the South End, I still go home to the suburbs. Where I live, I don't worry about bullets coming through the walls at night.

"Were you stressed growing up?" I ask.

"No, not really," she says, not giving it a thought. "I guess when you grow up in projects, the projects are all you know. I knew my neighbors, including the gang-bangers, and nobody bothered me. As long as I didn't walk in a strange hood, I was all right. But then, like most people in the projects, I never had the money to travel very far. And when I say travel, I mean like bus fare across town. So I didn't really know any other life.

"I'm a counselor in this women's support group," she says. "We help young, single mothers. You know, girls who get pregnant by fucked-up men who don't hang around. I was in that position once, but that's another story. Anyway, I go down to the projects now to talk with the girls, try and help them out. I try to be a role model for them. Just a week ago, I put three of the girls in my car to do some shopping in Torrance. Now, Torrance is not that far from the projects, maybe five miles. But only one of the girls had been to Torrance. It blew my mind. Then I took them to the beach. None of them had ever been to a beach before! Can you believe it? Three girls, all of them over seventeen, living in Los Angeles, and not one of them has ever been to the beach."

She has a big smile on her face as she remembers this.

"They went crazy," she says. "First they kicked off their shoes and ran through the sand. We were dressed for shopping, not for the beach. Still, they ran all over the place. I don't think they had ever seen such a wide-open space. Then one, Darleen,* goes down to the water and sticks her big toe in it. She starts fussing that it's so cold. So one of the other girls sneaks up behind her and kicks water all over her backside. We all started laughing and splashing water on each other. We got soaked. The people out sunbathing must have thought we were crazy, these four black project girls splashing water all over each other, laughing our heads off."

The fries are gone now. Cole grabs the paper bag and scrunches it into a ball.

"Darleen is still in high school," says Cole. "I asked her what she wants to do with her life. She tells me, 'I don't know.' So I push. I mean, there has got to be something, you know? What kind of job you want? I asked her. She says, 'Job? I can't do no work. I don't know how to do nothin'.' And she's serious. She has no skills—no real thought to ever get any. There is no college in her future. And I am telling you, she is a good kid with a good heart. Ain't no gang-banger. But she doesn't know any better. She says to me, 'I just want to have a place with my kids next to my mother's in the projects.' Which blows my mind. All she wants, all she knows, is to have a few kids and live close to her mother in the projects. Ain't nothing about having a man and a normal family. There is no thinking about moving out of the projects. She just wants what she knows. Her own place and a few kids to keep her busy."

She shakes her head.

"It's sad," she says. "But no one cares about the good kids in the projects. And there are many with good, strong hearts. But unless you are a gang member, no one wants to hear you talk. At least if you're a gangster someone may try to put you in a rap video, or give you a government check to be in on some gang truce. But the good kids, they don't get shit. It's like we reward people for being bad."

An hour later, Cole and I respond to a shooting call, this one on Exposition Boulevard, just across the railroad tracks from Dorsey High School. As we pull up to the residence, we see a blue Pontiac parked in the driveway. The passenger side of the vehicle is peppered with bullet holes, the passenger window and front windshield are blown out. Two males in their late teens stand next to the car, examining it.

When we stop, they turn and see us. They watch us cautiously as we exit our patrol car. We do the same. We don't know what we have here yet.

"What's up?" says Cole.

"We got shot at," says one of them. He is tall and thin, nicely dressed, as though he has just come from a party.

"Why you gettin' shot at?" asks Cole.

"I don't know," he says. "We don't gang-bang."

"You don't gang-bang?" says Cole. She looks at the other guy. "Where you from?"

Cole's not asking him his place of birth. She's asking him for his gang affiliation.

"I'm not from anywhere," he replies. "I don't gang-bang, either."

I look them over. Real *GQ*. One has on a black Italian dress shirt; the other, an expensive purple cashmere sweater. They do not emit the gangster attitude; they are clean-cut and athletic. But I have already learned that you cannot believe what anyone says. You have to take as much information in on your own as you can, then sort out the bullshit from the truth. I take in the "we don't gang-bang" information, and put it on hold, needing more information to figure out if it is truth or bullshit.

"Damn, man," says Cole. "They really shot up your ride." As she says it, she appears to be checking the windshield. By the way she tilts her head, I know she is looking inside it to see if there is a gun on the floorboards.

The front door to the residence opens. A distraught woman in her forties exits the house. "That's my son Brian," she says. It comes out like a plea not to hurt him. "He lives here. This is his friend Ricky."

"OK," says Cole, "I understand that, so be calm."

She turns back to Brian.

"What happened?" asks Cole.

"I go to college, man," says Brian. He seems ashamed to have been involved in this. "We were just driving home on Crenshaw from my friend's, when these two gang-bangers pull up next to us. One of them says, 'What's up, blood?' I don't want any trouble, so I just keep looking ahead. We drive a little farther, and they pull up on Ricky's side." He points to the more muscular youth who stands next to him. "Next thing I know," he continues, "Ricky's yelling, 'He's got a gun, he's got a gun,' and *bam, bam, bam*—he was just shooting for no reason," says Brian. "We didn't give him any reason. They were just lookin' for somebody to shoot."

"Where'd this happen?" asks Cole.

"Crenshaw and Thirty-ninth," says Brian.

"How long ago?"

"Ten minutes."

"What kind of car was it?"

"It was a blue Cadillac."

"A Seville," says Ricky. "Late seventies."

I immediately think of the youngsters I saw hovering around the OG. They were probably the OG's backup, and had gone looking for the kid in the purple sweater who disrespected them. Problem is, this isn't their man. Ricky wears the purple sweater, and he is definitely not the kid I saw on the sidewalk.

"You get a license number?" I ask.

"Nah, man," says Ricky. "I was too busy ducking."

We put out a crime broadcast, although I am sure that the blue Seville is already buried in some garage in the Rollin' 60s' hood. Then we examine the car. It is a miracle that neither youth was hit. There are four bullet holes along the passenger door and the front fender. One of them went through, burying itself into the side of the passenger seat, and both the passenger-side window and front windshield have taken a round.

Cole talks to the two victims while I scratch out a report.

"I know you saw the bullet holes when you drove up and thought, Oh, boy, two black gangsters," says Brian to me. "But that isn't what it's like." He looks at me as if he's trying to teach this white cop that not all black males are in gangs. But *I* already know that. There is no racism here. I have learned that when there are bullet holes in things, anybody nearby can be a suspect. And *he* has to learn that is how a police officer has to think.

"That's how we gotta walk up on you," says Cole cutting in. "We don't know what's up. Even though you're dressed nice, that doesn't mean anything. You tell me how a gangster dresses today?"

"Do they dress like this?" says Ricky, somewhat a challenge.

What do citizens think? That there is some official gangster fashion guide? Anyway, it is not just the clothing that an officer takes in when trying to determine if he is dealing with a gang member. It is clothing, it is demeanor, it is verbiage, it is location, it is time of day; all of these things are taken into account. Officers try to use common sense when appraising people they contact. Anyway, the determination of gangster status impacts very little; you cannot be arrested for being a gang member.

"They do if they want to get the fine-looking ladies," says Cole, responding to Ricky's question about wardrobe.

Brian tells us he is attending the University of California at Santa Barbara, where he's an engineering major. Ricky also attends UCSB, but his hometown is Bakersfield.

Brian's mother has been watching this scene quietly. Her face shows pain each time she looks at the bullet holes. She finally speaks as we leave.

"This is crazy!" says Brian's mother. "I sent my boy away to college to get away from the gangs. He comes home just for the weekend, and he nearly gets killed!" She looks at her son hard. "From now on," she says, "I'll come and visit you."

DEPLOYMENT PERIOD FIVE

With four deployment periods in the field behind me, I not only change partners this new DP, but I also change shifts; I have been moved from working P.M. watch to day watch.

Day watch is the shift when Los Angeles is at its most manic. The streets are clogged with traffic, the skies are covered in smog kicked up into the atmosphere after a night resting on the city's concrete, and the ears are filled with sounds. Buses, construction, sirens from emergency vehicles; it is a time when the senses can be overloaded.

Day watch is called the "poke" watch in LAPDese, because officers who work during the day are generally older ones with families, ones who like the nine-to-five schedule that goes with it. An officer can actually plan a life around this watch, which they do, setting times when they need to pick up kids after school or schedule baseball practices when they coach Little League. Because day-watch officers make schedules, they generally don't like to work overtime, which means they don't like to get involved in incidents too near end of watch. These officers can be slow moving "slowpokes," or in LAPDese, "pokes."

Los Angeles summer heat can be suffocating on day watch. When working this shift, it's easy to be reminded that the city is basically built in the middle of a desert. Anybody who has ever spent a summer in Los Angeles can attest to this. It's shorts and T-shirt weather—in uncomfortable conflict with the deep-blue wool uniforms required by the LAPD. The uniforms *are* as hot as they look. I can't help but be grateful to former LAPD chief Ed Davis, who in

1974 finally allowed *short* sleeves to be worn on duty. Before that, the only LAPD uniform was long sleeves *and* a tie. And I don't think the weather here was any cooler before 1974.

The summer heat can be especially stifling because of the bullet-proof vest some of us wear. A quarter-inch of Kevlar can really hold in the heat. We have been told to keep extra undershirts in our locker. On some hot summer days, many officers will change undershirts during watch, especially since our vehicles usually have ill-working air conditioning. Luckily, it's still springtime, and daytime temperatures are hovering in the high seventies, a low number when compared with the daily ninety-degree temperatures endured here during summer.

I am sitting in the roll-call room with Daryn Dozier and a thin P-I named Ed Hale, looking at a sheet of paper that has our new partner pairings. It is fifteen minutes before roll call and the only other person in the room is an older P-III who out of boredom is watching a soap opera on one of the televisions. Hale, Dozier, and I talk among ourselves, discussing our training officers for this deployment period.

Hale has Don Murphy. I tell him he will have an easy DP, Murph being not only an excellent teacher but a very easy grader. I wish I could say the same to Dozier. He has Richards.

"I didn't like her very much" is all I say. I hope that her attitude will be a little better with Dozier than it was with me.

My training officer is Mike Gurr, a tall white guy with a shock of dirty blond hair and pale blue eyes. During the four DPs that I've been at Southwest, Gurr has been assigned to the front desk. Usually, a stint at the front desk means an officer is either in trouble or on some sergeant's bad side, giving rise to the desk's nickname of "the penalty box." But Gurr's time in the penalty box was not the result of poor behavior; his right hand has been in a plaster cast, the result of an altercation with an *extremely* agitated domestic-violence suspect.

"He jokes around a lot," says Hale, a quiet guy who was an officer in the air force before joining the LAPD. "He's a prankster."

"Big pranks," adds Dozier "He's the guy they think put the chicken in the lieutenant's locker."

He is referring to a recent incident perpetrated against a supervisor, one who has since been transferred. This lieutenant had become very unpopular with the troops after initiating a rash of personnel complaints against officers for such "offenses" as arriving late to roll call, parking in the wrong parking space, and swearing in front of citizens. Now, I agree, these are "offenses" that officers should take care not to commit. But if committed, they can usually be resolved by a good talking-to from a supervisor—not by a personnel complaint, an action that usually means days off, with a bite out of one's paycheck.

That is rather upsetting to most officers. To register disapproval, on a Friday night, someone picked the lock on this supervisor's clothes locker and put a live chicken, along with ample birdseed and water, inside for a weekend retreat. By the time the lieutenant returned Monday morning, his clothing, to put it mildly, was rendered less than inspection quality. Not to mention, he had no small surprise when the chicken fluttered out as he opened the locker door.

The subsequent investigation has taken on Agatha Christie-esque proportions. It is rumored that Internal Affairs Division, called in to do the subsequent investigation, even attempted to fingerprint the chicken. But the "Mystery of the Cooped Chicken" has yet to be solved.

"Gurr is a funny guy," says Hale. "He'll talk about really deep stuff like why trees are green, and why we are here."

"You mean here as policemen?" I ask.

"No, here as in *here*," says Hale. "Like, why are we here on Earth as opposed to being Ice Men on Pluto? Ya know, things like that. Weird stuff."

"He also sings in the car," says Dozier. Dozier worked with Gurr his first DP.

"What?" I ask.

"He sings, man," Dozier continues. "You'll just be driving along, and he'll break out into an Elvis tune, or something."

"Really?" I say.

"Serious," says Dozier. "The dude is crazy, man."

As if on cue, I feel this presence towering behind me. I turn and look up. Mike Gurr stands there, looking past us, watching the soap opera quietly. Hale and Dozier now see him and they shrink, not sure if he has heard them, but he does not acknowledge it if he has. Then he looks down at me.

"Officer Dunn," he says, extending his hand, "I'm Officer Gurr. I will be your training officer this deployment period. But you can call me Gurr," he says, sounding out a growled *Grrrrr*. "Everyone else does."

I stand up, shake his hand. "Great, *Grrrr*," I growl. "Call me Dunn."

He looks at me and smiles, then looks over my shoulder at the television set where two soap stars are kissing. He nods to it. "Watch that closely," he says. "Police work is often like a soap opera."

"Uh, yes, sir," I reply, turning to look at the television. When I turn back to speak, Gurr is already walking up the aisle. I look at Hale and Dozier.

"He's a crazy man," says Dozier. "Nice guy, but crazy."

CODE X

Roll call today ends on an interesting note. After the reading of the lineup and run-through of the rotator, Sergeant Mike LaRue, a sharp-jawed former CRASH supervisor with a generally quiet demeanor, speaks up when Lieutenant Joe Germain, the day-watch commander asks, "Is there anything else?"

"Yeah, I got something," LaRue says dryly. I can tell it is something that he finds gravely annoying. "Last night, morning watch received a radio call of a shooting in progress at one of the motels near Adams Boulevard. Redd and his partner responded to the call and found some blood in the parking area. When they contacted the motel manager, he advised Redd that he only heard the shots, he didn't see the actual shooting, but after the shots he saw a man and woman get in a car and burn rubber out of the place. He had no further information. Redd and his partner searched the location and found some blood outside one of the rooms, but no victims or suspects."

LaRue continues, "Redd and his partner set up a small crime scene, and were about to call around to some of the nearby hospitals to see if they could find a victim, when two uniformed female officers from Wilshire Division arrived. They told Redd that they would handle the call, that it was related to an incident they had earlier. Redd didn't think anything of it—it was a busy night and we were down calls—and left the location without getting their names or unit number.

"About an hour later, I get a call from the Wilshire watch commander, asking me who was in charge of the crime scene for the *officer-involved shooting* up near Adams. I go, '*What? What officer-involved shooting?*' He says the one at the motel near Adams. The one that has put one of his officers in Westside Hospital with two gunshot wounds to the torso."

LaRue stops for a moment. He pinches his forehead between the fingers of his left hand. Obviously, this incident has caused him no small degree of stress, having some type of repercussions that are falling from far up the LAPD food chain.

"I tell him I had heard about a shooting-in-progress call near Adams, but that my unit had not informed me that it was officer involved. I advised him I would get back to him, and then I get Redd on a tac frequency. He tells me he has cleared the scene over an hour prior, and that some Wilshire coppers had handled it. So I got Wilshire back on the line, and the Wilshire WC tells me he *does not* have two females working a black-and-white!" There are a few chuckles from the back, but LaRue isn't laughing, and with a hard look from LaRue, soon neither is anyone else. "So I get Redd back on the radio. He swears up and down that two female officers from Wilshire took the call. His partner confirms it, as do Vera and his partner, who backed Redd. So I know my guys ain't lying." LaRue shifts on his feet. "We then find out that what happened was two Wilshire coppers, one male and one female, had gone to the motel after end of watch for a little *Code X,*" he says, using LAPD slang for a sexual encounter. "They had a bottle of vodka with them, and the male had gone to the motel's ice machine to get some ice. Some gangster, not knowing the male was a cop, tries to rob him for his wallet with a handgun. The copper draws his piece, and they exchange gunshots. Our copper takes two in the torso, the bad guy takes one in the leg. The copper runs back to the room, the bad guy runs off down Adams to parts unknown. When the female observes the male to have been shot, she throws him in the car and drives him to the hospital. Once he's in care, she calls someone—we don't know who—and sends them out to the crime scene to grab something. What, we don't know." The thought of what it might have been makes some officers giggle. LaRue continues.

"Her friends find Redd out there, and tell him to take off. They grab what they need, and then leave. Our crime scene, a very important crime scene, one where a cop has been shot, is now unprotected. And as would happen, the motel manager cleans the room, washing away the blood, completely destroying any evidence of the bad guy. About an hour later, the female cop decides it's time to let her watch commander know about the shooting on the border of our two divisions. And then he calls me."

The room is quiet now; no smirks or chortles. Everyone's serious.

LaRue asks, "Why did this happen? Well, one clue is that both the male and female coppers are married—but not to each other. Obviously, the female was taking time to try and think up a story, as well as have some incriminating evidence removed from the motel, probably to keep the truth from her husband. But in the meantime, we have a cop shot. And the only good evidence to finding the suspect is being washed down a drain.

"It is the stupidest incident I have heard of in all my years on the job. But then, every time I think I have enough time on the job to have seen it all, something else happens. There is a complete lack of thought here. If the female had called nine-one-one from the motel room, not only might we have caught the bad guy, but the male would have received better handling prior to his hospital arrival. Moving him and not letting him lie at the scene could have caused him an unknown amount of unnecessary damage.

"I hope that if any of you gets in a situation that is over your head, *you* will do the right thing, and take whatever lumps you have to take with some dignity—and *not* screw up things for others," LaRue concludes.

We all sit there quietly for a beat.

"Time to go to work" is all that Lieutenant Germain says.

As I rise, Mike Gurr is passing me, having walked down the aisle.

"Like I told you," he says, "police work is often like a soap opera."

*   *   *

After roll call, I am in the parking lot with our black-and-white, getting it ready. Prior to leaving the parking lot, officers have to check their vehicles to ensure they are in proper working order. First, overhead lights are tested, then the MDT. After that, the siren is activated in a short burst—generally just as another officer walks past, one hopes with a cup of hot coffee in hand.

The engine is then run and listened to for any irregularities, and brakes are checked for firmness. These mechanical checks are especially necessary. In my first four months, I have taken out of service, or "B/O'd" (for "bad working order"), at least one car each week for mechanical problems. I have even had to B/O two units in one night for improper working order. This is no reflection on the Chevrolet Caprice or Ford Crown Victoria, both of which are used by the LAPD. If anything, it's a credit to their engineering, because the LAPD is forced to work with police vehicles that have over *150,000* miles on their odometers! Those are *150,000* incredibly hard miles. We even have one unit, a Chevy Caprice, with *183,000* miles on it!

It's not hard to figure out why we work with ancient police vehicles. Our budget is pretty thin. Our city council has more important things to spend money on. What those things are, I am not sure. All I know is that we are still working with a street police force that is the same size as it was in 1972, even though the city has almost *doubled* in size since then.

After all of the above checks are completed, the interior of the car is looked into to ensure that officers on the previous shift have not forgotten anything. Drugs, as well as an assortment of other items, have been known to make their way from an arrestee's person to any crack or crevice found within the backseat area. Just last month, Dale Tanaka found a loaded .380 automatic under the front seat of one unit during his vehicle check, the weapon having been dumped without some arresting officer's knowledge.

Once everything is squared away with the vehicle, I pick up my equipment bag, which I had set on the ground next to the trunk. It is heavy, containing my riot helmet, extra shotgun and handgun ammunition, ten pairs of plastic handcuffs, and two notebooks filled with various report forms I may need during a shift. I move to put my equipment bag in the trunk on the passenger's side, which means I will be keeping books and running the MDT. If I were to put it on the driver's side, it would mean I would be driving. This is trunk etiquette. On whichever side your bag is placed, that is where you will be sitting in the black-and-white. I have yet to drive a black-and-white, so I just put my bag where I have always put it.

"Hey, hey, hey . . . what are you doing?" I hear Gurr growl as he crosses the parking lot.

"I don't know," I reply. Although I know I am putting my gear in the trunk, I decide to play dumb.

"Have you driven yet?" he asks.

"No," I reply. My first four DPs have been spent keeping books.

He grabs my bag and places it on the driver's side. Then he puts his bag in the passenger's side of the trunk. After taking his notebook from his bag, he walks over to the passenger door.

"You drive, and I'll keep the books," he says.

Yes! My first time driving a black-and-white. I cross my fingers, hoping to get into a pursuit.

"One thing," says Gurr.

"What?" I ask.

"Don't crash," he says.

People do the strangest things when they are driving in front of police officers. Emergency lane changes, four-wheel locked skids, and rapid, jerking turns are normal responses by citizens to having a patrol car pull in behind them. My favorite move is what I call the Inverse Speed Law. This is where the citizen reduces the speed of his vehicle in direct proportion to the amount of time a black-and-white has followed him. It generally takes about two minutes of following any vehicle for the driver to just pull over and stop, even if not signaled to do so.

Conscious of the public's fear of police vehicles, most officers try not to follow any one vehicle too long, unless there is a reason. They try to give people ahead of them a little extra room. People tend to hit the brakes hard when a patrol car is behind them.

With these things in mind, I'm driving northbound on Normandie, approaching Jefferson. I'm a little nervous, wanting to impress Gurr with my driving skills. Although I have had a California driver's license for over ten years, I now feel that I must prove myself, especially since driving a black-and-white is one of the criteria on which we boots are rated. So I am careful not to break any traffic laws, and I'm very alert to other vehicles. A traffic accident right now, even if not my fault, could have severe repercussions. I feel as if I were back in a high-school driver's training class. Only there are no pimply faced teenagers in the backseat popping gum and asking, "When is it my turn?"

So when a green light ahead goes yellow, I slow, even though I could easily make the light if I were to accelerate a little. The driver next to me, who has been paralleling my speed, suddenly realizes he is going to go through the yellow light without me. At the last moment, he decides this would be a bad idea, so he slams on his brakes, going into a full, four-wheel lock skid. The car behind him also probably could have made the yellow, but he now finds himself pressing his brake pedal through the floor. And finally, the car behind him—gently braking to stop for the light—now must stomp on his brakes to make a stop two full car lengths before he had planned. Smoke and dust erupt and tires screech, playing a high-pitched chorus. The third car ends up sideways, the driver wearing a complete look of bewilderment on his face.

When it's all over, I try to make eye contact with each of the three drivers. But they are fully cognizant of their actions and of me. All three look straight ahead like a group of school kids caught eyeing each other's papers during a test. Then I look over at Gurr, who is calmly leaning back in his seat, head on the headrest.

"A triple," he says. "And it's only your first day driving."

THE HARPY HILTON

"That's what we call the Harpy Hilton," says Gurr, nodding at the small house off to the driver's side. We're two doors down from it, stopped in the middle of the street. "If you're ever looking for a Harpy gangster, sooner or later, he'll show up there."

The area we are in is the northeast corner of the division, the section nearest downtown Los Angeles. The side street we are on is north of Adams and Hoover. The skyline of the city's center rises abruptly here from behind 1920s-style three-story tenements, and older weathered single-family houses that have held their ground since the turn of the century. A huddled Hispanic community populates these streets, one that is rapidly growing and expanding. Only ten years previous, this neighborhood had been 50 percent African-American. It is now 90 percent Hispanic.

I look closely at the "Harpy Hilton." Not exactly what Conrad Hilton had in mind when he started his famous chain of hotels. This is a *tiny* house, with a capital *T*. It sits wedged midblock between the rear fences of two large properties. The house looks as if it were being strangled. White in color with bulging chipped paint, it has two thin front windows squashed against the sides of a perpetually open front door. If there is a second bedroom, it must be no larger than a closet.

Harpys, the Hispanic gang dominating the area, is a branch of an older Los Angeles gang called East Side Harpys, *Harpy* being the name of a street in East Los Angeles. Some of the gangsters who run here are the children, and even the grandchildren, of original East Side Harpys. The number of Harpys in the division is relatively small, maybe a hundred. But their overall gang size, when including those in East Los Angeles, is pretty impressive, that number being somewhere near a thousand. That is more than double any of the large black gangs in our area, and could lead to a serious gang war in the future as other Harpy families move into the neighborhood. But there could be an even bigger war. Recently, some Eighteenth Street gangster families have been moving into parts of Southwest Division from East Los Angeles, mainly into the Jungle and the area of Forty-first Street and Hoover. Eighteenth Street is a gang that dates back to the 1920s and has an estimated eight- to twelve-thousand hard-core members. Eighteenth Street is also in solid with the Mexican Mafia. Many Mexican Mafia leaders are former Eighteenth Street members, so it is only a matter of time before the gang begins to seriously challenge not only the Harpys but also African-American gangs for the street drug trade in the area.

Five teenage Harpys sit on the cramped front porch of the house, nervously aware of our presence. They sport oversize white T-shirts and dark khakis that are two sizes too big for their small-boned bodies. They were laughing among themselves when we rounded the corner, but now they are silent.

"The one in the green pants is only fourteen," says Gurr, referring to a mid-size member of the group. "His name is Rainbow.*
He is one little nightmare."

Rainbow has deep black eyes, and he senses that we are talking
about him. He stares at us hard. The other gangsters seem nervous,
but not Rainbow. He has no respect for the police. In his mind, we
are an enemy, so he stares at us.

I think of what I was doing when I was fourteen years old. I know I
played Colt League baseball for the Encino Cougars. And I had four
close buddies with whom I hung out. We shot baskets after school and
went to the movies on weekends. I was at home by seven o'clock each
evening to do homework during school days. It was also at the end of
my fourteenth year that I experienced the pleasure of feeling a girl's
breasts for the first time, an act that would consistently hold me in
check until the summer after my senior year of high school. I was just a
kid going through the motions of being a kid. I had no anger inside of
me, only hope for the future. But these kids are much different from
that fourteen-year-old I once was. There is no Little League for them,
no movies, no homework. And feeling up a girl doesn't hold the mystery and excitement it did for me. I would imagine the average fourteen-year-old in this area is not a virgin. A few of them already have
children. These kids have lost their innocence. And worst of all, their
hope.

"Three months ago, I caught Rainbow in front of Oak Street
Middle School with a palm-size twenty-two auto, a six-round magazine in his pocket," says Gurr. "He had one bullet in the gun, which
is usually all you need to kill someone. But the workings were full
of lint. Thing would have blown up in his hand if he'd have fired
it. I probably saved his hand by arresting him." I look closely at
Rainbow. He has old eyes—cold, old eyes. He has seen too much
for any fourteen-year-old.

One of the Harpys is sitting on a rickety wooden railing. He
leans back, trying to look cool, and almost falls off the porch. This
causes the other four gangsters to laugh.

"You better tie homie there to the porch," yells Gurr. "Else he's
gonna break his neck!"

They laugh, their tension leaving with Gurr's joke. They begin
to talk among themselves, perceiving now that we're just talking,

not planning out how to jam them. The one who almost fell stands up and has to grab hold of his oversize pants before they fall down. They fit his body like a picnic blanket on a five-year-old—more clothes than boy.

I can't help thinking that the oversize clothing is more a defense mechanism than it is a fashion statement. All of these gangsters are rail thin, undernourished from poor eating habits and the stresses of street life. The baggy clothing they wear makes them appear larger than they are. I once saw a *National Geographic* special shot in Africa that showed tribal bush kids being told by their parents to hold their arms above their heads when confronted by hyenas. This made them appear larger, scaring and confusing the animal who refused to attack prey taller than itself.

"Who owns this house?" I ask Gurr.

"It's owned by an elderly white schoolteacher," says Gurr.

"What, he rents it to the kids?" I ask.

"No, he lives there," says Gurr. "He's just a weird old guy. He likes the gangsters. He lets the kids hang out and knock back a forty," *forty* being slang for a forty-ounce bottle of malt liquor. "He even lets them smoke dope and do their girlfriends in the bedroom. At first, we thought he was being forced to let them use the location. But one of the SLOs [senior lead officer, an officer assigned to handling ongoing community problems] talked to him. The old man told him he wanted the gangsters at his house. He loves them. Because he's some people's revolutionary party communist kind of guy, and he thinks that the gangsters are a liberation army for the poor and downtrodden. He also told the SLO that if any officers ever set foot on his property, he would sue for trespass."

Two more youngsters, dressed down, round the corner at the end of the block. They give us a quick glance before entering the house.

"He probably just likes the little girls who hang with the gangsters," says Gurr. "One of the *cholitas* told me he's always hugging on the young girls and feeling up their butts. Wouldn't surprise me if he was doing one of them."

"Wonderful," I say.

"We've had two drive-bys here in the last six months," says Gurr. "Two that have been reported, that is. There probably have been more. M/S [for La Mara Salva Trucha—a violent El Salvadoran gang] knows about this location. We get shots-fired calls up here all the time. But just the two had hits. Some day there's gonna be a blood bath here."

Rainbow is now standing in the doorway with a beer in his hand. I don't know where he got it from because I was not watching him that closely. He lifts it to us as if saying *cheers*, then takes a swig. He smiles at us and disappears into the house.

"Five years ago, we'd go in there and take that kid to the station," says Gurr. "Book him as a delinquent, and pop the old man for contributing. Now, if we enter that place, the ACLU [American Civil Liberties Union] would own our homes. Sue us for civil rights violations, even though common sense tells us this situation is not right. But common sense has been pushed aside by the letter of the law. Lawyers run everything using words printed in a book with no thought for what's really happening in any single situation. We *should* be able to shut this house down. It's a street gang hangout, and a menace to the neighborhood. People who live on both sides of it have to sleep on their floors at night for fear of being in the line of fire of a drive-by."

Gurr shakes his head. One of the Harpys waves to us. His friends laugh. Gurr then motions for me to drive on. "They're just punk gangsters anyway," he adds, more in frustration than in personal belief. "Nobody gives a shit anyways."

SLEEPY AND BLACK CROW

I run my gunsights over the car, quickly checking to see if there is an armed suspect inside. But there is no movement. I hold up a clenched fist to Officer Zedric Coleman, indicating the car is clear. "Very dead," I say.

His eyes agree with me. "I'm gonna still have the RA [rescue ambulance] respond," he advises.

I reexamine the scene before me. We're at the intersection of Vermont Avenue and Jefferson Boulevard. A dirty gold Buick Electra, stopped in the left-turn lane facing south on Vermont Avenue, is the car I have just cleared. It sits by itself, two full car lengths back from the intersection, in frozen defiance to the traffic lights before it now showing green. The engine is still running, the driver's foot jammed onto the brake, a nerve-shocked act that I am sure occurred in response to his body being riddled with bullets. I reach over the driver and put the car into park, making sure not to rub up against any of the blood or gray matter that is thrown about the interior as if some kids had a food fight. As I shift my weight, shattered auto glass from the blown-out driver's window crunches under my feet. I turn off the engine, leaving the keys in the ignition. It is noontime; students and faculty members from the nearby USC campus crowd the streets.

As I back away from the car I am greeted by the angry blare of a car horn. I turn and see a mean-faced old woman, hands tightly gripping the wheel of her red Cadillac, glaring at me, trying to drive past me in the opposite direction. She is oblivious to the situation, and must be in a hurry to go wherever she is going. Unfortunately, I am standing too close to her lane. I flatten against the Buick and motion for her to pass by.

I can hear the distant call of the rescue ambulance. I back away carefully, watching my feet so as not to kick any evidence such as shell casings. Officer Coleman, a pro lineman–size P-II whose nickname is Ballou, has been assigned to me whenever my regular training officer has a day off. He is already in our black-and-white, backing it into position to block off the street. I can also hear him request a supervisor and additional units for a crime scene as he drives. I take one last look at the Buick. It flashes through my mind that in essence, I am looking at a coffin, a Buick Electra coffin in gold. Quite the place to die. But I have other matters to attend to, so I turn away. I go and help Coleman begin to set up the crime scene.

The call came out as a shooting in progress. We were on the scene within a minute of the broadcast, patrolling a nearby neighborhood looking for truant gang members ditching school. On our arrival, the shooting was over. The victim's car sat by itself in the street; citizens driving past it in the curb lane avoiding the ravaged auto as if it were a crazy man preaching on a street corner. I could still smell the gunsmoke, a strong, bitter, sulfurous stench that poked at my nostrils. A crowd had already gathered on the sidewalk, and people were pointing. I knew there were two dead victims even before I approached. It just had that kind of a feel.

Our two victims are one "Sleepy," who sits upright in the driver's seat, and "Black Crow," who lies prone on the ground next to the open passenger door. They were both Harpy gang members from the Dead End clique, *clique* being a core subgroup of the larger gang who live in the same general area. (You get along with everyone in your gang, but you drink and party with the ones in your clique.) The Dead End faction of Harpys ravages the area west of Normandie and north of Adams, which is also Rolling 20 Blood hood.

Sleepy was a twenty-two-year-old male Hispanic, meaning he was classified as a *veterano* or a leader in the gang. He had done time in CYA for manslaughter as a juvenile, a plea bargain down from a drive-by 187. His shoulders and back are covered with gang tattoos that proclaim his loyalty to his homeboys. His left hand, the hand of cursing to gang members, has three painted dots representing the phrase *Mi vida loca,* "My crazy life," showing that he is *vato loco,* "a crazy man," meaning that he is down for his gang until the bitter end. The Dead End. Quite apropos, wouldn't you think? A hard-core gang member, he rarely held steady employment during his life. At the time of his death, he was on disability insurance for a back injury that occurred at his last job, that being a short stint as a warehouseman at a local market.

Many of the gang members I talk to who are over eighteen years of age are on disability. They get a job doing manual labor for six months, which is the minimum work time needed to obtain insurance coverage. They then come down with a bad back. They, of course, still have the strength to run from the police after doing crimes; jumping fences, dodging dogs, and wrestling with officers even though they supposedly have debilitating injuries. I guess the doctors who examine them must be doing so over the phone. Anyway, it looks like Sleepy's benefits can be canceled.

Black Crow was an oddity. Half Hispanic, half black, he could have gangstered with either Harpys or the Rolling 20 Bloods, both of whom coexist in mild tolerance of each other in his neighborhood. He chose to stand for the *barrio* instead of the *hood,* which appeared to be a smart move at the time. The Rolling 20s have been in some hellacious street wars when compared to the mild Harpys. But even the safest of roads has to be driven, and any journey can have a breakdown; now Black Crow has had a major breakdown, one that cannot be repaired. Also twenty-two, Black Crow had spent his life doing crimes and being a gangster. Often arrested but never convicted, he was currently a suspect in a drive-by shooting from a few months back. As in the majority of South Central homicides, today's victims are usually yesterday's suspects.

Our two Dead Enders were stopped in traffic next to a white foreign pickup truck loaded with eight to ten young male and female Eighteenth Street gang members, none of whom according to witnesses appeared to be much more than sixteen years old. Words were exchanged, and Black Crow, a large youth at over two hundred pounds, got out and slugged the driver. Big mistake. He sat back down in the Buick next to Sleepy just in time to be hit by a hail of bullets fired by both a male in the front passenger seat and a male who was in the bed of the truck. Stopped at the red light with vehicles in the front and back, Sleepy had nowhere to drive the car. So they just sat there and took it. Point-blank. Died in their car. When the light turned green, the white pickup drove off, leaving over twenty 9mm and 10mm shell casings littering the ground.

Other units now arrive, and we quickly get two of them to block off Vermont to eliminate the mean-old-lady factor. Then the rescue ambulance arrives and checks our victims. Sleepy has the right side of his face blown away. The RA leaves him for the coroner. Black Crow also has a head shot, but his head did not explode, so the paramedics pull him away from the car and hook him up to their equipment. The read-outs all show static lines. That's bad if you are Black Crow, because static lines are a good indication one is dead. The paramedics spend all of a minute on him before they leave him, too. Like I said, these guys are real dead. Coleman and I back off and await the detectives.

It is an odd assemblage of citizens that shows up at a crime scene. Most citizens will stop and take a look, a natural thing to do, because we are a curious species. I know that I myself will look whenever I see the flashing lights of a black-and-white. But that's all I do: I look. I don't stop and hang out—and I think that the average citizen does the same. There are more important things to do in this world than stand around watching a dead body for five hours. But crime scenes attract more than just the average Joe. When the yellow tape is up, a section of our society becomes an entranced mass that rings the outer edges. I have begun classifying this mass, and have so far found there to be three distinct groups of crime-scene watchers.

First there are those I call the *Complainers*. They are groups of old men—pensioner types—who stand at the back of the crowd and talk, examining the sheet-covered bodies from a distance, like judges at a beauty contest. They complain about how bad crime has become in this city, that the streets are not safe, that the cops take too damn long to respond to anything anymore—which I can understand. These are complaints that I think we all have. But they do not end their complaining there. Then they complain about any inconvenience that a crime scene may be causing, and they will step forward and utter their displeasure. At times, this can get a little distracting, especially when you are trying to look for witnesses and listen to the radio simultaneously. My favorite "Complainer" lines revolve around blocked pathways (i.e., sidewalks or roadways), which occur at any homicide scene: "You only need to block one lane of traffic"; "You can't put tape up to block the sidewalk"; and the oft-spoken "That police car is blocking *that* driveway over there" are a few of the more common complaints. I have found that this last complaint is the most easily deflected. You simply need ask, "Is that your driveway?" When the answer is "Well, no," you simply reply, "Then don't worry about it."

Second, there are the *Squenchers,* those who like to be at the front of the crowd where they can get a good view of the body. Oddly, they "squench" their faces in disgust a lot and say things like "I think that's part of his brain on the street" or "Officer, if I give you my camera, can you get me a close-up picture?" Even though they are disgusted, they stay for the full investigation, leaving only after the coroner has hauled away the body.

And last, but not least, are, of course, the gang members—whom I have simply classified as, well, the *Gang Members*. They flock to the scene as word of the homicide spreads like wildfire among both the victim's and the suspect's homeboys. They do not come very close, though, especially if they have knowledge of the crime, preferring to watch the scene from a distance, standing far beyond the Complainers.

"It amazes me how fast they hear," I say to Coleman, nodding to a group of Harpys who stand watching from a half-block away.

"The homie news service is quicker than CNN," replies Coleman.

The crowd always has one final swell when the coroner's wagon arrives. Even though it is an unmarked station wagon, people down south seem to be able to pick it out, and they know that when the wagon arrives, the sheet comes off. That is because the coroner has to examine the body, toe tag it, and transfer it to a plastic body bag, which takes some time and adds to the gruesomeness of the scene as the body is tugged and pulled—especially since there are times when built-up body fluids will flow and spill.

The sheet comes off as I am standing next to the crowd. The detectives mingle around the body, making notes as the coroner examines him. I feel a tap on my shoulder.

"Can you ask him to move?" It is an elderly, spinster-looking, black woman. She has on a church dress and thick glasses, and is poking me with one long, knotty index finger.

"Excuse me?" I reply. I look at her closely for signs of family resemblance to the little old lady in the Cadillac.

"Can you ask him to move?" she says, pointing to one of the detectives. "I can't see the body."

A typical Squencher. I give her a hard look. "No," I reply.

I remember seeing her an hour ago. She has waited a long time to see death, and now she feels that she is being cheated. This angers her, and she gives me a mild *humph*. I ignore her, and intermittently watch the crowd and the huddle of detectives, waiting for them to finish. Black Crow's corpse is stuffed into a body bag, the crowd of personnel around him never thinning enough for an uninhibited view before he is put in the coroner's wagon. Not much of a show for the crowd behind me.

"Officer?" I hear. I turn. It's the same elderly woman.

"Yes, ma'am," I reply.

"Fuck the police," she says, then turns and pushes into the laughing crowd.

DEPLOYMENT PERIOD SIX

The position of captain for the Los Angeles Police Department is one in constant turnover. Each station has two captains: the *patrol captain,* who oversees the uniformed officers; and the *divisional captain,* who is the commanding officer of the division and not only oversees the administrative and detective sides of the station but is the patrol captain's boss as well.

Captains change divisions with the frequency of the seasons. It is rare to have one stay at the same assignment for more than two years, because the goal of every captain is to make commander, and to make commander, one has to have experience with the myriad cultures throughout our city. So captains jump from division to division, making both departmental and community contacts as they go.

Our new divisional captain is Bob Kimble, who has transferred in from an assignment at the Police Administration Building (PAB), also known as Parker Center. He is a quiet, introspective man who even in his crisp LAPD blues has the sharp cut of an IBM executive. He has a master's degree from the University of Southern California in public administration, an advanced-education credential that is almost a necessity for movement into the upper echelon of this department. He is in roll call today to introduce himself.

After Lieutenant Germain finishes roll call, Captain Kimble stands before us and goes over his background. At this time, the LAPD still promoted only from within, and his journey through the ranks started where we all did: in the Los Angeles Police Academy as a recruit. The officers of the LAPD are picky; they don't like outsiders. That is because the LAPD has its own mind-set of what

142

it takes to police a large metropolitan area. It is a successful mind-set when compared with cities such as Chicago and New York. Throughout the 1980s, Los Angeles consistently had lower across-the-board crime rates than either of those cities—even though the LAPD was working with a uniformed force that was one half to one third the size, and the budget, of either of those cities! The LAPD was an efficient policing machine in the 1980s.

So even if you had ten years on the job of a major municipal police force attaining a supervisory rank, if the LAPD hired you, you still went through the Academy for six months and then spent a year in the field as a boot. The LAPD wants its officers to do things the LAPD way. Because the department promoted only from within, every recruit who entered the Academy had the added incentive of possibly one day becoming chief of police in the City of Angels.

After Captain Kimble finishes going over his career track, giving a captain's version of a "one minute, one second," he gets to the part of his introduction where he is to tell us of his expectations of how we should do police work. He begins by simply praising us for a job well done, noting, "I like what I see—keep doing it." Then he adds one last part.

"We always have to keep in mind one thing, and that is *professionalism* when dealing with the public, be it with citizens or criminals," he says. "I don't have to tell you that litigation against police officers, and the city, is on the rise. Especially with many citizens carrying around video cameras just so they can catch us doing something bad on film. Lieutenant Germain was just telling me about an incident in this division involving a minor use of force during an arrest. After the suspect was in custody, an officer, one who was definitely too excited for the moment, was captured on videotape yelling at bystanders: 'You better leave before I beat you, too.' Now, mind you, it was a good arrest *and* a good use of force. We had a violent felony suspect and witnesses who stated that they observed the suspect attack the officers. One of the officers *had* to use his baton twice to defend himself. We even had a witness who stated the officer showed *great restraint* in the use of his baton, and the moment that the suspect stopped his attack, the officer ceased the use of the baton. It was a textbook use of force. But the added theatrics were unnecessary. Just those words on tape, 'You better leave before I beat you, too,' even without any follow-up action, could put us in a situation where we would have to defend ourselves in civil court. Videotape is powerful, and if taken out of context without everything leading up to the moment viewed, can be utterly devastating."

It is an almost prophetic warning. Unfortunately, it was spoken in the wrong divisional roll-call room.

It is late February 1991.

MARCH 3, 1991

The implications of the Rodney King beating in Foothill Division on March 3, 1991, were not immediately apparent to the officers at Southwest Station. At that time, the LAPD still had a large number of veteran street cops with ten to twenty years on the job. If an officer had not been on the department during the Eulia Love shooting[1] in January 1979, he had been there during the Thirty-ninth and Dalton incident[2] in August 1988. Therefore, many officers had been through the ups and downs of public opinion, and few seemed concerned.

Both the Eulia Love and Dalton cases caused the department to receive much negative publicity. Lead articles denouncing the department splashed in banner headlines across local papers, and the individual officers involved were ridiculed and threatened with arrest and imprisonment. But each incident eventually sank away to the back pages of our newspapers, finally fading from public scrutiny. Both incidents, although using some department policy changes, had

---

[1] On January 3, 1979, two Southeast Division officers, one a male black with twelve years' experience, one a male white with four years' experience, responded to a call to assist gas company employees in turning off gas to Eulia Love's residence. An unemployed widow, Love had earlier in the day struck with a shovel a company employee who had tried to turn off her gas. When officers arrived at the scene, Love was in front of her residence with an eleven-inch boning knife. Two and a half minutes later, Love was shot by the officers while in the act of throwing the knife at them.

[2] In August 1988, Southwest Division officers staged a massive raid on four residences on Dalton Avenue just south of Thirty-ninth Street. All four residences were suspected Crip rock houses, confirmed both by citizens who had complained about activity there, as well as by narcotics officers, who had monitored the activity. After the raid, the residences were found to be "uninhabitable."

little lasting effect on the community's relationship with the department. That was true of most negative incidents involving the police, because there was always some subsequent event that brought the LAPD back into public favor.

After Eulia Love, the LAPD did an outstanding job with the 1984 Olympics. As the world came to the City of Angels, so, supposedly, would international terrorism. But there were no incidents; the department's security plan was a piece of perfection. The word *perfection* can be used here only in hindsight. The notoriety any terrorist act would have attained had it happened in the media capital of the world at the media event of the year must have had terrorists salivating around the world. But there were no incidents, because the LAPD was prepared.

To offset the Thirty-ninth and Dalton raid, the LAPD's successful war on South Central rock houses helped improve the LAPD's image. The campaign was highlighted by pictures of the police "ram," a converted U.S. Army personnel carrier with a thirty-foot battering ram crashing through the sides of fortified drug dens. There was also sympathy at that time from the public for the deaths of an unusually high number of police officers in separate incidents, reminders of just how difficult and dangerous the job of an LAPD street cop could be.

Consequently, officers had learned to ignore times of low public image, because something always came along to polish it up again. When I graduated from the Academy in 1990, a public opinion poll by the *Los Angeles Times* showed a 77 percent approval rating of the police by Los Angeles residents, a rating not seen since before the 1965 Watts riots. Even in South Central, the approval rating was over 60 percent! The LAPD was a positive entity in the minds of most citizens. My graduation was attended by over a *thousand* well-wishers and a legion of press photographers. When Chief Daryl Gates inspected us, Steven Spielberg was in his entourage, and Fred Dryer sat on the reviewing stand. My entire class was pictured on the front page of the *Daily News,* the second-largest paper in Los Angeles, throwing our hats into the air. When I graduated in 1990, citizens would actually wave hello to me with all of their fingers extended.

So the initial reaction to media coverage of the tape of the Rod-

ney King beating was one of only mild interest by officers at Southwest. To them, Foothill Division was a "Valley" division, over
twenty miles removed from the daily violence that officers in the
South End faced. Few officers at Southwest even knew officers at
Foothill. I myself had just one classmate, Dave Love, who was assigned there. So Foothill and *its* problem did not have an immediate
impact on us at Southwest. It would take about one week.

When I first saw the beating of Rodney King on tape, three days
after the incident, I was shocked. What I saw on my television set
was ten powerful seconds of uncontrolled baton swinging on a man
lying almost prone on the ground. I had never seen anything like it
before. In the five months I had been on the job, I had been at the
termination of seven LAPD pursuits and had yet to see any physical
force beyond arm twists and wrestling—never any baton action, not
even a punch thrown by an officer, even though I had seen suspects
take a few swings. As far as use of force was concerned, it had been
far below my expectations.

Having been an avid fan while growing up of television shows
like *Police Story* and later *Hill Street Blues,* I had joined the LAPD
expecting a fair amount of fighting. I figured we would have to clear
out bars full of rowdy drunks, get into wrestling matches with
crazed husbands, and fight to put the cuffs on any number of criminals. I really thought altercations were in the job description of an
LAPD officer. But truth is different from fiction. The average use of
force (which, before Rodney King, happened at most four or five
times a month for an *entire* police division, even one as busy as
Southwest) involves two officers grabbing a suspect, wrestling him
to the ground, and then handcuffing and sometimes leg restraining
him (and I mean *him*—I have yet to see a use of force on a woman,
although it does occur). The average use of force involves two elements: twist locks, encompassing arm and wrist holds, and combined body weight, like dog piling when you were a kid—*not* baton
blows.

So I had not seen *any* baton swinging prior to March 1991.
Many of my fellow officers, especially the older ones, did not even
take their batons on radio calls. They left them in the car, already
fearing lawsuits from baton use even before the Rodney King tape.
Street cops at that time were a tough breed anyway and had no fear

when it came to a wrestling match. I even had one partner who left his baton in his locker, stating that such a weapon was nothing more than "the lawyer's best friend."

So given the circumstances and attitudes toward the baton, my experience then in observing its in-field use was nil.

Before I continue, I should note one other item that we carried on our belt in 1991: aerosol teargas, also known as Mace. Mace was the single most useless item a police officer could carry. As far as that little can on our belts was concerned, it was there for decoration. All training officers, and I mean *every single one,* told me that if I Maced a suspect, they would shoot me. The Mace we carried then (as opposed to the oleoresin capsicum spray the LAPD switched to in 1994) was highly selective as to whom it affected, as well as highly toxic to a discriminating few. Only 70 percent of those suspects sprayed were seriously impeded by it. And Mace had a habit of forming a thick cloud that wafted over the immediate area, hindering not only the suspect, but also both officers. Combined with the 70 percent suspect-effective rate, you could easily have situations where suspects were not affected—but both officers were. That, clearly, is bad.

It was also found that suspects on the drug PCP were *completely* unaffected by Mace. Because a large number of suspects arrested at that time smoked "sherm" (plain cigarettes dipped in PCP at about three dollars a hit), using Mace generally did more harm to officers than to suspects. Added to this were many cases where officers suffered violent allergic reactions to Mace, developing total body rashes, as well as severe lung damage. Some officers even had to be pensioned off due to reduced lung capacity from their reactions to Mace. So, I had also not seen anybody Maced.

In summary, my experience with uses of force were minor, even though over the past five months I had already arrested almost forty suspects for felony crimes. The actions seen on the Rodney King videotape were a new experience for me—and for many officers on the LAPD as well.

BACK THEN

I am seated in the Boulevard Café, an African-American–owned coffee shop on Martin Luther King Jr. Boulevard near Crenshaw Plaza.

A large portrait of Malcolm X adorns one wall, while photos of jazz greats Billie Holiday, Thelonious Monk, and others are spotted around the room. I am having breakfast with five other officers. They are Ernie, Darius, Ron, a P-III nicknamed Hondo,* and my former partner Zedric Coleman. I am the only white officer present. The other officers are African-American. The topic of our breakfast conversation is the same thing everyone else is talking about: the fallout from the Rodney King videotapes.

It is now two weeks after March 3, and we have all realized the magnitude of the situation. Every night on the news, the "Rodney King Beating" is the lead story. Perfectly coiffed anchorpersons punctuate their stories with stern, disgusted facial expressions, their anger seething as if it were they who were struck. Their images are always backed by the same grainy photo of Officers Laurence Powell and Timothy Wind standing over Rodney King—batons at the ready. The newspapers are also headlined by anti-LAPD stories, stories filled with quotes of prisoners and past arrestees who claim that they too were "victims" of the LAPD. The media are dedicated to the stance that the beating was not a singular, isolated incident—but a department-wide epidemic of brutality!

What is worse is the war of words being waged in the media. Semantics are powerful. An example is Rodney King being portrayed as an innocent "motorist," an average citizen out for a drive who was bewildered and confused when police stopped him. Now, no matter how you view the beating, one must admit that calling King a "motorist" is a stretch. Yes, the dictionary does define motorist as "one who drives or travels by automobile." But our culture further associates a "motorist" as someone out on a leisurely Sunday drive. A motorist is a librarian driving a Honda in the slow lane. You would never call someone driving like a maniac a "motorist," would you? But King is being portrayed as such. Even though he was first observed driving in excess of one hundred miles per hour[3] when the

---

[3] I know, I know—he was driving a Hyundai, a cheap foreign car that *couldn't* possibly go a hundred miles per hour. But the stretch of freeway he was first observed on—the 210 freeway westbound approaching Sunland Boulevard—is a long, steeply sloped 7 percent grade. A few years ago, a teenager lying flat on a skateboard, riding it like a luge, was clocked at sixty-five miles per hour on a nearby identical grade.

California Highway Patrol (CHP) first observed him, then crossed three lanes of traffic to make a freeway curve, then led both the CHP and the LAPD on a 7.8-mile pursuit during which he was clocked at eighty miles per hour on a city street with a posted thirty-five-mile limit. Even if you think that the police are completely lying about the speeds, King's own passengers state that when they saw police lights behind them on the freeway at the start of the chase, they continually urged King to stop the vehicle for the remaining seven miles. Words are powerful, and those used by the media in regard to this incident are seemingly not meant to describe, but to incite.

I don't think "motorist" applies here, unless you want to start calling the incident the Rodney King "Use of Force."

Anyway, as a result of this negative tidal wave of publicity, citizens are turning on us, and turning quickly. Only two weeks after the incident, the LAPD's approval rating has already fallen under *50 percent,* an almost 30 percent drop! Just one day earlier, I had received my first (of many) "LAPD salutes." My partner, a white P-III, and I were stopped at a red light on Martin Luther King Jr. Boulevard. An African-American citizen standing at a crowded bus bench gave us his middle finger as casually as if he were waving hello. Embarrassed and confused, we ignored it and drove off, the crowd on the sidewalk cheering. *Cheering.*

It was an alien situation to us, one we did not know how to handle. Not only did we have an idiot flipping us the bird, but a crowd of about ten average citizens cheered him on. A crowd that did not have a single gang member–looking fool in it. Just a bunch of normal working stiffs taking the bus to work.

Only a month prior, if somebody had given us his middle finger, we would have stopped and talked to the individual. It is just *too* strange behavior to let go uninvestigated, because one would generally have to be intoxicated or mentally ill (and thus in need of our assistance) to make such a signal. Either that, or he was one stone-cold, fearless asshole-type criminal out looking for trouble. And I guarantee you, he would have found it, because LAPD officers did not take that kind of shit. So before King, we would have jammed the guy, and jammed him thoroughly—meaning, he would have been identified, run for warrants (arrested if he had any), and then given a citation if there was any criminal offense also committed, such as spitting on the sidewalk.

Not beaten, though. That's movie trash. But we would have let him know that we saw him and his aggression toward us *and* the authority of the citizens we represent. But not now. Not today.

"All this shit is because we lost the damn choke hold," says Hondo in the café. The choke hold, an upper body control hold which pinches off the carotid arteries of the neck, causing a temporary block of blood flow to the brain, was banned from police use in 1981 after a rash of lawsuits. "If this had been the old days, they'd have knocked King to the ground and then somebody would have put a lock on him," adds Hondo. Hondo is a grizzled Vietnam vet. He rolls a thick, unlit cigar around in his mouth, the end of which has been thoroughly chewed. "And that would have been it. It doesn't matter how crazy he was or if he were on PCP. That hold would have put him down."

"I don't know about that," says Ernie, a rail-thin P-III with over twenty years in the street. "If this had been the old days, I think they would have broken a heckuva lot more bones." Ernie looks at me, Darius, Ron, and Zedric. Only Ernie and Hondo are old enough to have been around in the "old days." None of the rest of us has over four years on. Ernie continues, "There was a time on this job when you didn't run from the LAPD, otherwise you'd go to the hospital. Officers didn't put up with any kind of resistance to arrest. When I came on in the late sixties, I saw stuff that made Rodney King look like nothing. It could get real ugly at times. People had a reason to fear the LAPD."

"But it worked," adds Hondo. "Back then, we didn't have half the fools running from us that we do now. Seems every time I pick up a newspaper, I see an article about some suspect blowing a red light running from the police and killing a family of four. We didn't have that when I first came on, 'cause if you ran from us, you got whipped."

"I saw a lot of shit that wasn't right," says Ernie. "Not very often, but I still saw some shit. And management condoned it. If somebody beefed you over a choke out, you were protected. You couldn't sue the police back then the way you can now. And some officers abused that protection. If you even looked at them the wrong way, they'd either throw a choke hold on you or poke you in the belly with the straight stick," referring to the straight billy club officers carried before the introduction of the side-handled baton.

"Hey, there wasn't anything wrong with that, Ernie," says Hondo. "Back then, we kept the assholes in line because they feared us. If they gave us any shit, they got thumped. And that's 'cause we had to. Backup has always been so fuckin' far away in this town. This department has never hired enough officers, and the size of this city spreads us so thin. It's always been a couple minutes before you could get other officers to your location. And these streets have always been some of the meanest in this nation. Back then, we didn't have rovers on our belts to call for help. Wasn't any button at our fingertips to summon the troops. It was just you and your partner. The radio was in the car, and when you stepped away from that black-and-white, you were away from your lifeline. You were on your own. You had to protect yourself and your partner. And you did it through fear. If any asshole even thought about fucking with the LAPD, they knew that they had better be ready to die, because we would definitely take it all the way. If they mouthed off to us, we'd choke them out. If they got physical, they got beat with a stick. If they pulled a knife, they got shot. And if they pulled a gun, they got shot dead. Plain and simple. We protected ourselves with fear."

"But some took it too far," says Ernie, holding up a hand to Hondo, a gesture that knives his words into Hondo's. "Some officers were choke-happy muthafuckas. They'd choke anybody. Choke out mouthy speeders. Choke out regular citizens. We had some officers choking out people just to practice, especially some training officer working with a boot. First thing a T.O. would do with a boot coming out of the Academy was take him out and find someone to choke. They'd see some asshole they arrested before and sic the probationer on him. Choke him out. Some would even do choke outs just to see if they could get the suspect to piss in their pants. Now they were a small group, mind you. But every division had a couple of choke-happy fools. And they fucked it up for the rest of us. So we lost it. We lost it because we had some fucked-up policemen. Which really hurt us as a force. Because the choke hold is a necessary tool. With it, you can take down aggressive suspects—no problem. If we'd have had it today, Rodney King would be in jail. And those four boys would be working the field."

"I don't know where this whole thing's gonna go," says Ernie. "I hear on the news they're talking about taking away the baton. And did you see that video from Washington, D.C.? Where that policeman punches that asshole? I heard one newsman say that if an officer uses his fist, he should go to jail. What kind of use-of-force scale would you have then? Verbal requests—and then straight to gun?"

Ernie settles back in his chair. "I'm just glad I'm retiring soon. You young ones are gonna be screwed. It's soon gonna be where if you use any type of intermediate force like your hands or baton, you're gonna get sued. They're putting you in a way that says, 'Use your words or use your gun. Or stay the hell out of the situation.' "

THE RUSSIAN

Even though Rodney King is going hot and heavy, police work still must be done. And I am still trying to learn how to do it. Fortunately, I have been partnered with a P-III who not only enjoys police work, but also enjoys teaching it.

Aton Milosov* is of Russian descent. He has a thin, almost gaunt face and a shock of red hair that is never quite combed right. He looks more like a nuclear physicist than a police officer. But it's a good thing for the citizens of Los Angeles that he is not in the scientific field, because he is an excellent police officer, thorough and conscientious.

In the modern LAPD, most officers are report takers; they simply write out a preliminary investigation report and move on to the next call, which is understandable, because of our call load. In the case of a burglary, many officers simply note the point of entry, the property taken, and not much more—no real "investigating." They expect the follow-up detective to call the victim the next day and get all the details, which is not too effective, since people forget facts quickly. But Milosov has a little bit of Sherlock Holmes in his blood. He will search the premises and its surroundings for clues, then go door to door in the vicinity afterward, talking to neighbors, seeing if anything or anyone out of the usual was seen. We will then drive through the area looking for suspicious persons, knowing that most burglars travel on foot and generally commit more than one crime per day. Because of this, he makes a large number of key felony arrests, even though he is a day watch copper.

Milosov and I are driving down Normandie Avenue toward the end of our shift. We see a male black transient pushing a shopping cart full of new stereo equipment midblock across a busy street. The transient looks everywhere but in our direction.

"I'll bet that equipment is stolen," says Milosov, his voice simple and flat.

"How do you know?" I ask.

"I just know," says Milosov.

The transient is jaywalking, pushing his cart through traffic, far from any crosswalk. This provides us with a convenient reason to jam him, which is necessary because we have been told in so many words by supervision not to have consensual encounters until the fallout from the Rodney King video dies down. Not that it ever will.

But at this time, we don't know that. We've just been advised to greatly lessen our citizen contacts, because *all* citizen complaints that cannot be easily resolved will be taken in the form of a 1.81 Personnel Complaint, a complaint form that stays in an officer's package throughout his or her career. So, no more stopping Bloods just because they're in a Crip hood; no more searching juveniles in all-black clothing out on the streets past midnight; no more talking to groups of men who stand around a pay phone for four hours at a time—because if they complain, it goes in one's package. Even if they are the lowest ex-con, gang-banging, coke-slinging type of fools on parole for murder and rape, and drunk off their asses and common sense dictates that they are engaging in criminal activity.

"If a *citizen* complains in writing, you *shall* be burned" is how one supervisor put it. "The motto is no longer 'To protect and to serve.' Now it's 'Let them do whatever they're doing and we'll pick up the pieces afterward.'"

But waiting for crime to happen is not the way LAPD officers were taught. We were taught to be proactive, to look for crime before it happens. It's difficult driving down the streets of South

Central, seeing bad guys who you know are up to something, and being fearful to stop and talk to them because of a political climate. Real difficult—frustrating to where it turns a good officer's stomach.

But with this transient we *have* good reason to stop and talk with him. We even have a lawful detention because we want to write him a jaywalking ticket. So we wait until he reaches the sidewalk, then approach him.

"Good afternoon, sir," says Milosov his voice cordial. "What are you doing, may I ask?"

"Nothing, Officer," he says in a calm, matter-of-fact tone. "Just pushing this stuff home. Some guy down the street left it out next to his trash cans so I thought, hell, looks good to me!"

"Well, I did not stop you about the items in your cart," says Milosov. "I stopped you because of the way you crossed that street."

The transient looks about forty-five years old, although he is probably younger. His body, once very athletic, has been withered by heroin. His eyes, although full of lies, have the ex-con "don't mean nuthin' " attitude. His clothes are dirty, but not thick with filth like many of the South Central street community. He has not quite reached the point of being a complete bag person. He still probably has an address nearby; maybe his mother's home or a garage in which someone lets him stay.

"Oh, I'm sorry," he says. "I guess I missed that crosswalk. But my stuff's so heavy, I just didn't want to go down to the end of the block. Can you give me a break?"

"No," says Milosov simply, but firmly. "What you did is very dangerous, not only to yourself, but for those driving down the street. I'm afraid that I'm going to have to issue you a citation."

I look at the stereo equipment. It's new, expensive, and a full system: CD player, graphic equalizer, cassette player, and tuner— not the type of stuff someone would just kick to the curb. Then I notice there are no speakers. Probably too bulky to steal. There is also dust on the components in a way that suggests they were until recently stacked as a system.

The transient has a knife in a sheath on his belt, so I do a quick search for other weapons. In his front pocket, I find some spark plugs, which is significant. Burglars break off the ceramic covers of spark plugs to use as projectiles to break windows. These pieces will not shatter a window, just spider it. A burglar can then quietly push in the glass. There is no sound for neighbors to hear other than a short *ping*—kind of like a rock hitting your windshield.

"I need to see some identification," says Milosov.

"I ain't got none," he says.

"Then how are we supposed to know who you are?" asks Milosov.

" 'Cause I'll tell you," he says. He begins acting real annoyed, as if we are wasting his time.

"OK," says Milosov. "What's your name?"

"King," he says. "Rodney King."

This is, of course, not Rodney King. But it is just one of what will be literally hundreds, of needling comments about Rodney that I would receive from suspects.

"Sir," groans Milosov, "I need *your* name. Otherwise, it's down to the station with you for interfering with a police investigation."

"I'm sorry," he replies. "Smith. John Smith."*

"Smith. Is that the English spelling with a *Y,* or do you use an *I?*" says Milosov with a perfectly straight face.

"With an *I,* dammit," he huffs. "Don't you try to trick me."

"I would not think of it, Mr. Smith," says Milosov. "When were you born?"

"January first, 1960," he replies.

"And that makes you how old?" asks Milosov.

Bad question for Mr. Smith. He thinks for a minute, but cannot do the arithmetic.

"I don't know," he says. "I'm in my thirties. You can't arrest me for not knowin' my age."

"That is true, partner," says Milosov, looking at me as if he were teaching me something new. "Where do you live, Mr. Smith?"

"I'm homeless," he says. "I'm living on the streets."

"Where did you used to live?" asks Milosov. "What address did you have on your driver's license?"

"Ain't never had no license," he says. "Ain't never had no ID card, neither. Been homeless all my life."

"I believe you may not be telling us the truth," says Milosov, smiling. "How am I supposed to write you a jaywalking ticket if you do not tell me the truth?"

"I don't know, Officer," he says. "I am who I say I am."

I run the name John Smith over the MDT, a truly amazing device, giving us instant access to driver's license records, parole status, and any *wants* or warrants for the person. The name John Smith is a common name, and it comes back with numerous arrest warrants. There are a few that come close to matching our transient.

"Well, those warrants are probably you," says Milosov. "Partner, put the cuffs on him. We'll take him down to the station for further investigation."

"You can't arrest me," he says. "I ain't did nothing."

"You are not being fully arrested," says Milosov. "You are being transported to the station so as to be eliminated as a warrant suspect. If those warrants are not yours, we'll bring you back."

I move to put the cuffs on him.

"Wait a minute," he says.

Then he gives us his real name. He tells us he was just afraid because he was on parole.

"What are you on parole for?" asks Milosov.

"Uh, burglary," he replies.

I run him, and find out he is telling the truth. He is on parole for burglary, but he has no warrants. But we still hook him up.

"You can't arrest me," he says. "I ain't did nothing!"

"Section Thirty-one of the Vehicle Code," says Milosov. "Giving false information to a police officer after committing an infraction upon a public roadway is a misdemeanor."

We transport him to the station to book him for the misdemeanor traffic section. His bail will be only one hundred dollars.

"Now we know he has done a burglary," says Milosov when we're in the report-writing room, out of our suspect's hearing. "We also know *he* knows we know. If he gets out, he will disappear into transientdom, becoming very difficult to locate, and thus prosecute—not to mention he will be out in the public doing more crimes. So we have to work fast."

We tell the burglary detectives what we have. One of them, a D-I, wants to book him for receiving stolen property, which carries a five-thousand-dollar bail. This is far short of the thirty thousand dollars that goes with residential burglary, but should still be out of our suspect's price range. But the D-I's supervisor will not go for it.

He tells us to go back out to the neighborhood and find the burglarized residence.

So Milosov and I hit the pavement, walking the street we think he came from, checking for open doors and windows, but our search comes up empty. It is now two o'clock in the afternoon, and we will be off duty soon. We had skipped lunch, running into our suspect just before we were going to request Code Seven. We decide to take our break now, hoping that some resident will come home and find his house broken into in the interim.

We go and eat. When we finish Code Seven, there is a message on our machine from Steve Heglar and Foster Rains, a pair of P-IIs assigned to work a midwatch car. They had heard about our transient and were driving in the area of our arrest when they were flagged down by a citizen who advised them he had just returned home to find his residence ransacked. It's less than two blocks from where we found our transient pushing his cart.

We respond to their location, which is a block farther north than the residences we had checked. We find a white-and-brown GI Bill tract home with three bedrooms and a large shade tree on one side which cools half of the house, as well as obscures the east windows from view of the street. One of these windows has been shattered and is the point of entry for the burglar.

"Here's what was taken," says Heglar, a tall white male who rides Harley-Davidson motorcycles. He hands Milosov a short list of items that the owner knows are gone.

"There may be other things missing," says the owner, a middle-aged black man who works as an engineer for Chevron in El Segundo, and who is visibly shaken by this incident. "I just have not had a chance to look for everything. I am so nervous."

Milosov looks over the list. He holds out the paper to me.

"Look at items three through seven," he says.

Those items list stereo equipment just like the system we found on our transient. But our victim does not know the brand of his system, which could be a problem. Fortunately, the victim advises us that he still has the factory box for the CD player in his garage, having been using it to hold Christmas ornaments. We retrieve the box, which has on it the serial number of the component it used to contain. It matches the CD player in the transient's shopping cart.

We go back to the station and book our suspect for burglary. Milosov is informed by the jailer that our suspect's brother is en route to the station with the hundred dollars to bail him out.

"Too bad," says Milosov. "He's gonna need about three hundred times that now."

TERRORISTS

"Have you ever heard of the Stockholm Hostage Syndrome?" asks Milosov.

Milosov and I are driving in the Jungle. It is going to be a smoggy day, and the surrounding hills already have a foggy tint to them. There are very few people on the street, which is the norm here. The gangsters and drug dealers are the only ones who are not afraid to stand at length outside of their fortified apartments. They will not start showing up until after school is out. I mull over Milosov's question.

"Yeah," I reply. "That's where those people in a bank were held hostage by a group of terrorists so long that they began to identify with them, to sympathize with them."

"Correct," says Milosov.

The event, which occurred in August of 1973 at the Sveriges Kreditbank in Stockholm, Sweden, is an often-cited case involving the psychological effects on hostages of prolonged imprisonment. Four hostages, all young female employees of the bank, were held captive for 131 hours while their two male terrorist captors made various political demands.

"Did you know," asks Milosov, "that when police finally stormed the bank, the hostages actually tried to attack the police in an effort to protect the terrorists?"

Up the street, two teenagers see our police car and run between the apartments. Milosov does not notice them, and I do not alert him, because it's nothing, anyway—just two kids ditching school, trying to get us to chase them.

"Some of the hostages even corresponded with the terrorists while they were in prison," he continues. "They would send them birthday cards, cakes, sometimes even go and visit them. This, even though the terrorists repeatedly threatened and physically abused the hostages during the siege."

As we pass the spot where the kids disappeared, I look up the walkway. One of them peeks from around the corner, like he's playing hide-and-seek with me. I point my index finger at him as if to say, "I see you." He gives me back his middle as if to say . . . something else. We drive on.

"You could almost say that is what's going on here," says Milosov. "Look around you. What do you see?"

We are now northbound on Nicolet Avenue from Pinafore Street, the very center of the Jungle. It's P-Stone Blood hood. All the apartment buildings are heavily fortified, thick steel bars on all windows and doors. Gang graffiti, although not on the street-facing walls, cover most alley and driveway-facing surfaces with a cacophony of script that silently numbs the senses. Only those surfaces protected by high fences with razor wire have a chance to remain bare, and even some of those have been brazenly infected.

"I don't know," I reply. "I see the Jungle. Burglar bars and spray paint."

"True," he says. "But what you also see are cells, prison cells. And people live in them. Some really good people, too. Hardworking and honest. But they're trapped with the bad. Who knows how many gangsters and parolees live in this little square-mile area. Must be hundreds. And they are in the good people's faces constantly. They live on top of each other in a small space. One that is getting more and more crowded. Good people here cannot go outside without seeing a gangster, cannot drive past a street corner without seeing a drug dealer. Many of them sleep on the floor for fear of stray rounds being fired into their homes. Their minds have taken in so much negative information that they overloaded a long time ago. They are numb to the violence."

We cruise past four male blacks sitting on a wall, gangsters, sporting gold chains and dark, pressed clothing. One of them is a big three-hundred-pounder with a bald head and a Buddha body, whom Jackson pointed out to me as being a bodyguard for one of the neighborhood drug dealers. He silently watches us, his head slowly tracking as we pass. One of the bad people.

"Good people know the bad," continues Milosov. "Bad people know the good. And the good people just try and get along. So they bend for the bad. It is to the point where the good people know not to leave their homes once the sun goes down for fear of getting robbed or shot. And they accept it. Because they have been hostages so long, they've come to know their tormentors. They would actually think it was *their* fault if they went out after dark and got shot. It is part of the culture down here. If you go out after dark, you know you are fair game for the predators."

Milosov continues as we cruise the area. "Look at how the media portray people from South Central. They're all gang members. You never hear about the good people, about their accomplishments. You don't hear about the ones who go on to college and successful careers. Unless they do sports. The newspapers and TV are big to push stories of kids from the South End who make it in sports. They make it seem like the only way out is through shooting a basketball or carrying a football. Can't do it in school. Not in the South End.

"The politicians are worse. They do not even acknowledge that there are normal citizens in the South End. When the mayor talks about building South Central, who does he talk to? Not to the good people. Not to the hardworking average citizen. He talks to the Crips and the Bloods! He openly tries to get them to open businesses or start charitable organizations with government money he is only too happy to give out. He acts as if they were the saviors of South Central. And they're glad to act that way because they're getting paid. But to me, all those grants are just extortion payments. And those payments, and the elbow rubbing with politicians that goes with them, just make the gangsters more powerful."

We turn into an alley and slowly cruise. I see a streamer of yellow police crime scene tape attached to a fence. Must have had a homicide here last night, I say to myself. I scan the alley for patches of blood, but find none.

Milosov continues, "When they talk about revitalizing, they don't talk about bringing in more jobs or getting people off of government money. They talk about more low-cost housing, which really means smaller boxes to live in, more housing that puts one on top of the other, that confines the people who live there to a minimal area of living space. It's like they're putting families in cement coffins. Heck, South Central is turning into one big housing project mausoleum! No place for kids to play, no parks to stretch back and relax in peace. Just a bunch of cement boxes.

"It's junk like this that has forced the good people to accept the violent lifestyle the bad have drawn them into. Their minds have been molded over time, their senses dulled. They no longer will fight against the loss of freedom, because they don't remember what freedom is like. Nothing in the South End, especially areas like the Jungle, is the way it should be. The inmates are running the asylum."

Milosov pauses, and I think about what he's been saying. It is a world gone wild. But it is a much deeper problem than good people versus bad—one that with barely six months in the area I cannot comprehend.

"I am not trying to justify people's actions here," Milosov concludes. "There is no way to justify allowing your children to run wild like some do. What I am trying to say, though, is that I do not want you to get burned out when some of the good people down here bite your head off on a radio call. Because, deep down, they still are good people. It's just that they have been so conditioned by the bad that they do not always act the way they really want to. And with this Rodney King stuff going on, the good are even more confused than they have ever been."

DEPLOYMENT PERIOD
SEVEN

S pring in Los Angeles seems extraordinarily long, and is not the same season that we see marked off on Hallmark wall calendars. It stretches from the end of dramatic January rains—a time when busy street intersections are flooded to the top of one's whitewalls, and expensive canyon homes slide down muddy hillsides—until the cool, smoggy-eyed days of May. Then the end of spring and the beginning of summer comes to Los Angeles with the suddenness of sunrise and sunset over a barren desert. The line of demarcation is as thin as a day.

The first suffocating heat wave arrives promptly in either the third or fourth week of June. Like an anvil, it crashes down on the city, driving air conditioner sales rampant and sending canyon dwellers into a state of perpetual panic as they watch the hillsides for the first sign of a wildfire. Summer rages until late September, its boiling days working on the psyche of the city, the long, hot spell slowly simmering on the minds of the inhabitants of the City of Angels. By mid-July, South Central is in a state of perpetual anger, the nights rarely cooling to a comfortable state for slumber before eleven o'clock. It is a time that touches something animal in the human soul, something that is awakened by the heat of the day, but lumbers long into the night. It is a time when the humans of South Central should migrate from the domain, just as birds leave the north before the snows of the winter. Even in your house, behind thick walls, the heat invades your core and you feel an uneasiness that there is no safety. For you can stand on your front porch in the evening and listen to the sounds of gunfire, like firecrackers at a

Fourth of July picnic, and watch the shadowy huddles of gang members as they invade the street corners and alleys. You can drive down the boulevard and look for the police barricades and flashing amber lights of patrol cars as they guard the crime scenes. Then you can inspect the patches of blood after they have gone.

THE CANADIAN

I am sitting in Mikoshi with my partner for this DP, a P-II just off probation named Kent Pallister. Lieutenant Farrell, the new P.M. watch commander, informed me yesterday that I had completed Phase II of probation, and am now Phase III, which means I will be rated only on a bimonthly basis as opposed to a daily basis. Dozier, Banderras, and Tanaka have also been reclassified to Phase III. Unfortunately, our classmate having problems has termination proceedings going against him and has already been relieved of active duty. If terminated, he will be the tenth member of my graduating class of eighty-three to separate from the LAPD. And we're only six months out.

My uniform shirt is soaking wet, the Kevlar vest I have on acting as a furnace in the intense midafternoon heat, cooking my heart and stomach like boiled meat. I tug on the front of my undershirt, pushing my vest and uniform away from my body. A ball of steamy air rises from my chest. I blow down, a coolness running over my skin as the puff of wind hits perspiration. I tug on my shirt in a fanning motion, hoping that some of the restaurant's air conditioning will have effect.

Even with the heat, P.M. watch is my favorite shift because it builds in intensity like a Mozart symphony. It begins slowly, although noisily, in afternoon rush-hour traffic. The radio calls come out in a gentle trickle as citizens scurry home for dinner. Officers actually have time to have coffee together between the calls for service.

Then it builds as the evening falls, bad guys first stirring from hazy alcohol- or drug-induced slumber, venturing outside as a cloak of darkness falls over the city. Then comes the night, and the majority of criminal activity in the city. The crime curve bends sharply skyward between the hours of six and nine. After nine, the city runs wild. Almost 60 percent of homicides in Los Angeles occur in the six hours after nine o'clock at night.

The only problem with P.M. watch is that it starts around three in the afternoon—the hottest time of day, which can be especially uncomfortable during the one-hundred-degree weather southern California sometimes experiences.

"Man, I don't want to work today," moans Kent. "This is really uncomfortable."

I agree with him, but the amount of energy it would take to reply has long since been sapped out of me. Our patrol car, an ancient Chevy, of course has a broken air conditioner, as do about a third of the units at the station. So we handle the one call dispatched to us, a minor domestic dispute involving an argument only, then head straight for the air conditioning of Mikoshi, advising the RTO to voice us our calls, as we would be out of the vehicle.

"Man, I cannot get used to this heat," says Kent.

"It wouldn't be so bad if the air conditioner worked," I reply.

Tall and thin with a blond handlebar mustache, Kent has just wheeled in from West Valley Division, a predominantly white, upper-class area covering the western end of the San Fernando Valley. Even though West Valley Division is considered a "slow" division by LAPD standards, it still averages about twenty homicides a year in an area of forty square miles.

"I can't believe this," Kent says. "Here we are, laying our lives on the line, and we can't even get a little cool air."

"Just be glad you're not stuck in the station," I say. "They have it worse."

That is true because, when purchasing environmental equipment for the station, the city has apparently acquired cooling units capable of sustaining a working space only half the size of the average station. Like any municipality, Los Angeles is given to spending too much for too little. So most LAPD stations turn into concrete furnaces during summer. There are rooms in Southwest Station that I am convinced could be used as a kiln for pottery, which means it can be pretty unpleasant, especially when everyone has to wear wool uniforms.

The waitress brings us each a glass of water. By quickly emptying my glass while she stands there, I make it known that we will need a pitcher. We both order something light and cold, a pair of salads. Not very macho food for a cop, but anything else would put us on the nod. We eat in silence, the only sounds being those of water gulps.

Slowly, we are revived and soon in shape to get back into the black-and-white. But this is our first day working together, so we sit and talk. I don't know anything about Kent other than that he is just off probation from another division, which means he was a boot like me only last month. He must have had some good ratings to be put with a boot after having so little time on the job.

Because he is just off probation, with only a few more months on the job than I have, he has advised me we will be on a first-name basis. That's good, because I am two years older than he is and I would feel odd calling someone younger than me "Sir."

"How did you like working the Valley, Kent?" I ask.

"We weren't near as busy," he replies. Raised in Calgary, Alberta, he speaks with a slight Canadian accent. "We didn't have near as many calls. And all of this obs crime is amazing," he says. *Obs crime* refers to "observational crime," arrests made by officers who actually see the crime, such as driving up on a robbery in progress. "I worked last night when you were off. Two different units chased stolen cars, and another unit heard gunshots, then found some guy shot in a nearby alley!"

"Amazing, huh?" I say. "But the reports are the same, and so are the bad guys. I just think you have a helluva lot more bad guys on this side of the hill," I add, referring to the Santa Monica Mountains, which divide the San Fernando Valley from the rest of the city of Los Angeles. "So we stay busier."

"No kidding," he says. "I can't believe the amount of gang members. They're everywhere. But I'm looking forward to working here. I've always wanted to be a *gunfighter*."

I grin at that part about being a gunfighter. LAPD officers are paid the same the city over (there is no hazard pay for working a fast or dangerous area), so officers who work in the Valley (which is considered slow compared with the rest of the city—but still *fast* compared with the rest of the country) call officers who work Southwest, Southeast, Seventy-seventh Street, Rampart, and Newton

Street divisions "gunfighters." They work in the "Wild West" parts
of town.

"Well," I reply, "we'll see if we can get you your spurs tonight."

Kent's enthusiasm is uplifting. Ever since the Rodney King video,
officers at Southwest have been in a slow mode, which is understandable, because citizen-initiated personnel complaints have increased by over fivefold. Before Rodney King, there were five
separate incidents of misconduct by officers under internal investigation at our division. Since the video, there are almost thirty separate incidents under investigation! Some of the beefs are ridiculous.

A case in point is one in which I have become involved (my first).
A black man stated that he went to the front desk of Southwest
Station in an attempt to file a forgery complaint against a former
employee who had forged his signature on a number of checks. He
stated that the officer he spoke with, a male white with light blond
hair, told him to file his report downtown with Bunco-Forgery Division.

That response is misconduct right there. Forgery is a crime re-
portable at a divisional level. But the reports are long and difficult
to complete, and some officers will try to get out of doing a forgery
investigation. So it is conceivable some officer unfairly told this man
to go downtown because the officer wanted out of a lengthy report.
It does happen. Rarely, I hope, but a fact of life. And if an officer
told the man to go downtown, instead of taking the report at the
desk, it is misconduct. Not major misconduct, but still misconduct—
generally, a slap-on-the-wrist type of thing.

But it gets worse. The man has stated that when he protested
having to drive downtown for service, the officer stated, "Get out
of my station, *nigger*."

As you can see, this is a serious accusation. Terminology such
as this can lead to termination, so someone could be in hot water if
this did indeed occur. Unfortunately, that someone could be me,
because through a departmental investigation, it has been determined that I am a *possible* suspect in this incident. Because the man
cannot remember the specific day it happened, the incident is being
investigated over a one-week time frame. Unfortunately, I was as-

signed the desk the third day during this period and am thus viewed as the possible perpetrator. *Fortunately,* the complaint isn't as straightforward as it may seem, for a number of reasons.

First, the incident happened three months *before* the Rodney King video, and the man is reporting it two months *after* the video. So five months have elapsed. If the incident was as serious as he claims, why did he wait so long to report it? Second, because the incident occurred while Operation Desert Storm was going on in Iraq, three officers were assigned to the desk at all times because of the possibility of terrorist action against the station. During the one-week span in which he claims the incident occurred, only two white officers—myself and a P-II named Sciam*—worked the front desk. Sciam and I never worked the same day, meaning there were always two nonwhite officers assigned the front desk with us. On the one day I worked, there were two black officers with me, one of whom was a grizzled old-timer with a foot injury which kept him practically glued to the desk. He advised the LAPD investigator that if he had heard any racist term used in his presence, he would have shot the perpetrator himself. Third, both Sciam and I have brown hair, not blond, and mine is dark brown. Fourth, the man was shown pictures of both Sciam and me (without our knowledge, I might add), and the man stated that the perpetrator was neither of us.

But they are still doing paperwork against me even though the man has cleared us. I have been interviewed by Sergeant Jones, a black female who truly seemed upset by the unfairness of the complaint. Twice she apologized to me and stated any number of times, "I can't believe this." She even advised me that she had spoken to the man since the initial complaint, and that he had backed off of the statement that any racist term was used, now stating that the officer simply gave him the phone number of Bunco-Forgery Division and told him to call there for an appointment, which means he lied in his initial complaint (a lie for which there is no penalty for him, I might add). Still, the powers above Sergeant Jones want paper on the incident, and they want my and Sciam's names on it. So Internal Affairs Division will have my name in its file as being involved in an incident involving racism, even though the man no longer alleges the term was used. That file can be reviewed anytime I attempt to promote. They will see I was involved in an incident involving racism. I cannot have it expunged from my record. I have no recourse in the matter. Once a complaint is made, it goes on your record, and stays, whether you are innocent or not. It is a no-win situation. And we still have to deal with the second item of misconduct, that being the failure to take a police report.

I am not somebody who takes false accusation lightly. If this had happened a year prior, while I was still in the business world, I would have demanded my right to face my accuser, as well as threatened legal action against anyone who took part in this incident. But I am no longer in the private sector. Becoming a police officer, I have apparently lost many of my personal rights and freedoms, rights I did not know I had lost. The city will not give me my accuser's name, and they will defend his privacy with city attorneys. It appears that now that I have put an LAPD badge upon my chest, my back is open to any slanderous knife a citizen wishes to stick into it.

This is frustrating, because I am not a bigoted man. I have my views on life and people; they are far afield from the definition of bigotry. One of my best friends in high school was African-American, and another friend I roomed with for almost a year after college was also African-American. I do not throw these friendships out as some badge of racial heroism. I remember them now because I may to call upon them should I need character witnesses at a trial board!

My frustration is compounded because I can only sit back and let supervisors do their investigation and then present a determination to my captain. I cannot cross-examine. I cannot present evidence. I can only rely on an investigation by others within the system. I do take solace in the fact that I am not alone, because my frivolous complaint is not an isolated incident. Since the Rodney King video, they seem to be departmentwide.

Officers have done a major work slowdown since the Rodney King video because of the drastic increase in personnel complaints. Monthly arrests are down over 50 percent! I can understand why. An incredible amount of stress goes with a personnel complaint. I myself do not want to be involved in any citizen contact that might result in a similar untruth from a citizen. Imagine what would have happened if some angry gang member had walked into Southwest

Station after interacting with me and also lied, stating that I had called him the *n* word! Two racist complaints at one time! I would have been under intense scrutiny whether they were true or not.

The false accusation by the citizen with the forgery complaint left me completely exposed. And I feel it. I feel that my statement of noninvolvement meant nothing to the department, and that if Sergeant Jones had not cared and done the follow-up interview that she did, I could have faced a serious problem. The city of Los Angeles seems to have a witch hunt mentality, and officers are getting burned at the stake on innuendo and outright lies. It is an ugly time.

But Kent's enthusiasm is addictive. He is putting me back in a working mode. "Spurs, huh?" he says. "Yeah, I'd like to get some spurs."

SPURS

Kent is enjoying himself. This is the busiest he has ever been, and the busiest I have been since the Rodney King video. We have handled eight radio calls so far and we still have four hours to go. Two of the calls have involved shots fired, which is a month's worth for a car in the Valley.

We are on Thirty-ninth Street at Arlington Avenue, waiting for the light. Thankfully, the sun has gone down. Bare slivers of orange and red are visible on the horizon silhouetted behind the low-lying bungalows that line the street we're on. Belatedly, and as if to tease us, our air conditioner is now pumping out slight wafts of cold air which combine with the evening cool to make the temperature now tolerable.

"I want to get a G-ride," Kent says, using LAPDese for a stolen car. "I've never had one where we caught the guy who was driving. Just came close once. We got behind a stolen IROC Camaro on Sherman Way. But he hit the gas and smoked us, then disappeared around a corner before we could even light him up. We found the car empty about five blocks away."

"Yeah, it would be sweet to get a stolen," I reply.

It is amazing how sometimes the spoken word can materialize before your eyes. I am watching traffic as Kent is typing on the MDT. A blue Toyota Celica passes in front of us northbound on

Arlington, and it shudders as the driver shifts gears. It occurs to me that he does not know how to drive it.

"I think that's a stolen car," I say absently as I turn into traffic, punching the gas to get behind the Celica.

"Where?" says Kent.

I just nod at the car, which is now in front of us. As if on cue, the car shudders as the driver again misses a gear, emitting a grinding sound like a roller-coaster car being pulled to its summit. I read off the plate so Kent can type it into the MDT. He sends it off for confirmation.

"You think it's stolen?" says Kent.

The driver watches us nervously in his rearview mirror. He now runs a red light while turning to eastbound Exposition.

"Yeah," I say, the traffic violation confirming it for me. I'm patting myself on the back for picking it out. I feel like a veteran. Problem is, I'm not acting like one. We should be letting other units know what we have, but Kent has to see it on the MDT screen to believe it, and the computer system is slow in returning the information we have asked of it.

"It still hasn't come back," says Kent.

If either of us were a more seasoned officer, there would be a broadcast going out right now about our situation. But we are not. We are a pair of young officers just watching the situation unfold.

The Celica turns right on the next street and picks up speed. I am driving a very fast 1989 Chevy Caprice and easily stay on his tail. Even though I can now see he is trying to pull away, I still do not tell Kent to broadcast.

"Still no return," says Kent, staring into the MDT. We both continue acting like the brain-dead. The Celica now sharply turns west onto a dirt street, which ends in a cul-de-sac. The driver of the Celica realizes the street is about to end and he brakes. His door then flies open, the vehicle still in motion. The driver hops out, a frog-bodied Hispanic man with an untucked black polo shirt. He never looks back. He just runs from the car.

"It's a stolen, it's a stolen!" yells Kent, the MDT finally returning.

The driver runs for a chain-link fence to his left. The Celica rolls forward toward a brick wall at the end of the cul-de-sac. Now, finally, Kent and I pull our heads out of our you-know-whats and take some action. First, I have to stop my car. But before I can stop, Kent is out in a dead sprint after the driver. So I throw the still-rolling Chevy into park, a sharp *clunk* rattling through the engine to let me know the car hadn't finished moving yet. Because my door is open, it swings hard, and I get a lesson in rebound motion, the door bouncing back sharply and striking me squarely in the chin as I exit. *Ow!*

Seeing stars, Kent and I crisscross, me after the still-rolling car, Kent after the driver. I catch the Celica, jumping in and hitting the brakes just before it bulldozes into the wall. I turn just in time to see Kent disappearing into the darkness beyond the chain-link fence. I run after him, and as I run, I now put out our first broadcast.

"Three-Edward-one, we're in foot pursuit!" I say into my rover. And that is all I say—which is not good.

Because I am trained to stay with my partner, I completely forget to finish my broadcast by saying where we are. The frequency is now on stand-by, and everyone has frozen in their tracks, waiting for more information, such as where to respond. All that anyone knows is that there are two officers in foot pursuit somewhere within the nine square miles of Southwest Division. Just running after someone is not how we are trained; we are trained to broadcast and *then* pursue. Not just straight pursue. But I am desperate to catch up to Kent, not wanting him to confront this fool by himself. So I run instead of talk.

I hit the fence and flip over into darkness. There are no lights in the yard, so all I see are vague shadows of movement. I reach for my back pocket, but this time, there is no flashlight. It's still in the car.

Kent and the suspect are making noise crashing through the darkness ahead of me. I come to a brick wall and hop up on it. I pause for a moment to listen for Kent and the suspect, who are somewhere ahead of me. But I also hear the chatter on my own radio.

"Three-Edward-one needs help," says the radio tansmission operator, a little panicked. *"Unknown location, Air-Eighteen responding."*

Damn. Because we never rebroadcast, the RTO has assumed the worst, that we have been involved in an incident of violence, and has upgraded our backup to a *help* call. I pick up my rover to broadcast our location, but I realize I do *not* know where I am! I remember passing through the intersection of Arlington and Exposition. After that, we took a few turns, and I didn't look at the streets.

Great! I try to get my bearings, thinking, *Let's see, if I turn there, and then there . . .*

"Three-Edward-one," I puff. "We're running through the houses southeast of Arlington and Exposition; suspect is a male Hispanic with a black shirt." I pat myself on the back for remembering to add in the suspect description. Then I freeze.

Off in the darkness ahead of me, I hear the low, hard growl of a very big dog. I cannot tell where it is, other than in the yard before me. I am still on the brick wall, so I hop off it into the yard I'd been in. Then I hear it barking—thunderous sounds, its teeth trying to tear at something near it. Suddenly, Kent comes over the wall, landing on the ground in a heap. I go to help him up. Then, *bam!* The suspect also comes over the wall. I try to grab him, but he is nimble, and he hits the ground running.

I follow. "Edward-one," I say, as we run down a driveway into the street. "We're running out onto Arlington midblock south of Exposition."

I'm out into the light, under a streetlamp, and I finally get a good look at him. He is a young Hispanic with a ponytail and a thickly muscled body. He has a frame built for power, not for running, and he is tiring. In an attempt to hide, he dives into some bushes in the front yard of a yellow house. He must not have expected me to be so close, because he's surprised when I reach in after him. I grab his ankle and try to yank him out with one hand, but he kicks himself free and frantically crawls away, getting deep into the underbrush. I pause to catch my breath, my quarry now trapped in a maze of bushes. I draw my gun.

"Get out of there!" I yell.

The suspect glances at me from between the bushes, then looks around for an escape.

"Get your butt out here!"

He still ignores me. Kent is now next to me, breathing hard.

"Where is he?" asks Kent.

"Right there," I reply, pointing into the darkness at the rear of the bushes. "I'm gonna grab him."

Kent flashes his light, and I can see the suspect balled up. I push away a mass of branches and reach for him. The bushes brush up to a driveway where a large motor home is parked, and I can see one of the wheels through a leafy tunnel. I just about have him, but he crawls through the tunnel like a little rat, then under the motor home. "Shit!" I say. And I mean it.

Kent and I run around the motor home just in time to see him now climbing up the vehicle and onto the roof. He lies down, a lame attempt at concealment.

"Get down from there!" I yell at him. "Get down from there now!"

He slowly stands up, like King Kong on the Empire State Building, looking down at us from his perch.

"*Get down!*" I yell again. My voice cracks, the air blasting out of my lungs causing a flutelike whistle.

"*No comprendo,*" he replies, looking as if he is completely surprised by our presence. "*No speaky Englis . . . speaky Spanis?*"

He looks at me as if he has no idea why I am talking to him, as if he changed identities crawling under the motor home. He points to the house.

"*Es mi casa!*" he says.

"Get down now!" says Kent, and he makes motions like he's jumping. The suspect just looks at him.

"*No comprendo,*" he says.

That's it. I have had enough. I leap, catching the top of the motor home with one hand to support myself, grabbing the suspect's leg with the other. I pull him off the motor home and onto the grass. He immediately tries to run, but Kent and I swarm him and muscle him to the ground, quickly cuffing him. I then sit on him, too tired to try to hold him down, because he still wants to get up and run. I grab my rover.

"Three-Edward-one," I say, "Code Four—suspect in custody."

"*Code Four on the foot pursuit,*" replied the RTO, a disgusted tone in her voice. "*Suspect is in custody.*"

I am embarrassed. There is a certain amount of professionalism expected of you when you are an LAPD officer. When you are following a stolen car, or are in foot pursuit, the first thing you do is calmly, and I mean *calmly,* let everyone know where you are. You always think of coordinating with other officers to catch bad guys. LAPD officers are taught to hunt in packs. None of this lone-wolf stuff.

To make matters worse, I now look north up Arlington toward Exposition and see eight units all clustered at the corner, all waiting to find out where we are. With our Code Four, I hear some of them screech off, their tires burning in anger. Our fellow officers are a little upset with us. But the worst is yet to come. I hear a supervisor get on the air.

"Three-L-sixty," he says, *"could you ascertain from Three-Edward-one their exact location for a meet?"*

Uh-oh.

"Three-Edward-one," says the RTO. There is a hint of glee in her voice, satisfied that I will be getting a much-deserved butt chewing. *"Your exact location for a meet with Three-L-sixty?"*

"Uh, Three-Edward-one," I mumble. "We're on Arlington south of Exposition, about midblock on the east side of the street."

About ten seconds later, the supervisor rolls up. It is a new sergeant to Southwest, Sergeant Mike Fanning. An old-timer who spent over fifteen years at Seventy-seventh Street Division, he slowly exits his car, a bent frown on his face as though he were looking into the sun. I can tell he is trying to categorize all the comments he is going to make on our now-completed incident, as well as suppress a few swear words.

"So," he begins, "this is the suspect?"

I then realize I am still sitting on him. I stand up.

"Uh, yes," I reply.

"I ran your last request," he says. "You had a stolen?"

"Yeah, and this is the guy!" exclaims Kent, a big smile on his face. Kent is way too happy, not knowing that even though we got a stolen ride with a body, the way we did it is a screw-up in the South End.

"You know that broadcast was pretty poor?" He says it slowly, keeping his disappointment low-key.

"Yes, sir," I reply. "It was."

He nods and looks around some.

"I've been in over sixty-five vehicle pursuits in my career," he says. "The most important thing I have learned is communication. That is communication not only with your partner, but with the other troops. If we don't know *where* you are, we can't get there to help you. I have seen way too many officers get injured because they confronted a violent suspect either by themselves, or with only their partner, when they easily could have had other units there to help them if they had only taken the time to broadcast. I would rather that you let the suspect get away than not broadcast your location. Do you understand?"

We both nod in agreement.

"Do you know where your car is?" he asks.

I try to answer, but—

"On the other side of the block," Kent cuts in, still smiling. "I'm not sure where."

Doh!

"You at least know which *street* it is on?" asks Sergeant Fanning.

Doh!

Kent and I stand there, real quiet, our brains are working as hard as they can. We must look like a pair of morons contemplating some abstract mathematical theorem. But we do not answer.

An A-car pulls up behind the sergeant with Teri Bennyworth and her P-I, Brian Johnson. Bennyworth just shakes her head, while Johnson gives me a deriding smile that seems to say, "Officer Dunn, *you* are a dick."

"May we transport your suspect to the station for you, Officer Dunn?" asks Bennyworth, a very polite smile on her face.

"That would be a good idea," says Sergeant Fanning before I can answer.

After Bennyworth and Johnson take our suspect, Fanning drives us back to our car. Bad move. We should have walked. As we pull up, we see that the headlights of our vehicle are on with both doors wide open. *And the engine is running!*

Doh!

"You know," says Sergeant Fanning too calmly, "some suspect could have driven away with your car."

This fact had not escaped me, but to hear the sergeant say it sends a chill down my spine. Thoughts begin to run through my mind. What if someone had taken it and stripped it? Or if some criminal had stolen my car and then committed some heinous crime in it? Or, worst of all, if some gangster had grabbed it and then been caught in the backseat copulating with his girlfriend? I can see it now, Folsom Prison, twenty years in the future, a group of pumped-up cons telling tough-guy stories. "Oh yeah," says Little Chuy, "I'm so bad, my daddy stole a police car just so he could knock up my momma!"

"Pallister," says Sergeant Fanning, "make an entry in Dunn's log that he left his keys in the ignition of his vehicle, with the motor running, while not in the vicinity of his vehicle."

"Yes, sir," says Kent.

Fanning looks at both of us, an English general looking over mere tribal warriors. He shakes his head.

"Enough said," he finishes, pushing the words out as though there were a weight behind them. He gets in his car and drives off.

Kent and I now stand alone. I feel quite stupid, thank you. Only with the LAPD could you catch a car thief and still feel like an idiot. Kent still does not grasp the fact that we screwed up. All he knows is that we got a stolen car, his first. He turns to me, all smiles, enthusiasm gushing through his veins. He looks like he's just been to an Amway pep rally. He puts his hand up, a high-five. I give him a half-hearted slap.

"That's a spur for *one* heel," he says. "Let's go find the other."

Kent and I redeem ourselves three nights later. Again Kent is having wishful thoughts.

"I want to get in a pursuit" is the first thing he says to me when we sit in the black-and-white. From his mouth to the pursuit-god's ears.

We are driving north on Crenshaw Boulevard at Exposition Boulevard just snooping around to see what we can see. Kent is randomly running the license plates of vehicles around us, hoping to find one that is stolen. Looking for stolen cars this way is a crap shoot. Most stolen cars are taken straight to a chop shop, and thus are off the road by the time they're reported; or the stolen car has a license plate from another vehicle that has no *want* out for it. The only way to find these types of stolens is by a traffic stop for a vehicle-code violation, and then doing an investigation. But there are thousands of vehicles stolen in Los Angeles each year that are recovered with their proper license plates still attached. So randomly running plates *will* turn up stolen cars.

The more common crimes found when running license plates as Kent is doing now are nonpayment of registration fees (an infraction) and Department of Motor Vehicle (DMV) fraud (a felony). You can find these violations in about one in a dozen plates because registration fees in California are some of the highest in the nation. South Central is especially plagued with this type of activity because of the high unemployment rate.

So when Kent runs a jet black 1976 Cadillac Seville for DMV status, we are not surprised to find that the vehicle has not been registered in over a year, even though the plate shows a current registration tag. This just means that the tag on this license plate is stolen from another vehicle's license plate, which further means that some other citizen is unwittingly driving a car with no registration tag and is open to parking and traffic tickets, not to mention having to buy a new tag from the DMV.

"I hate these guys who do this stuff," says Kent. "Let's cite him and impound his car."

I can only see the upper torso of the driver, but he has the body of a power lifter. He wears a bushy, outdated Afro, as if he doesn't know current hairstyles. I can see his eyes watching us coolly in the rearview mirror, and I immediately know I am dealing with an ex-con. I inform Kent of this.

"Yeah, I think you're right," he replies.

I light up the Caddy around Thirty-ninth Street. When the lights come on, the con puts his hand under the front seat.

"Did you see that?" I ask Kent.

"Yeah," he replies, then waits a beat. "See what?"

"The guy went under the seat," I say. "He may have just grabbed a gun."

"Oh," says Kent.

Kent gets on the radio and requests an additional unit for our impending traffic stop. I take in my surroundings. There is a lot of traffic. We are in the middle of rush hour, and Crenshaw is a main artery. Still, we have been behind him for two blocks now, and I know he has seen the lights, but the Caddy does not pull over. Instead, it continues with the flow of traffic. I hit the siren at Stocker, with no response, and then again at Forty-third. Kent is about to put out a backup when the con stops the car. Right in the middle of traffic.

Kent and I exit. I unholster my handgun, holding it behind my thigh. At first, it looked like the con was going to get out of the car fast, but he got hung up in his seat belt, so he still sits behind the wheel.

"Pull the car around the corner and stop," Kent says over the loudspeaker, attempting to get the Cadillac onto a street with less traffic. If this guy does have a gun, we want to confront him on a side street away from the citizenry. Even if he had not made the movement of reaching under the seat, traffic stops on busy streets are to be avoided. It is not much fun walking up on a driver when there are cars driving thirty-five miles per hour only three feet behind you. Especially when you could get one who is drunk or crazy. I don't want to end up somebody's hood ornament.

The sound of Kent's words over the loudspeaker echoes off the squat storefronts that line Crenshaw. But the car does not move. Kent orders him around the corner again, but the car still sits there. Traffic is now backing up behind us. Shoppers on the sidewalk stop to watch, and a smart ass with a video camera comes dashing out of a shoe store and begins filming us.

Kent repeats his command for a third time, and the con complies, slowly pulling the Cadillac forward. We reenter our vehicle and follow.

The con pulls the Cadillac around the corner onto Leimert and stops. But he does not cut off the engine, and his rear tail lights are lit, his foot heavy on the brake. Again we exit our black-and-white, but I stay behind my door. I don't like the way this man is acting at all. Kent begins to walk up on him.

"Kent, wait," I say. "Don't walk up!"

Kent stops, gets back behind his door. I shout at the guy in the Caddy. "Turn off the eng—" I never get to finish. The Cadillac's engine roars. Its tires screech. Smoke and dust kick up from its rear. And the Cadillac is screaming down the street like a funny car dragster. He fishtails around the next corner, which means only one thing:

Pursuit!

Kent and I jump in our black-and-white, my foot pressing the gas pedal to the floor, the thrust forward closing both our doors with a resounding thud. Kent, not knowing the area yet, is a little disorientated, so I do a Julie Richards. In one move, I hit the lights, activate the siren, and grab the microphone.

"Three-Edward-one," I say, "we're in pursuit, northbound Victoria from Leimert, possible man with a gun requesting a backup and an airship!"

The RTO comes back.

"All units on all frequencies stand by," she says. *"Three-Edward-one is in pursuit."*

I now flip Kent the microphone, but he's not sure what to do with it. He's not nervous or scared, though. This is his first high-speed vehicle pursuit, and he's unsure about the radio procedure.

"Kent, give them a vehicle description," I say. He calmly does.

I now concentrate on the Cadillac, which is really moving down Victoria. He crosses the intersection at Homeland, a street with two deep gutter dips, the street engineered to handle a heavy flow of water during January rains. The Cadillac hits the first dip in a shower of sparks, its suspension system weakened by years of Los Angeles driving. The vehicle is then catapulted upward as it hits the road crown, straining the axles as the tires extend to where only the outer edges are barely touching the ground. The sedan then slams down hard on the second dip, emitting another shower of sparks as the vehicle pancakes under the heavy weight of its full-size frame.

"Whoa!" is all Kent can say.

Our travel through the dips is not as dramatic. The Chevy we drive has a heavy-duty suspension system, and although we feel the bumps, we glide through without any bottom rubbing.

"Southbound Victoria from Homeland," Kent says over the radio.

As we approach Stocker, a Mercedes is stopped to make a left turn. Normally, that's not a problem, but this is a narrow street, one lane going each way, with no room on the right of the Mercedes. The driver of the Cadillac does not seem to notice this. He steers straight for the back of the Mercedes. I think he is going to hit it. "Oh, shit" is all I can say.

But at the last minute, the Mercedes pulls forward into the intersection, hearing our siren and aware of the trouble behind it, leaving room for the Cadillac to pass. The Caddy squeezes by on the right, its hubcaps sending sparks pinwheeling skyward as they scrape the curb.

"This guy is nuts," says Kent.

We slide by on the left after clearing traffic. This gives the Cadillac a little bit of a lead, but it's the safe way to do it.

"We're eastbound Stocker," says Kent, which means we are headed right back at Crenshaw—and a sea of commuter traffic. The Caddy slows, the driver blowing his horn as he picks his way across Crenshaw against a red light.

"You see that!" yells Kent.

I do not reply, my concentration being on the traffic ahead. As we pass through Crenshaw, I see a brown sedan pull out of traffic. I look into it and see that Moe Landrum, from the drive-by shooting team, is driving, a partner next to him. We already have backup!

"Three-William-sixty-two, we're with the unit in pursuit," says Landrum, pulling his unmarked police car into the chase.

The Caddy, moving at a high rate of speed, takes the next right southbound. The street is clear and residential. The air unit now announces its arrival.

"Air Eighteen over the pursuit," the pilot says, which brings something back to mind.

"Kent, tell the air unit to take over the pursuit," I say, thinking *déjà vu.*

"What?" he asks, unclear of the concept.

"Let the air unit broadcast," I say. "They have a better view."

"What, just tell them?" he asks.

"Yes, just request they broadcast," I reply. And he does.

"Air Eighteen, the pursuit is now southbound McClung from Stocker," says the air unit.

This thing is going picture-perfect: I have my backup, I have my air unit, and I am driving.

The Cadillac now takes a number of turns, an attempt to outmaneuver us. Trees and trash cans zip past as we race through the back streets of Leimert Park. Citizens exit their houses, coming out to watch the spectacle. One house we pass twice, the second time finding a group of kids on the front lawn. They wave at us as we pass.

The Cadillac now heads back toward Crenshaw Boulevard. The citizens traveling home on Crenshaw whom we see this time must be the same ones we've been by before, because they are frozen still when we approach, waiting for us. As the Cadillac passes a red Corvette, a middle-aged black man sticks his torso out the window and shouts some expletives at our suspect. He punctuates his words by giving him his middle finger.

"Get that muthafucka," he shouts as we enter Crenshaw and turn.

"*Crenshaw southbound passing Leimert,*" says the air unit.

The Cadillac stays on Crenshaw now, the driver attempting to use the wide boulevard to see if he can outspeed us. Before I know it, we are ten blocks south at Fifty-fourth Street—still right on his tail. Not a very good attempt. But the attempt to outrun us does produce one major result, and it involves the suspect's car. The Cadillac begins to bellow smoke, a thick black steam cloud which signals imminent engine failure.

"He's burning up!" says Kent.

I try to remember if I saw a fire extinguisher in the trunk. All the black-and-whites are supposed to have one, but with our budget you never know what's in your trunk.

The Cadillac's speed decreases. I look in the rearview mirror and see that there are two other black-and-whites behind the homicide unit, both probably from Seventy-seventh Street Division, as we are in their area.

The Caddy turns onto Fifty-fourth and slows almost to a crawl. But the con still does not stop. Even though his engine is dying, he keeps going with what he has. I guess he feels that as long as he's moving, he's not caught. We continue in pursuit for four more blocks this way, with the other units bunching up to our rear. Soon the Cadillac is slowed to where we could go in foot pursuit of it. Kent gets on the P.A.

"*Stop your car and put your hands on your head,*" he says. "*Do it now!*"

Finally, the brake lights come on, and the Caddy stops. But once again, the brake lights don't shut off; the engine is still running with the vehicle in drive.

"Put it in park and turn off the ignition, then put your hands on your head," says Kent.

The driver thinks for a moment, then puts it in park. The brake lights finally extinguish. I am already out of the car, gun in hand.

"Driver, open the door from the outside with your right hand," I say. He does.

"Get out with your hands up," I say. He attempts to, rolling out of the vehicle. But the problem is, he still has on his seat belt and shoulder strap. He hangs out of the vehicle like a puppet on a string and looks back at me. "I'm stuck," he says.

Soon we have him unbelted and in custody. Kent checks under the front seat. He finds two grams of cocaine, each gram individually bagged, and a box of ten factory-fresh hypodermic needles stuffed far back under the seat.

"There may have been other stuff under there, because of the way this stuff was placed," says Kent. "And we did lose sight of him for a moment when he made some of his turns. So he may have thrown something out."

That is probably true, because we find out our driver is on parole for drug violations. He is looking at heavy state prison time for being in possession of the cocaine, which is a felony. If the parolee had been able to dump all the drugs without our detection, he would have had to deal only with an evading charge, which is a misdemeanor, and although a violation of parole, not an offense that would generate heavy state prison time.

Sergeant Fanning is the supervisor who will be doing the pursuit report for our chase. Back at the station, he pulls Kent and me aside.

"That was an excellent broadcast, Pallister," he says. "And Dunn, both the air unit and the homicide detectives said your driving was outstanding."

He has a thin smile on his lips. "Pallister," he says, "make an entry in Dunn's book that he is an outstanding driver."

"Yes, sir," replies Kent.

* * *

The drug case against the parolee was later thrown out. Because Kent recovered the drugs from under the seat, he was the only one who could testify to paralee's being in possession of them, even though I was there when he came out of the Cadillac with the bag of cocaine and needles in hand.

But Kent was on a prescheduled vacation with plane tickets and itinerary already set when the court date arrived. I was in court, but the attorneys would not do the preliminary trial on my testimony alone. And they would not continue or refile the case until a date when Kent was back in town. So the parolee was set free on the drug case.

DEPLOYMENT PERIOD EIGHT

It is a bright, clear day in Los Angeles, what I call a Three-Range Day, a day when not only are the low-lying Santa Monica Mountains visible, but also the snowcapped peaks of the San Gabriel Mountains and the more distant San Bernardino Mountains. Three-Range Days are becoming more plentiful as we roll through the 1990s. The smog-choked 1970s, when the city each year averaged thirty smog-alert days (when outdoor physical education for schoolchildren was prohibited and industries that produced fume by-products were shut down), are becoming a memory.

It is a Friday, normally a busy day, but we are two hours into watch and have yet to handle a single radio call. It is a rare day, an aberration from the norm of five calls waiting on the computer screen. We are enjoying the calm. We have driven the streets telling war stories, trying to outdo each other.

Laura Gould is a feisty twenty-four-year-old from German stock. A P-II, like Pallister, she is just off of probation, her boot year spent at Rampart Division, a dangerous place to work. Although the second smallest division at eight square miles, Rampart has the fourth largest population, almost 230,000 people. (A whopping 28,700 people per square mile!) Rampart is consistently a leader in homicides and violent crimes, and is a hotbed for criminal gangs from Central and South America. The officers there are tough, and the boots they train learn in a gunfighter mode. Gould is a definite gunfighter, full of swagger and confidence—deserved confidence, because she does her job well.

I am getting used to working with P-IIs. Because I have learned the job quickly, the supervisors have all but quit pairing me with regular P-III training officers. I like it, because I enjoy working with younger officers. Some of the older P-IIIs are so angry and frustrated by events surrounding the Rodney King video that they have all but given up on doing any effective police work. Many of them will only respond to radio calls, and that they do slowly.

I especially like working with Gould. Because of her Rampart "upbringing," she *sees* an awful lot. And I don't mean looking out the car window and taking in the trees.

"Those two guys there," she says to me. I'm driving, and I glance from the road and follow her finger, which is pointing down the street to two men in dark jogging suits walking away from a pay phone. "I'll bet they're dealing from there."

She tells me to go down two blocks, and then take a few quick rights. When we drive up on the pay phone from the side street, the two men are at the phone again. Only this time, they walk away from the phone in the opposite direction.

"You want to jam them?" I ask.

"No, because we don't know where their dope is," she says. "The only way we'll find it is if we watch them make a sale."

"You want to find a place to watch them from?" I ask. I'm into it. The only other officer I worked with who liked to take down dealers was Jackson—and that was months ago.

"I'm hungry," says Gould. "Let's get something to eat first, give them time to think they're cold, then come back and find a place to watch them from."

"Sounds good," I reply.

Because she's new to Southwest, she doesn't know where to eat. I try to think of a place nearby. We're on the northern edge of the USC campus, so there are numerous eating spots within a minute's drive.

"What do you feel like eating?" I ask.

"I don't know," she replies. "What did I eat for breakfast?" she mumbles to herself.

We are stopped at the light southbound on Hoover Avenue at Jefferson Boulevard. I look past Gould to the entrance of the Bank of America on the northwest corner. USC students are walking in clumps to and from afternoon class, so the sidewalk is crowded. But still I notice him.

He is now walking down the sidewalk away from us. He is very much in place, a casually dressed man in his early forties wearing a polo shirt and a nice pair of slacks. His right hand carries a leather executive satchel. He looks as if he has just made a bank run from a business that he owns. But when I first saw him—just in an instant—I observed him stick a small handgun into his left front pants pocket as he exited the doors of the bank.

"I think the bank just got robbed" is all I say.

Gould looks at me, smiling, then she sees that I am not kidding. Her head swivels, following my eyes.

"Older male black, blue shirt, he has a gun," I say.

"I see him," she replies.

Things speed up now. I turn the corner slowly, and he runs full speed down the sidewalk. He is trying to yank something from the satchel. I immediately think he may have another gun. But . . . *boom!* The man temporarily disappears into a cloud of red smoke.

"Dye pack," says Gould evenly, referring to the bank security device which has just exploded in the man's hands.

We continue to follow him in the car. The man is running parallel to us, a cement wall prohibiting his running anywhere but down the sidewalk. I know he'll tire quickly—no need to chase him on foot yet. And we may need the car as cover should he decide to shoot it out.

The load on his lungs from fear and physical exertion has caused him to overload. He is soon running as if he had lead weights on his ankles. City-planted trees and bushes have thus far separated our roadway and his sidewalk, but the trees end ahead, and now it's just cement sidewalk to street. I pull onto the sidewalk behind him and stop. Gould and I are out of the car, running, and quickly catch up to him, shoving him to the ground. He tries to resist—never going for his pants pocket, though. But he is exhausted, and we easily cuff him up.

"Damn," he huffs, his face smeared with red splotches of dye. "I knew she gave me the damn dye pack."

I look over at Gould. She has a big grin on her face. I reach into his front pants pocket and remove the handgun, a blue steel .25 automatic. Then I look into the leather satchel. It is filled with money—close to five thousand dollars.

"Three-A-fifty-five, we are Code Six, Jefferson and Hoover, on a bank two-eleven suspect," says Gould into her rover, giving our first broadcast of the incident. Like I said, it happened fast. "Show a Code Four, in custody."

The suspect sees that I am examining the handgun. "That's just for show," he says. "I would never use it."

A crowd now gathers, not sure of what is happening. Two security guards from the bank, unarmed, come running up to us.

"Was your bank just robbed?" I ask. But they both shrug uncertainly. One adds, "Not that I know of, but we were both outside." Gould then sees money strewn on the sidewalk back along the sidewalk to where the dye pack blew. "I want you both to go guard that money now!" she orders. "Nobody touches it. Leave it there." They hustle off.

As I lift the suspect to his feet, my rover gives three beeps, the warning that a hot shot is about to be broadcast.

"Any available Southwest unit, two-eleven in progress, Bank of America, Jefferson and Hoover, any unit available, respond Code Three."

I look at Gould. Her grin is even bigger, probably as big as mine. She keys her rover.

"Three-A-fifty-five, send us that call," she says smugly. "And show a Code Four . . . the *bank robbery* suspect *is* in custody."

"The Alligator-Bag Bandit," says the FBI agent.

Gould and I are in the downtown offices of Robbery-Homicide Division, discussing the bank robber we have just brought in with an FBI agent who has responded.

"The *what*?" I ask.

"He's called the Alligator-Bag Bandit," says the FBI agent, a sharp, precise black man in his early thirties named Primus.* He opens a briefcase he has laid on a conference table and pulls out a fold of pictures, very much like one a proud father would carry to show off photos of his kids—except this one holds dozens of black-and-white photos taken from bank surveillance cameras. He opens it, letting one end drop to the floor, holding the other end above his head. Then he twists the fold from side to side, and I see that *both* sides have photos. Each one is different, but in angle and setting only. They all depict the same neatly dressed black man wearing sunglasses, carrying a small leather satchel and in some of them a handgun.

"These are just the robberies he has done *this* year," says Agent Primus. "Thirty-two. Today would have been thirty-three if he had pulled it off. And that's only this year. He's been active for the past three years."

"*Jeez!*" I reply, impressed. Primus then produces a computer printout.

"Each job he did by himself," he says, running his finger down a list of banks along with a list of dollar figures. "And he did pretty well. He always made off with at least twenty-five hundred, but no more than ten thousand. That's because he never went for the vault, which is smart. In and out, with a max three tellers ever knowing the bank was being hit. A real pro."

I look at the bottom of the page where the dollar figures are totaled. It is in excess of one hundred thirty thousand dollars—which is his take for *this* year only.

"*Jeez!*" I reply again, even more impressed.

"We had no idea who he was," adds Primus. "And he wore only sunglasses as a disguise. But we couldn't match him."

"Here's who he is," says a second FBI agent, a leather-skinned southerner named Tomkins* who has the bearing of a twenty-year homicide detective. Tomkins seems more "cop" than Primus, who bears a closer resemblance to an attorney. "Name is Wright, Carl Lee Wright."

Carl Lee Wright *is* a professional bank robber. He is forty-two years old, and has been robbing banks for more than sixteen years, minus a single seven-year stint in a federal prison for his career choice. He has other arrests, just a few, but no convictions. A very short, very clean rap sheet.

"You and your partner caught yourself a good one," says Tomkins. "We would have never made him through investigation. But now that we know who he is, we can hook him up to all of these capers. Mr. Wright will be spending the rest of his life in federal prison."

Gould and I grab cups of coffee from a machine in the corner of one of the detective areas of the building. We're still giving each other pats on the back for our big arrest, but I feel somewhat subdued. Tomkins's words hang in my head: *Mr. Wright will be spending the rest of his life in federal prison.* What an ominous thought.

Agent Tomkins then asks me to sit in the interview room with Wright while he and Primus discuss the case with an LAPD detective. The room has the usual three soundproof walls with a two-way mirror on one side. A heavy wood table and four heavy wood chairs are the only furnishings.

Wright sits across from me, handcuffed, as we are in the room by ourselves. He has the eyes of an intelligent man, and his hair, thin mustache, and tight goatee are neatly trimmed. If I had not spotted the gun when I saw him walking down that street near USC, I would have kept on driving.

He seems resigned to the fact that he is caught; there is no anger in his eyes—just deep thought.

"So, why'd you do it?" I ask, hoping to learn a little. "Why'd you rob banks?"

"Because that's where the money is," he replies, thinly smiling, quoting Willie Sutton, the most famous bank robber this side of the James Brothers. Then he refocuses. "I use heroin. Been using it ever since I was twenty-six. And it's expensive."

"Heroin," I say. "How often do you use it?"

"Whenever," he replies. "Twice a day, maybe more, maybe less. I'll start hurting in a few hours."

I look at his arms. The polo shirt has short sleeves, but I don't see any needle marks.

"I shoot in my legs and my feet," he says, acknowledging my curiosity. "Keeps people from noticing."

"Oh," I reply, and nod my head in agreement. Appearances are important.

"I'm a pro," he says, shaking his head. "I mean, I saw the teller give me the damn dye pack. I knew what it was. I can spot 'em a mile away. And usually they're no problem. I took it 'cause I'd already put my fingers on it. Figured I'd just walk it out the doors and let it activate, then toss it and let it explode so it would get rid of my prints. But then I step outside, and there you were. Looking right at me. I panicked. I just panicked. Like some punk just on the

streets. I cannot believe I took off running with that damn pack in
my hands," he says, smiling at his mistake. "It must have been some
sight when it blew. Red everywhere, all over me. I should have worn
a red shirt, 'cept that's one rule of robbing banks—don't wear bright
colors," he says, his mind momentarily sidetracked. "And the money
was flying . . ."

"How long you been robbing banks?" I ask.

"Since I was twenty-six," he replies. "That's when I started to
use drugs. Lost my job over 'em, and could never get back on my
feet. Before I got hooked, I had a regular job. I was working with
computers just when they were becoming usable in general business.
I could have made a lot of money if I had stayed in the business
world. But I messed up with the drugs. I really ain't a bad guy."

"Well, you're not a good guy, either," I add.

"I never hurt anyone when I robbed a bank," he says seriously.
"Never shot anybody, never punched anybody. I just wanted the
damn money. That gun I had, it won't even fire. I had it strictly for
show." He lowers his head, scratching his nose on his shoulder. He
rubs hard and long, a slight sheen of perspiration forming on his
face, the first sign of the impending drug withdrawal.

I feel sorry for him. Yes, he is a bank robber, a true bad guy.
But it hits me that I have just arrested a human being who, because
of the gravity of his numerous federal crimes, will be spending the
rest of his days in a six-by-twelve cement room. My actions, as
lawful as they were, have resulted in the effectual end of this man's
free life. Tomkins's words go through my head again: *Mr. Wright
will be spending the rest of his days in federal prison.*

I am human, and do not savor putting people into small cement
rooms. I get no feeling of accomplishment by taking away someone's
freedom. But I do savor separating the bad from the good, keeping
the predators away from the flock, so to speak. I want to be a piece
of that "thin blue line" between the good and the bad. I have so far
separated the action of arrest from the action of incarceration. When
I put those cuffs on a bad guy, I do not think of where he could be
going. I just think of the good it will do taking him off the streets.
I understand the need to incarcerate. It must be done if we are to
retain some semblance of order in all of this chaos. I am just glad

that all I have to do is arrest, because if I also had to incarcerate, if I had to look at imprisoned human beings, I would not do this job.

I try to push the sympathetic thoughts out of my head.

"I just wanted the money," he adds quietly.

JOINING TO LEAVE

Gould has entered police work in Los Angeles with one goal: to gain experience with the LAPD and then join a department in her native Indiana. This is a common goal for many young officers on the force today, who later return to their hometowns to continue police work there.

"At first, I was gonna do five years," she says. "Ya know, get some specialized experience like working a vice unit or something. But with all of this Rodney King stuff, I'm already applying back home. I have my application in with three different departments around my hometown."

The Los Angeles Police Department has the tradition and the training. It is a prestigious place to work, known throughout the world for the quality of its officers. The city provides a great training ground for police work. Because of the violence of its streets, and the "thin blue line" that stretches throughout the sprawling city, LAPD officers will be confronted in one year with as many different and difficult situations as street cops in other big cities will face over a ten-year period. As such, LAPD officers are a valuable commodity in the law-enforcement community. They can go to any city in any state and quickly become a department's hardest-charging crime fighter.

"I have a feeling I'm gonna have a pick of departments," she says. "Now, back where I live, they hire maybe ten people each year per department. But the people they have to choose from don't really have any experience. And I did my probation in Rampart Division, which is a real junky place. I've told a couple of the recruiters some of the things I've been involved in. They seem amazed, 'cause the places I'm looking to work are *real* small towns. If they have two murders in one year, it's a crime wave."

Throughout the 1960s, the LAPD's pay and benefits package

ranked first in California. At that time, the city of Los Angeles spent the majority of its budget on such necessities as police, fire, schooling, street maintenance, and sanitation. But in 1991, police pay ranked fifty-third in the state, at a time when the city budget allocated more funds to its Arts Council projects, miscellaneous studies, and government office redecorations than it did to law enforcement. The LAPD is truly run on a shoestring budget with a skeleton crew. Couple this with the negative and hostile attitude of some of the the citizenry (one that has worsened tenfold after the King incident), and the city has created a horrendous working environment for its police. But its Academy is still one of the best in the country, so many officers, like Gould, join for the training—and then leave.

Gould's departure will be the department's loss. She is a good cop. Her telling me of her plans reminds me that Kent Pallister is in the same mode. Currently going through the application process with a city in Canada, he will be flying there on his next vacation to take their physical test. By this time next year, he will be gone, as will another P-I named Nucholls, who is applying for the West Covina PD. And Sergeant Roberts, who is applying to a number of departments. And the list goes on.

THE WESTWOOD INCIDENT

The officers involved in the Rodney King incident have been indicted and ordered to stand trial. Officers Laurence Powell, Timothy Wind, Ted Briseno, and Sergeant Stacy Koon have been charged with battery under the color of authority, as well as filing a false police report, charges which could land some of them in prison for up to eight years.

The indictments have had a devastating effect on the department. Almost overnight, proactive police work, the very heart and soul of the LAPD system of policing, has come to a grinding halt. Yes, it had slowed some in the weeks since the Rodney King video was made public. But with the indictments, police work has stopped. Because the majority of officers I talk with simply do not understand *how* those officers could be charged with a crime. They see the four as acting in the course of their employment with no malice aforethought, especially since even some media do not question the *need* to have struck Rodney King with the baton at least a few times. Where the problem arises is the number of times he was struck, which many officers regard as a subjective question and decision. What is too many strikes? Even if they did hit Rodney King too many times, police officers view it as an "in-house" problem, one that should be taken care of through internal disciplinary channels.

To the average LAPD officer, indictments with possible criminal punishment seem far out of line for the act with which they are being charged. After all, they were making a felony arrest of a hostile, aggressive ex-convict who outweighed any one of the four officers by at least forty pounds. At six feet one and one hundred ninety pounds, Laurence Powell was the tallest and heaviest of the four officers. Rodney King's height is described as being anywhere from six feet two to six feet five with a weight between two hundred thirty pounds to two hundred sixty pounds.

With this new threat of indictment, officers are working scared right now. Many feel that they too could become the victim of a video camera, that a slight shove or a harsh word caught on tape could mean time behind bars. Officers could understand the Thirty-ninth and Dalton trial and its possibility of criminal prosecution because there was destruction of property and the probability of prior planning. But Powell, Wind, Briseno, and Koon were just making a felony arrest! That's all! If they were really an unruly mob with planned malice, why didn't they also beat the two passengers in the car with King?

So there is much confusion among the street cops. And fear. And it is manifesting itself in the way the LAPD works. A case in point is an incident that recently occurred in the Westwood area of Los Angeles.

Westwood is a small enclave of low-lying shops and preppy bars on the southern edge of the UCLA campus, and is where the premiere of the film *New Jack City* took place. Starring rapper Ice-T and actor Wesley Snipes, *New Jack City* is the story of a black youth's rise to power in Harlem's drug underground. When the late show sold out of tickets, those citizens who did not get in became upset. They began milling in front of the theater, a seething mass. Soon, members of the crowd began shouting, "Black Power!" and "Fight the Power!"—and made references to the Rodney King video.

The crowd began to swell as passersby joined in. At this point, merchants in the area became fearful and called police to the location. When officers arrived, they were met by a large, rapidly swelling and unruly crowd.

According to eyewitnesses, "One guy then picked up a rubbish can and threw it into the street. Another picked up a traffic barricade and threw it. Then people just got braver and braver from there." A multitude of youths "began smashing windows and looting stores." A full-scale riot ensued. Estimates placed the crowd of rioters between six and eight hundred, with almost a hundred officers responding to the scene before peace was restored. It was days before many of the stores reopened, and damage tallied into the millions of dollars.

But the worst number is *zero*. That's the number of rioters arrested. Even though the LAPD had a force of almost a hundred officers at the scene, not one arrest was made! There was extensive vandalism, riotous actions, and numerous assaults on police when the crowd began throwing rocks and bottles at officers. But still, not one arrest was made.

The LAPD cannot be blamed for this zero, because as fast as officers responded to the problem, so did the media. The newspapers are full of photos of *rioters*. They are captured smiling as they smash store windows. They are shown yanking stereos, clothing, jewelry, and whatever else they could carry out of local stores. Yes, the papers are full of photos of the incident, but not one picture is of an LAPD officer.

Not one picture of an LAPD officer trying to strike a rioter with a baton, or grabbing a rioter to make an arrest, or even standing near a rioter. Because with the way popular opinion is swayed right now, supervision at the scene wisely did not allow officers to engage the crowd, an activity that surely would have resulted in massive uses of force, no matter how defensive those actions would have been.

The King video is a piece of selective journalism. It shows only the end result of the incident; it does not show how it started. It does not show King drinking earlier in the evening (which he admits). It does not show him speeding on the freeway. It does not show him evading police. It does not show him dancing when officers attempted to order him into a handcuffing position. It does not show him throwing four officers off him when they tried to dog-pile him. It does not show him getting electric shocks twice with little effect. And it does not show him attacking Powell. It just shows the aftermath. And there is fear that if officers moved in after taking rocks and bottles at the movie theater, the media would only be showing footage of the arrests, not the actions before, because the media are perceived by police as being biased against police. Plain and simple. That's because there is no commentary on Rodney King's actions; just on the reaction of officers. King is a motorist, and LAPD officers are thugs. And it is perceived by police that this type of biased reporting will continue with any future police activity.

So LAPD officers kept their distance, moving in only after rioters tired themselves out. Stopping a riot is just not worth going to jail for.

WOLF PACKS

A week after the Westwood riot, Gould and I are stopped in a gas station on the south side of Leimert Park at the junction of Crenshaw Boulevard and Vernon Avenue. The park is small and flat, no more than a dozen trees thrown over a square green expanse that is about half the size of a football field. It was once the heart of a fashionable shopping area; at its center are four ancient wooden benches that were once a resting place for weary shoppers. But that was in the 1950s. It is now a dangerous place, especially in the early afternoon when high school lets out.

Students are looting the businesses before us. But we just watch them from a distance, unable to take action until we get some backup. It is a helpless feeling, watching as citizens we are sworn to protect and to serve are attacked. But we can do nothing. If we move in now with just the two of us, we will definitely have to take physical action, possibly using deadly force. But the crimes we are observing are property crimes only. Add to this that the majority of our suspects are students under the age of seventeen: juveniles. So we stand by waiting for backup, hoping that a strong show of numbers will be enough to disperse the crowd, allowing the juveniles to continue, the latest in a series of daily disturbances the local media have called Wolf Packing.

"Wolf packing," I say. "This looks more like a riot."

The Los Angeles School District in a cost-saving measure has taken "slow and/or problem" students from Crenshaw, Manual Arts, and Dorsey high schools and put them into one program using vacant facilities at nearby Audubon Junior High. Unfortunately, many of the slow and/or problem students from Crenshaw are Rollin' 60s and Rollin' 40s Crips; from Manual Arts they are Five Deuce Hoover Crips and Fruit Town Brims; from Dorsey they are P-Stone Bloods and West Boulevard Crips. So now we have kids from six different major gangs going to school together, and it is causing some problems—like complete chaos around the park every afternoon this week.

"This is a riot," says Gould, scanning the scene before us. "This really is. We should have teargas and we should have rubber bullets."

Students are running everywhere. Through the streets, through the park. Hundreds of them. They knock over trash cans and throw trash. They spray-paint walls and etch their slogans into storefront glass. They act as if they are completely out of their minds. Many have stormed the Korean-owned shops near the corner of Denker and Forty-third Place, running inside the businesses en masse and stripping the shelves bare like a swarm of locusts in a wheat field. Others have tried to break the bullet-proof glass of a pawnshop a block away. More than a few have run within a hundred feet of us and flipped us off, trying to get us to chase. But we ignore them and wait for backup.

Soon we have six units, just as we did the day before and the day before that, and we form a line with the cars. We break the rioters into small groups, herding them in different directions. Some board the buses that have stops at the park. Others just run off down the street. Some hurl bottles at our patrol cars, but we do not chase them down. We are all cognizant of the current climate and how a baton-wielding battle would look in the newspapers. Rodney King, the sequel, is a movie none of us wants a part in, so we move slowly, ignoring the rocks and bottles. In ten minutes, the area is clear, the only signs of the kids being the strewn trash and the spray-painted walls.

We make no arrests; we do not even try to. We are all of the same mind. Unless an officer is injured, we are not sticking our necks out; not to put a few juveniles in jail who will be released to their parents in a few hours; not with a hostile media. Officers are beyond paranoia when it comes to using force. Our police force has been effectively emasculated. These juveniles sense that. They have complete confidence that we will do nothing, and they are right. They can wolf pack all day, and we will do little else in response than herd them out of the area.

We return to the stores around Leimert Park to take crime reports for damage and theft.

"I cannot take this anymore," cries one Korean woman who owns a beauty-supply store on the corner of Forty-third and Denker. "I had a group of twenty girls come in here. They stole everything, pay for nothing. I saw so many faces, I cannot remember one. They just came in, screaming, then grab things and run. When I try to grab one, three of them shove me to the ground."

I scratch out a robbery report for her.

"This will not do me any good," she says, holding the paper. "I have no insurance, no money to replace the things taken. I think I will take my store someplace else. Someplace where kids have respect."

She thinks for a beat.

"I think I will go back to Korea," she says quietly.

DEPLOYMENT PERIOD NINE

On my vacation, I go to Colorado for a wedding of two friends named Doug and Gayna. I have some time before I need to be back to the streets of South Central, so I drive.

On the first night, I stay in St. George, Utah, a quiet Mormon town at the spot on the globe where Arizona, Nevada, and Utah all meet. I pull off of the freeway about nine at night, and drive through the downtown area. The streets are quiet, just a few cars rolling, and that's all. I see no one on the sidewalks. It is a cold night, so I can understand the lack of pedestrian traffic, but still it seems that most people of this community stay home at night.

It feels odd, not seeing people out, especially since I'm used to driving through Los Angeles after dark. I'm used to seeing crowds of men standing around pay phones or sipping cheap wine near liquor stores. The most noticeable missing feature is the absence of juveniles on the streets. There are none. I see no groups of teenagers walking in close formation, clothing dark, with stern looks on their faces. Apparently, the kids of this town have better things to do.

I find only one restaurant open, one of a small local chain, and I stop in to get a cup of coffee and a slice of pie. I buy a newspaper to read while I snack.

The restaurant is clean and constructed in true "diner" fashion, a throwback to the fifties with polished white-and-red tile, lots of stainless steel, booths with billowy red-cushioned seats for families to sit in, and red wheel-like stools along a white tile counter. Behind the counter are shelves of pies and cakes with slanted mirrors so that you can get both a side- and topview of the desserts.

I sit at the counter. There are a few patrons: two old cowboys in heavy denim jackets puffing on cigarettes down the counter from me, and a smattering of couples and families seated at tables around the restaurant.

The waitress comes by and I order. I go to the rest room, feeling secure that no one will take my newspaper, which I leave at the counter. While I'm washing my hands in the rest room, I look at the tile next to the mirror and see *Crips* scrawled in black felt pen, with the dot over the *i* in an X shape.

"Someone wrote some graffiti in your rest room," I say quietly to the waitress when I return to the counter.

She just shakes her head and sighs.

"Hey, Mike, someone made a mess in the john," she calls to a tired-looking man wearing a white apron.

"OK," he replies as he walks past me toward the rest room.

I open the newspaper and look for a story to read while I eat, settling on one about families who had moved to St. George from Los Angeles and the problems that they are having assimilating.

In the story, they interview a local law-enforcement officer, one who is starting the area's first gang unit. The city has seen juvenile gangs forming at the local high schools, and there was recently a drive-by shooting which has caused tremendous concern.

The article continues:

In California, their kids are victims of the violence. They get beat up and stepped on, and the parents say, "I need to get my family away from this." But when they get here, the kids find out that they are celebrities to a lot of our children. Because these new kids are from the mean streets of LA, and some of our kids have watched too much television. So these new kids find out that they're expected to act like gang members here. And they do. You have the kids who were victims in Los Angeles turning into the lead gang members here in St. George. They even name the gangs after the ones they know of back in Los Angeles.

The article goes on to interview the mother of a boy accused of knifing another youngster after school. She is raising two teenagers by herself, and has been in St. George for only two years. There is a picture of her accompanying the article. She is heavyset, and white. The gang members she discussed in the article are also white.

> I moved here to get my kids away from the problems at their schools in California. We lived in Hawthorne, and it got so bad I was afraid both of my kids would be dead before they reached sixteen. But they came here, and they started hanging out with kids who wanted them to act bad. The other kids looked up to mine. I still don't think my son knifed that boy. But I guess he was around when it happened.

Mike comes out of the bathroom, a darkened washcloth in his hand. He sees me watching him and smiles, having heard me advise the waitress of the defacement.

"Little bastards been doing that a lot lately," he says. "If I catch 'em, I'm gonna give their fannies a pretty good paddling."

That is, of course, if they don't shoot him first.

I think about finding the graffiti in the bathroom of this restaurant. I wonder if *Crips* was placed there by some displaced white kid from Los Angeles with delusions of being the ghetto star of St. George, Utah. The thought strikes me as funny: white Crips. I can think of a few Rollin' 60s who must be rollin' in their graves.

THE SMALL-TOWN COP

"We had some Crips come into town a while back," he says, "but we got rid of them."

He is a police officer named Tim who works in a small municipality of about sixty thousand people just north of Denver, Colorado. He is a neighbor of the friends with whom I am staying while in town for Doug and Gayna's wedding.

We are in the backyard of a modest ranch house with a large shade tree. We sit in low-slung lounge chairs, beers in hand, George Strait crooning from a CD player with large speakers. The Rockies stand before us, mammoth cathedrals of rock exploding out of the farmlands of northern Colorado. It feels a million miles from the streets of Los Angeles.

"You had Crips here?" I ask. "How do you know they were Crips?"

" 'Cause they *told* everyone they were Crips," he says with a smile on his face. "And they looked like the ones we see on television. You know, black guys driving purple and green Chevys and stuff."

"What were they doing here?" I ask. "They move into town to live?"

"Kind of," says Tim. "But they weren't really families. Just one guy who rented a house near the college, then moved in about six other guys with him, along with some girls. And next thing we heard, people all around the neighborhood are calling us saying they're selling drugs out of this house. We couldn't believe it. We actually had what you call a 'crack house' here in town."

"What did you do?" I ask.

"Hell, at first we didn't have the faintest idea what to do," says Tim. "We had a couple different officers go up to the house to buy drugs, but that didn't work. None of us had ever bought drugs before, didn't know how to. Ain't one of us who speaks street slang, so we'd be saying stuff like, 'Got any crack for sale?'—which didn't go over too big. They'd just look at us funny, ask us if we had any tickets to sell for the Policemen's Ball, not that we have one.

"They sniffed us out like a bitch in heat. So we started writing them traffic tickets and stuff, a little harassment, which did do something, 'cause we found out one of them was wanted in Los Angeles for selling drugs. So we picked him up and shipped him back to your neck of the woods. But we still had all these other guys to deal with.

"We didn't know what to do," says Tim. "Then one night, we get a call of a big disturbance at the house. By the time we get there, it's over. All we have is one of the Crip girls, I guess you'd call her a Cripette, tellin' us a bunch of cowboys in pickup trucks came over to their house and just started smashing everything. Including the Crips, 'cause two of the males are laying on the sidewalk, all beat to shit. And their cars, like I said, real nice Chevys, and a new BMW, had baseball bats took to them. All busted up. Windows smashed, tired slashed. A real insurance nightmare. And the house was beat up, too. Not a window in place. At first we thought it was a drug deal gone bad. But then some neighbors tell us that when the cow-boys left, and there was a good dozen of them, the cowboys was yelling at the Crips to get out of town. Else next time they'd bring shotguns instead of ball bats. So we think it was a little vigilante thing. Actually, we know it was, 'cause of gossip around town now. Some folks in town just got fed up and called in some mean-assed cowboys."

Tim takes a slug of beer and continues. "So the house was vacant the next day. But I don't think it did much good, 'cause all they did was replace the black faces with white ones. After the Crips left, a similar operation opened in a condominium near the college, this one run by some local white trash. We got a few too many rednecks around here for a bunch of out-of-town gang members to come here and open a crack house. But they can get some local white people to do it for them, which they have.

"We don't get near as many complaints about these white boys selling crack. And so far, ain't a cowboy set foot in town to take care of business. And we can't buy drugs from them any better than we could from the Crips. So I guess the Crips have won. 'Cause as long as they don't cause too big of a commotion when they sell, people don't make a big deal out of the white trash sellin' it.

"Even if we could get rid of this crack house, I don't think it would do any good anyway. 'Cause all we're doing is fighting the selling. And the problem that needs to be addressed is the buying. We need to put people who buy this stuff in jail."

Tim shifts in his lounge chair and sums up.

"But I think that will never happen. I mean, when they're open-ing crack houses in towns as small as ours, you know that the de-mand is *real* widespread. 'Cause we don't even have a Walmart, but we do have a crack house."

Near the end of my vacation, I get together with a group of my classmates at a night club called The Red Onion in the Marina Del Rey section of Los Angeles. It is basically the same group that would get together during our Academy days, although the numbers have dwindled some.

I stand off to one side talking to Banderras and Jeffri Norat. Norat is a muscular Puerto Rican, an ex-marine boxer, who was our class leader. A strong family man, he has called his wife twice since his arrival, feeling guilty at leaving his spouse home with the kids so he could meet up with his classmates. Norat scans the room, shaking to the beat of the disco-style music the club plays. I myself am taking in Banderras, who looks incredible out of uniform, a black stretch dress fitted tightly over her. I can eye Banderras, because Kelly and I have split—not because of my job, though. I think that officer-involved relationships shattering apart because of job stress or unusual scheduling is not as common as is portrayed in the movies. Love conquers all—it's the truth. Kelly and I broke up just because it was not working out. If we wanted to be together, we would. My being a police officer was a non-issue.

"I hear Sanders quit two weeks out of the Academy to join the Secret Service," says Norat, yelling over the din, referring to a classmate. "And Moore joined a fire department in Seattle."

"I guess there are probably others," I say. It's difficult to keep track of eighty-three officers and their movements throughout the department. "But I think most are hanging in, even with all of this Rodney King stuff. I just feel sorry for Dave Love."

Dave Love is one of our classmates. He was extremely popular, having a warm, outgoing nature. But he was at the scene during the Rodney King beating. And with all the publicity, any attachment to the incident by an LAPD officer is like the kiss of death. Although he arrived at its conclusion and had no involvement in the incident other than having exited his black-and-white, he has been pulled from his patrol duties and is under investigation by the FBI for possible misconduct, and possible future prosecution. To make matters worse, Dave Love is an African American, the only African American at the scene, and the pressures of this added issue I'm sure are suffocating. One of King's attorneys is quoted as calling Dave a "house nigger," which is sickening.

"I called him," says Banderras. "We should keep him in our prayers."

The thought quiets us for a moment. "Ann Hayes quit after Tina Kerbrat was killed," says Banderras. "I gave it some thought myself, you know. I mean, that's a pretty heavy thing when an officer goes down. You really have to examine your job. But I know staying with the department is the best thing."

I think about our conversation for a moment.

"There are so many pressures right now to leave the LAPD," I say. "I mean, there is Rodney King. There are officers getting killed. Then, we have the media, which in our city seem to be trying to make life as miserable for us as it can. This is a terrible employment situation. None of us deserves all of this bullshit that we are being put through. Right?"

I lift my bottle of beer, tap it to the glasses of my classmates.

"Why do we stay?" I ask. "And I mean with the LAPD—because we can make more money elsewhere, and live in better areas. All we have to do is apply."

I look at both Banderras and Norat. They think for a moment.

" 'Cause it's fun chasing the bad guys here," says Banderras.

I look at Norat. He nods in agreement.

"And that's it?" I ask. I am somewhat amazed, because our answers amount to staying with the LAPD because it has the best bad guys to chase: most murderers per officer; most robbers; most car thiefs; most overall surly individuals.

"Yeah," shrugs Banderras after some thought.

And that's it. " 'Cause it's fun chasing the bad guys here" is the only reason we can come up with. Unfortunately, the more I think about it, the more truthful it becomes. I begin to laugh. "We are some twisted individuals" is all I can say.

Banderras grabs my hand and pulls me toward the dance floor. "Dunn, I think you need to dance," she says. "And not think so much."

DEPLOYMENT PERIOD TEN

It seems that in the South End, you cannot leave your home for any extended period of time without the neighborhood burglars taking advantage. Unfortunately, a three-hour shopping trip to the mall sometimes qualifies as an extended period of time. Citizens take an especially big risk going away for the weekend, because come Monday, they may not even find their homes' foundations still there.

Because I am a Phase III probationer, I am "street certified," which means that I am approved to work a one-officer report-taking car on the streets of Los Angeles. The report car I am working is nicknamed the U-boat because it has a call sign of Union One.

"The U-boat's job is to write reports and stay out of trouble," says Sergeant Reese to me during roll call. "If things go sideways, don't hesitate to ask for other units."

This is a typical South Central Monday, which means the report car will be very busy. Burglars and sneak thieves looking for a weekend high have perpetrated many crimes. A dozen different citizens, just home from weekend vacations, have called the front desk to report break-ins. The desk officer's report log, the "Storm Log," is full. I copy down the first five and call the citizens, making appointments.

When people think of crime in South Central, they always think of shootings. Those are what we read about in the newspapers. They are more bloody, more spectacular than other crimes. Gunfire with the thought of murder is quite intriguing to us. But for some, a burglary can be as devastating as being shot, having the same nightmarish quality, the same sense that you've lost the ability to protect yourself. Your home has been violated and some unknown intruder has gone through your most personal belongings. To make matters worse, theft insurance in South Central is prohibitively expensive, so very few have it. When someone is burglarized and something of great value is stolen, it will be a long time and much hard work before it is replaced. The theft of a television could mean not being able to watch your favorite shows for six months. That is why we read of people dying over the protection of a sports jacket or a wristwatch. Luxury items take hard work to obtain. People are willing to die for their property because they have invested so much into getting what they have. And if they do not fight for it, they may never get it again.

My first call turns out to be rather pleasant. I find myself sitting in the living room of Miss Sophie Jones,* an elderly, dainty black lady with wispy white hair. Her home has been ransacked while she was at a church luncheon. From what I can see of the living room I am seated in and the dining room, the house is full of very old, very elegant cherry-wood furniture. It is a little disheveled right now, drawers pulled out and their contents strewn, cushions overturned. But Miss Jones seems more worried about my having enough cookies to eat or cream for my coffee than the events of the day. Every few moments she is up again trying to tend to my comforts.

"These are my favorite," she says as she puts two more sugar cookies on the plate of goodies already in front of me.

"Thank you, ma'am," I reply. "But really, I am fine."

"It is my second time being robbed," she says. "They keep coming in through the windows in the back. And I keep forgetting to get bars put on those things."

"How many years ago was your first?" I ask.

"*Years ago!*" she exclaims, a smile flashing across gold-inlaid teeth. "It hasn't been *years* ago. It's been, oh maybe three *months*. I am sorry, I must be confusing you. When I said this was my second time being robbed, I meant my second time being robbed this year. I have been robbed well over a dozen times in the last twenty-seven years I have lived here."

With us is her neighbor, Miss Beatrice Washington.* She could be the twin sister of Miss Jones, down to the floral-print dress and pins holding back her hair. Miss Washington saw the suspect from her home across the street.

"I knew he was up to no good," she says. "He went up her driveway and looked in her windows, like he was a Peeping Tom or something. But my daughter called me on the telephone, and by the time I was finished, I didn't see him anymore. I figured he had just left. I'm so sorry, Sophie."

"That's all right," says Miss Jones. "He didn't get much. Just some costume jewelry. At least he didn't get my television. I had my grandson bolt it to the floor."

Bolting your television to the floor? This is not something I would think to do. Only in the South End . . .

Beatrice Washington is a good witness. She gives me a detailed description of a skinny male black in his thirties wearing a red shirt. It sounds like he might be a rock-cocaine smoker. I write it all down, and am just about finished. The women sense this and decide to do what all grandmothers can do so well: embarrass.

"Your job is so hard," says Miss Jones.

"That's true," says Miss Washington. "You young men don't get enough credit."

"Well, thank you," I reply.

"And you're all so handsome," says Miss Jones. "Why, if I was forty years younger . . ."

"Ain't that the truth," says her friend. "And this one has the cutest dimples! Like a peach pit."

Now I am starting to blush. The badge is no armor against the tongues of little old ladies.

"Well, thank you," I say. "My mother thanks you, too."

I hand the report over to Sophie Jones for her signature, and she gets in one last compliment. "Your mother must be so proud," she says as she slowly scrawls her name in elegant penmanship.

Then . . . "*Hey!*" exclaims Beatrice Washington. She seems startled. I look up. She is pointing out the front window. "That's him there! That's the skinny little weasel right there! Coming down my driveway from my house!"

I follow her finger out the window and see him across the street. He fits her description to a tee: skinny, in his thirties, and still wearing that red shirt. Definitely our burglar, and a very bold little bastard at that. I watch him as he nonchalantly walks out to the street, looks both ways, then goes down the sidewalk toward my police car, which is parked quite prominently at the curb.

"Ladies," I say, "stay here."

I am out the front door. The suspect walks right past my black-and-white as if he were on a Sunday stroll, hands in his pockets, looking into the trees as if he's bird watching.

"Three-U-one," I say into my rover. "I need a backup, four-five-nine suspect, Juliet just north of Adams, male black, thirties, red shirt."

"Three-U-one is requesting a backup," the voice comes back. *"Four-five-nine suspect."*

My body is filled with adrenaline, along with a short burst of fear. I am by myself, with a burglar not fifty feet from me, one who is possibly armed; one who is possibly crazy; one who may have no fear of the police. And I am still just a boot.

But they've hired me to handle these types of situations. The only problem is, how do I handle *this*? Do I wait for backup? Do I approach him? And if I approach him, do I approach him as if he is an average citizen, try to bluff him until the troops arrive? Or do I put his ass to the ground? I'd better think quickly, because he's moving down the street away from me.

I make a decision, one that is more instinctual than thought out: I'll put him on the ground, felony prone, and if he's armed, I'll find out now.

I move toward him quickly, hand on gun. As I close in, he looks over his shoulder—too late. I already have a full head of steam. "Get on the ground!" I yell.

"What?" he begins to say. He tries to react, run up a driveway, but I put him on the ground.

"Bury your forehead, man," I growl. "Don't do anything with those hands!"

"But I ain't did nuthin'," he yelps, trying to get to his feet.

"Down, now!" I reply. I put a knee in his back. I grab his left wrist and twist up and in. He struggles for a moment, but I twist hard. He quits struggling, and I handcuff him.

I stand up over him, leaving him prone on the ground. A unit reports back that they have a one-minute ETA, so I leave him on the ground, as I want to put him in their car for transportation. Then I hear something behind me, and I turn to find both women standing there.

"Shoot him!" says Miss Jones.

"Shoot him right in his pointy head!" says Miss Washington.

"Ladies," I say, "go back in the house."

"Gimme your gun," says Sophie Jones. "I'll shoot him."

"Get those bitches away from me," says the suspect.

"Shut up," I say to the suspect.

"Can I kick him?" asks Miss Jones. "Just once in the behind?"

"Ladies," I say, "will you please go back into the house!"

The women are distracting me. The suspect sees this, and starts to get up. I again assist him in lying prone, a quick expulsion of air exploding from his lungs due to this assistance.

"I said, *stay on the ground!*" I yell, this time keeping my knee on him.

Suddenly, *pop!* Miss Jones stomps him on the ankle.

"Hey," I say to her, "knock it off!"

"She kicked me," moans the suspect. "She can't do that!"

"Man, shut up!" I say.

Beatrice Washington now tries to maneuver for a blow.

"You!" I say, pointing my finger at her. "You will not kick him!"

She stops for a moment, frozen by my finger. Then, *pop!* right into his hip.

"*Ow,*" says the suspect. "She kicked me, too."

I now have a pair of 415 grannies on my hands, and it is all I can do to keep them from tearing up my suspect.

"Ladies," I command, "into the house, now!"

"Just one more," pleads Miss Washington.

"Knock it off!" I bark. "You're making my job very difficult. Now back into the house with both of you!" They look at me sheepishly. "Don't make me ask you again!" They turn away. I refocus on the suspect. From out of nowhere: *Bam!* Beatrice Washington strikes again, sneaking a kick to his left ankle with her pointy-toed shoes.

"*Ouch!*" cries the suspect. "Bitch kicked me again!"

I look at her hard.

"Just wanted one more," she says like a six-year-old schoolgirl who has gotten her way. With that, the two women scurry off across the street and into the house.

"I think I need to go to the hospital," moans the suspect. "I might be disabled. I want a lawyer—"

"Oh, shut up," I cut him off.

Sergeant Laughton, a midday-watch supervisor, arrives, and soon we get the suspect searched. Not only does the suspect have some of Beatrice Washington's property just taken from her house in his pockets, but he's wearing one of Sophie Jones's rings on his pinkie finger, as well as a ring taken from another burglary earlier in the day.

At his trial four months later, I find out the suspect is already on parole for burglary. The two women are there, looking sweet and innocent. The judge drops a heavy sentence on our burglar.

"I'm glad they put him away for a long time," says Miss Jones afterward. "I was so scared of him, why I went and bought me a gun."

"Really," I say.

"Yes, sir," she says. "It's a three-fifty-seven magnum, a Dirty Harry special."

I wonder if I should tell her Dirty Harry uses a larger gun, a .44 magnum?

"I also got me some of them hollow-point bullets," she says. "Just let some sucka climb in my bedroom window now. *Pow!* Right in his pointy head!"

Uh, better not tell her.

NATURAL-BORN KILLER, PART TWO

Two days later, I am U-boating it to a burglary report call when I hear a report of a "drive-by shooting—just occurred" at a residence on Hobart Avenue just south of Adams Boulevard. I'm not far away, so I back Don Murphy and his boot, a male named Ponce, who are the primary unit that takes the call. It's a call that will introduce me to the most cold-blooded killer I have met, Eric Buford.

The residence is a common three-bedroom, brown-stucco California bungalow. A big shade tree squats out front, its heavy thick branches arching up, holding clumps of leaves, like a weightlifter's dumbbells. There are rosebushes in a side garden. It's not much different from the houses around it, except as I walk up the front steps, there are bullet holes running in strafing patterns all along the front of the house. I stop counting at fifteen.

"Dunn, you working the U-boat?" says Murphy, as he comes out the front door.

"Yeah," I reply, knowing what will come next.

"Can you take the report on this thing?" he asks. "It happened about two hours ago and we're loaded down with calls."

"Sure," I say. I thumb one of the bullet holes. Pulverized plaster smears my digit. "Why wasn't it called in sooner?"

"They weren't going to report it at all, but one of the rounds hit their stereo," he replies. "And their homeowner's insurance only covers it if they file a police report."

"Oh," I reply.

"I count six rounds fired this time," says Murphy.

This time? Now I look closer at the front of the house. As I said, I quit counting at fifteen, but most of the bullet holes look weathered. A few have even been painted over.

"Some of these holes seem old," I say.

"They are," says Murphy. "I've been here before on shootings. They need to start dating the bullet holes."

Dating the bullet holes? Murphy sees that I am a little more than amazed.

"This is nothing," he says. "There's an apartment building over on Manhattan Place and Twenty-seventh Street that has to have over a hundred rounds that have been fired at it. Thing would probably collapse if you put a magnet on one side of it."

I look into one of the holes. I see a faint spec of light from the other side.

"The victims are inside," says Ponce.

Murphy and his partner leave as I go inside of the house, which is a sharp contrast to the bullet-riddled exterior. The aroma of freshly baked oatmeal cookies with a pinch of apple in them wafts through the air. Family photos are placed neatly about. There is a large stone flower vase filled with red roses resting on a doily atop a vintage cherry-wood table. When I step farther inside, I see a slender black woman in her fifties with a tint of gray in her hair and a worn expression on her face. The woman, who is named Mrs. Buford, wears a floral-print dress, and looks as if she just came from church. I feel like I have walked into a Norman Rockwell home complete with loving grandmother, except for the numerous bullet holes on the outside and the two gangster-looking guys who are sitting in the living room with her.

One of them is her son James. In his early twenties, he has a full chest and wears a thick web of gold chains around his neck. He looks too soft to have been in the joint. But the other one, a pumped-up cousin in his midtwenties named Cliff, I can tell right off has done time. He has a blue paisley handkerchief wrapped around his left wrist, which I associate as being a flag declaring his Crip affiliation. James sits next to his mother, trying to be helpful. Cliff sits away from us, staring at the television, ignoring me.

"Ma'am, can you tell me what happened here today?" I ask.

She is slow to answer, as though the life had been sucked out of her long ago. She seems resigned. I get the feeling I am talking to a prisoner inside her cell.

"Someone drove by out front," she says. "They shot up the front of the house."

"You see anyone?" I ask.

"No," she replies. She speaks slowly and softly. "I was laying down in my bed, takin' a nap. I usually take a nap in the afternoon 'cause I get tired. I guess I'd been down maybe fifteen minutes when it happened. I just heard the shots, like firecrackers. Then the tires screeching. That's all." She thinks for a moment, painful thoughts. "That's all I ever hear. I never know why they do it."

I look at James. He gives me the smile of an insurance salesman. "We don't know why anyone would want to do this," he says absently. "They may have mistaken our house for somebody else's."

I look over at Cliff. He is watching a rap video, one with youthful, gangster-looking performers in it.

"Just as they mistook your house before?" I ask.

"These are some violent times we live in, Officer," says James. "It's hard not to get shot at."

"You might want to ask Eric about it," says Mrs. Buford.

I notice that Cliff's eyes shift. He is now paying attention to us, although his head is pointed at the television. I get the feeling he is here simply so that he can report back to this Eric.

"Who's Eric?" I ask.

"That's my other son," she says. "He lives in the back."

"Why would Eric know something?" I ask.

James's eyes run over to Cliff, then back to me. Cliff still looks ahead.

"Well, he may have just got in a fight with some guy in the back alley," says James.

"Who?" I ask.

"I don't know him, I didn't see the fight," he replies.

"You know why they were fighting?" I ask.

"No," says James. I am about to press him for more. Mrs. Buford sees this and cuts me off.

"You better ask Eric," she says.

I look at her eyes. They are very sad. I could exert a little command presence here, push James for a little more info, but it would only make those eyes sadder. It is not worth it to me. "Where is he?" I ask.

"I'll show you," says James.

I follow James. I glance back at Cliff, who still stares at the tube. He is back in a television mode, shutting out the rest of the world, now that the discussion of Eric is out of earshot.

James first takes me to his mother's bedroom. He points to a fresh bullet hole that has torn through the wall just above the headboard.

"My mother was laying here when the shootin' started," he says. "They coulda killed her."

He indicates she was lying not a foot from the hole. Then he points across the room at a four-drawer stereo system. It is all black, so black that you would not notice the bullet hole in the tuner unless it was pointed out to you.

"Cost us almost eight hundred dollars," says James, "but the insurance will cover it."

Then I follow him through the house and into the backyard. A baby rottweiler greets us on the steps. He wags his tail and licks at our knees.

"Hey," says James. "Down. You're gonna get the policeman dirty."

"What's his name?" I ask.

"Gangster Jack," says James.

Wonderful name. I wonder if he has taught the dog how to sniff out Bloods. James pushes the dog away, then turns to me. "Hey, man," he says, "I just want you to know I don't gang-bang. I go to college, man. I'm a musician."

I normally would not answer, not really caring. I have quickly learned on this job that preaching to those citizens that we come into contact with has little effect. People who call the police are generally a screwed-up lot. But I am curious as to what he has to say.

"Then how come you gangster name your dog, and you dress like a target?" I ask.

"Eric named the dog," he says. "And what's wrong with my clothes?"

"What do you think?" I reply.

I say it not being a smart ass, but to be real. The guy is dressed like a gangster: black T-shirt and brown khakis. All the gold around his neck makes it look like he is applying for OG status.

"Man," he says, "you think *any* black man is a gang-banger."

"Not true," I say with a frown. I think for a moment. "If I drove you over to the P-Stone Blood hood, could you walk down the street and live?"

"Naw, man. Some fool'd bust a cap in my ass," he says seriously.

"But if I go over to USC," I say, "grab some Joe College African American and drop him off there, P-Stones wouldn't do shit to him. Am I right?"

"Probably," he answers. "Might sweat him."

"Might sweat him, but wouldn't just walk on up and pop a cap in his ass," I add. "And how could they tell? They could tell by his attitude he wasn't a gangster."

"You're talking about attitude, man, but you're looking at my clothes."

"Your attitude is conveyed in your clothes," I reply. "And in the way you carry yourself. It's subtle stuff. But I take one look at you, and I read *gangsta*."

He does not reply.

"Where is Cliff from?" I ask, curious about his cousin's gang affiliation.

"He don't gang-bang no more. He just out of the pen," says James, using the slang term for penitentiary.

"What was he in for?" I ask.

"I don't know," says James. "But whatever he did, he was in for a long time."

"What was Cliff, a thirty?" I ask.

"Naw, man, I think he was TSH," says James, using the gangster slang for "Ten Seven Hoover," or 107th/Hoover Street Crips.

"He's a long way from home," I say.

"Thirties kick with TSH," says James. "Ain't no disputes."

James now leads me to the rear garage, which has been turned into a small apartment. The garage looks as if it should be on its own piece of land, separate from the front house—or its own planet, for that matter. The front house and its garden are under the watchful eye of a woman, clean and fresh. But halfway through the backyard, the grass becomes overgrown. There are weeds. And the area immediately around the rear structure is littered with beer cans, flat tires, and anything else the occupant was too lazy to walk to the trash cans in the alley only a few yards away. It is as if I have crossed a border and entered a third-world country; one that is forbidding.

James knocks on the side door of the garage. Weathered paint cracks out from it, and I half expect the chips to shake off from the pounding. After a moment, I hear the occupant stirring. Something falls and hits the floor. I hear a few "muthafuckas," then feet shuffling toward us. Somebody is having a hard time waking up.

"Eric usually sleeps during the day," says James.

"Tough life," I reply.

The door opens, and out comes a yawning, shirtless male black in his early thirties. Eric Buford has the body of a long-distance runner, a body without an ounce of fat. I immediately notice two crude tattoos: HARLEM is inked in a dull blue on his right shoulder, and 30s is inked on his left. They look uneven and self-inflicted.

There is another one, larger, the kind only imprinted if one has been in the pen.

"What's up?" he asks, the *what* coming at the end of a yawn.

"Someone just shot up the front of your mother's house," I say. "You know anything about it?"

"I heard some shootin'," he says, "but I was in bed."

"You didn't get up to look?" I ask.

"I hear shootin' around here all the time," he says. "Ya' know, it's a black thing."

He says it between yawns. His yawning seems affected, like he is trying to show me how little he cares about my presence. He fixes his eyes on me for the first time. They are totally black, almost like a comic-book character's. His eyes repulse me. I have seen them before. Vincent Hubbard had this kind of eyes, soulless and deeply disturbed.

"You get into it with someone in the alley earlier today?" I ask.

"Yeah," he says. "Some fool down the street come up here, said I was messin' with his girl. I jammed his ass."

He is lying to me, plain and simple. Why, and about what, I do not know. He is just lying to me. He is a typical ex-con; since his time in prison, lying has become part of his nature.

While in prison, lying is bred into men. Cons score points with other prisoners by putting one over on the guards, and the easiest way is to lie. They lie about being sick so as to get out of work; they lie about their pasts so as to gain sympathy; they lie about their guilt so as to gain a sentence reduction; and they lie just to lie. They do it straight-faced, or with emotion. And they do it well. It is a game to the ex-con, one he plays even after he leaves prison.

That's what I have here. An ex-con who is lying to me. So I am already going to disregard just about everything he says to me. But I still have to play it out.

"You think this person did the shooting?" I ask.

"Maybe," he replies.

"What's his name?" I ask.

"Don't know," he replies. "I only know him by sight."

"What does he look like?"

"Kinda big, like you," he says. " 'Cept he's black."

"How about his clothes?" I ask. "What color shirt did he have on?"

"I don't know, man," he says. "I ain't a fashion-conscious person."

"You fought this guy, and you didn't see his shirt?" I say. Even to him this sounds lame. It forces him to find a better answer.

"A white T-shirt," he says.

"Any slogans or sayings on the shirt?" I know I am not going to get anywhere with this conversation. He has no interest in talking to the police. But his insolence strikes a chord within me. I want to talk to this guy all I can, get a feel for him. Because I know I will be dealing with him again. He is a true "bad guy." Hard core. And he further embeds this summation of his being by giving me a real hard *"Fuck you"* look for about a quarter-minute before he answers my last question.

"It was a clean, white T-shirt," he says slowly.

"Anything special about him?" I continue on. A look comes over his face. He can't believe I'm still asking him questions. But this guy fascinates me.

"Like what?"

"He have any scars or tattoos?" I ask.

"I don't look for that shit, man," he says. "I wouldn't know it if he had 'em. I just began bustin' rights and lefts. I was lookin' for hurts, not for tattoos or shit." He says the last words as if he were throwing the punches at me.

"Where's he live?" I ask, and a further look of disbelief comes over him. James shifts uneasily next to me.

"Up the street," he replies. I am about to ask him to show me. He senses it. "But I don't know which house."

I think hard, trying to come up with another question that I could reasonably ask. But I can't think of any. Like I said, this basically was a worthless conversation from an informational standpoint. But I wanted to embed him in my memory, because I know there will be a payback on this incident, one that may result in a serious crime like murder. I look at him carefully for future identification just in case he becomes a suspect. "Anything you can add to this?" I ask.

"No," he says.

It hits me that not once has he asked about his mother. "You know your mother was almost killed?" I ask. "A round hit near where she was sleeping."

"Ain't that a bitch," he replies through a yawn.

He just wants to go back to bed.

"Thanks for your help," I say. I turn to walk back to the front house with James.

"No sweat, man," he says. "I love helpin' the po-leece."

I write a "Shooting into an Inhabited Dwelling" report, listing Mrs. Buford as the victim. As I am leaving, James tells me he knows the guy Eric fought with, and where he stays. He points out a house about a block away. Great. I know the house, as does everyone else at Southwest Division. No one lives there. It's a rock house narco has not been able to get to yet. So this whole situation probably has its roots in some kind of drug dispute that Eric was involved in. I thank James and his mother for their help, and I leave.

DEPLOYMENT PERIOD
ELEVEN

Morning watch! *Damn.* I've been put on morning watch.

It is every officer's obligation to take his turn working in the early hours of the morning. It is an inevitability, and is part of a police officer's life. All officers are duty-bound at one time or another to work at night and sleep during the day.

But the human body does not understand duty. It understands when it needs to sleep, which is during the night. So the body rebels against the morning-watch officer. Red eyes and deep yawns are plentiful, and a tired, run-down mind-set overtakes one to the very soul. I truly believe morning-watch officers age two days for each day worked, and thus should receive double pay.

Besides the body being rushed toward early decrepitude, the citizens you deal with from the witching hour to dawn are, to put it lightly, strange. Many of them seemingly coming out of the sewers or other unknown, secret places. Quite possibly even the bowels of hell. When you hear of some strange or exotic crime occurring, it is usually a "morning-watch caper."

Yes, there are some officers who prefer morning watch. There is a core group of pale-skinned officers who stay on it year in and year out. Some work it because it gives them ample time to work a second job. Others feel that it's easier to sleep during the day, which is unfathomable for me. Whatever their reasons, I do dread working with them.

Car 3-A-57 is assigned to cover the center of the division. It is the most ethnically diverse section of Southwest, the population being an almost homogenized blend of African Americans and Latin-American immigrants. It is also the most economically depressed area.

My partner, a black P-III named Milt Thompson,* is a typical "morning watcher." Pale and peculiar. Yes, he is black, but he is a pale black. Thompson has held down this car for almost two years. He is a man of habit, a man in a rut, his daily routine rarely changing. He arrives at the station an hour early each night, carefully polishing his gear. He is in roll call ten minutes early, always sitting in the same seat, an aisle seat in the last row, with a cup of coffee in hand and the front page of the newspaper spread out before him. He drives the same black-and-white, shop 056, and will wait in the parking lot a great length of time should a unit on a previous watch have dared to check it out. He brings his meal with him, and we eat promptly at 3:00 A.M. We take extra care to ensure that we are off on time each morning, holding all nonurgent reports so that we can go out to the station to avoid late radio calls, because Thompson likes to be home in bed promptly by 9:00 A.M.

Like all officers, Thompson has his peculiarities. And generally, officers's peculiarities are not a problem for me. I have grown used to different officers and their habits, from ones who like to sing in the car, to ones who have to run to the bathroom every five minutes. I have learned to deal with them.

But Milt has one habit that may force me to use my gun. He does not talk. No idle conversation; no chitchat; no "How are the wife and kids?" And it is not that he has some physical disability that has caused his vocal cords to fail. It is just that he does not like to use his powers of speech.

Yes, I like calm, quiet partners. But quiet to a point. Thompson is beyond that point. We're talking a man who has taken a vow of silence—which is not good. I have been told by other officers that he can go an entire watch without uttering a word to his partner. Should be a barrel of laughs on those long, cold mornings when the radio is dead and all we do is drive around.

Now, he *is* a good guy, and a good officer. Don't get me wrong; the man knows his police work. I am real comfortable with him when it comes to tactics and common sense. He has been an officer for eleven years, all in the South End, and he has definitely earned his stripes. But he doesn't talk. *Ugh* . . .

Really, I think I'm just bitching because I don't like being on morning watch.

We get a stolen car right out of roll call our second night.

Not two blocks from the station, Milt sees two young gangsters in a black IROC Camaro stopped at the curb at Denker and Thirty-ninth Street. A group of five other gangsters circle the car. They all look at us like a herd of deer frozen in our headlights after we turn onto the street because we know something's up. We do not even get a chance to run the car before both passenger and driver throw open their doors and are out running between the houses.

Thompson is a runner, so he takes the lead while I broadcast. Both the driver and the passenger run together, in a pair. This is different, because usually, suspects run in opposite directions.

We hit some fences, go through some backyards, knock over a few trash cans, and generally cause the dogs in the neighborhood no end of barking in sharp protest. Before I know it, I hear tires screeching all around us—and flashlight beams are probing the yards. I now realize officers from two different watches are here. Morning watch is here because roll call has just let out, and all of P.M. watch is also here because they were en route to the station from the field for end of watch. So we are deep, real deep.

It is now like watching the Keystone Kops. A pair of partners runs here, another there, all chasing our two teenage suspects. The suspects try to jump over a tall brick wall only to find four officers on the other side. Then they try to come back over only to find me, Thompson, and two others on their tails. To make the odds even worse for them, the air unit now arrives overhead, its thick beam of light bolting down from the sky. So they sit on the wall, hands raised, a crowd of officers beneath them like drooling patrons at a strip show.

We take them out to our car. Thirty-ninth Street looks like the station parking lot. Units everywhere. I feel like ordering a few pizzas and having a block party. Catania walks up to us.

"Damn, man. All this just for us?" says one of the suspects, the passenger, a kid named Def.*

"Yup," says Catania without missing a beat. "You shouldn't have stole Chief Gates's car." Milt looks at me sideways, a wicked smile on his lips.

"You so full of shit," says Def, unbelieving. "You're tripping."

"Look around you," says Catania. "You think we'd have this many units for a plain old G-ride?"

Def surveys the scene. It is overwhelming. Police cars are packed into the slender street for the entire length of the block. Then he looks at the two stripes on Catania's arms, and the edges of gray hair on Catania's head. He feels he must be dealing with someone with authority.

"Boobe,* you so stupid, man," says Def, looking at the other youth. "I told you we shouldn't take that car. It had a homing device in it, right?"

None of us answers. We stand there straight-faced.

"I told you, man," scowls Def at Boobe. "You so fuckin' stupid!"

"Oh, m-man," says Boobe. He is thin and shy, and he has a speech impediment. He speaks with his eyes on his shoes. "Ch-chief of police don't live in South C-Central, m-man."

"Yes he does," says Catania. "He keeps a house down here so that he can throw parties on the weekends."

They look at Catania, not sure.

"Officer C-Catania," says Boobe, laughing, getting Catania's name from his name tag. "Y-you just b-bullshitting us."

Boobe is a Rollin' 40 and is our driver. He tells us they had taken the car not fifteen minutes before.

"W-we ain't h-hurt no one," he says. "We j-just wanted the car so we c-could meet some g-girls." His speech impediment is heavy, and it is accentuated by his nervousness.

"Except the owner, who is going to have to pay some bucks to fix his ignition," I reply.

Because the owner lives just a block away, we drive the car to his house. After we get a few handshakes from him and a written statement that no one had permission to use his car, we go back to the station to book our suspects. Even though it is an open-and-shut caper, I interview Boobe just to try to learn a little about him for the reports. I do not even try to interview Def.

"Fuck the police" is all Def says when I ask him if he wants to talk. "I'd have kicked yo' ass if there weren't so many cops!"

Boobe is willing to talk, so I take him to one of the interview rooms, a small six-by-six-foot space with soundproofing and a thin wooden table and two chairs. It has the feel of being an oversize phone booth, with pen marks and scratchings left on the walls from unattended prisoners. Boobe acknowledges that he was the driver, and that he took the car. Def was just along for the ride. He is willing to sign a statement, fearful that Def will go to jail. He is sixteen years old, a tenth grader at Los Angeles High School, and he knows his juvenile status and minor record will keep him from doing any hard time. But Def is eighteen, and could face time. Boobe wants to protect his homie, so he is cooperative.

I look at him. He is tall, almost six feet, with creamy brown skin. His face is boyish, with baby-fat cheeks and close-cropped hair. A mansize body with a baby face. When I ask him to write out his statement, he tells me he is unable to.

"I got d-dyslexia," he says. "Things I write come out sideways."

"What do you mean?" I ask.

"M-my words get all m-mixed up," he says. "They look all right to me, but my t-teachers say it ain't English. They c-can't understand anything I write."

"You don't know how to write?"

"No, I know how to w-write. I know how to draw all my ABCs, it's just I m-mix them up all over the place. C-can't nobody understand it but me."

As he talks to me, he watches his shoes. He never looks me in the eye. His hands fumble slowly in front of him, his fingers twisting around and around. His speech is a bare whisper.

"Where are your parents?" I ask.

"I ain't seen my m-mother in two w-weeks," he says.

"She out of town?" I ask.

"O-out of her m-mind," he replies. "She using r-rock. She f-fuckin' old men for ch-chips," says Boobe, using the slang word for a five-dollar piece of rock cocaine.

"Where's your father?" I ask.

"D-don't know him," he says.

"You go to school?" I ask.

"Ain't b-been to s-school in t-two years," he says. "Ain't no m-money in it."

He tells me he's been staying with a group of Crips who live in a house near where we found him with the G-ride. Then he changes his story about why they took the car.

"We were gonna c-cruise for just a little, then t-take it to a place I know to chop it," he says.

He is referring to a "chop shop," a place where the car would have been stripped clean of engine and usable parts.

"I can get two hundred d-dollars for an I-IROC," he says. "That's c-cash, and they'll take all the I-IROCs I can g-get."

"How long you been doing this for?" I ask.

"Not long," he replies. "I still can only s-start a c-couple kinds of c-cars. But one of my homies, he knows how to s-start a Range Rover. He can g-get a lot of money for one."

He will not tell me where the chop shop is, even though I ask him forcefully and repeatedly. He does not want to hurt future business. So I decide to go back to asking him questions about himself.

"Why aren't you going to school?" I ask. "Don't you want to make something of yourself?"

"I'm s-something," he says. "I'm something to my h-homeboys."

"There's more to life than hangin' with the homies," I say.

"N-not to me," he says. "Th-they all I got."

"What are you gonna do, steal cars and gang-bang the rest of your life?" I ask. "It's just gonna get you killed."

"I-I know," he says. "But I ain't got long t-to live, anyhows. God hates me."

"Not true," I say. "God doesn't hate. He makes it so that people can do whatever they want to. There's a lot available to you besides gangstering."

"Like w-what?" he asks.

Oops. Good question.

"I don't know, man," I reply. I think for a beat. "You're going down for some time on this, you know it. So instead of pumping iron and hangin' with the homeboys in jail, why don't you try reading some and learning. I know you have troubles with them. Ask your counselor to get you a special teacher. Knowledge is power. Knowledge is what helps you make decisions on your own. It helps you work your mind and helps you apply some purpose to your life. Knowledge gets a future."

I sound like my father. But I want this kid to understand me.

"F-future don't mean nuthin' t-to me," he replies.

"Why?" I ask.

" 'C-cause I'll be dead before I'm t-twenty," he says.

"Why?" I ask. "Someone trying to kill you?"

"No," he replies. "I mean, no one in p-particular. B-but I know I'll just be d-dead, soon. Either that or in j-jail."

And I stop. Something inside me makes my mouth quit working. Because as I watch him talk, I know that he honestly believes with all his heart what he has just said. And my little five-minute pep talk, although not falling on disrespectful ears, has fallen on deaf ears. Or should I say ears that could hear, except that they have been tightly plugged.

And unfortunately, he is right.

THE OLD GUARD

We have a new lieutenant who has just transferred in from West Los Angeles Division. He is tall, about fifty, with dark German features. He has a neatly trimmed mustache, hair turning silver at the temples, and eyes as black as CHP sunglasses. A large tattoo adorns his right bicep. Faded red and green, it depicts a knife thrust through the center of a heart, drops of blood falling onto a banner containing a Latin quotation. It is the insignia of the army ranger unit with whom he saw action in Vietnam. One of the sergeants reads off the line-up, then introduces him: Lieutenant John Akers.* A southerner from Georgia, he speaks in a drawl as soft as velvet. Because he is new to the division, he gives us his speech about his work philosophy and what he expects from us.

"I want my officers to go out and do old-fashioned police work," he says. "I want crime in this division to be nonexistent. I want to see the benches full of suspects, and I want to read a lot of reports. I also do not mind a justifiable use of force every now and then if the suspect's not going with the program. I want criminals to know we know them, and that we are not going to take any crap. I want the citizens of this division to deal with the bad guys as little as possible, which means I want crime to be stopped before it happens. I want the citizens of this division to feel we can protect them."

He stops for a beat. Sounds good so far in theory, but with the political climate in Los Angeles, impractical. I hope he is not some idealist who is going to get us all thrown in jail.

"That's what I want," continues Akers. "What I'll get is totally different, I know. I understand that we cannot really do any of this right now. As we all know, these are hard times we live in. When I first came on the job, you could choke out any belligerent, criminal scum-bag on the street and just leave him there. No Use-of-Force report, no notifications. It was up to our discretion to interface with whomever we felt we needed to, and it worked, because we knew who the assholes were. And if a bad guy mouthed off to you, no problem: down he'd go. Choked out cold. And Lord help him if he took a swing at you. Why he would be black-and-blue for days. And it really kept the criminals in line. They had an awful lot of respect for us. Very few ran. We did not have anywhere near the amount of car chases we have today. They did not dare. But now, if you use any force, you must call an RA, write a Use-of-Force report, and not only face departmental review, but you will most likely be sued. Sorta takes the fun out of it."

Akers shifts in his seat. "Guess what I'm trying to say," he continues. "You really need to watch yourselves now. On the one hand, attacks on officers have tripled over the past decade. On the other, lawsuits have increased tenfold. So I would not rush into anything the way we used to. Unless you have an officer getting his butt kicked, I would not be in any hurry to get to any of these calls. Code Two means Code Two, no busting traffic lights, even if the comments of the call tell your heart otherwise. Citizens will just have to fend for themselves a little bit longer now, because I will not have you risking legal problems by rushing to some citizen's aid in a manner quicker than the manual allows.

"And when you do run into someone with a mouth, stand back. Do not be in a hurry to prove yourself. There should not be a soul in this room who has to prove his or her toughness. Hopefully, we have all been in enough altercations prior to taking this job that you do not have to get into any now. I mean, yes, in any given situation, we can always win. Doesn't mean we have to.

"My job as a lieutenant is a tough one. On the one hand, I have to keep an eye on you guys; make sure you guys are not getting out of hand. That you are not kicking too many asses. On the other, I have to make sure the fallout from Rodney King is not making you guys a bunch of slugs. That you are not kicking too few asses. See, basically, you cannot trust a lieutenant. Even if I was willing to back you guys up like we used to, a lieutenant in this department just does not have enough steam anymore to get you out of serious trouble. There are too many police officers on this job above me who are no longer police officers. Captains and above, far as I am concerned, have turned politician on us. Most of them are out for themselves. The more street cops the politician cop burns, the higher he goes. It is as if we were a bunch of adult animals eating our young during a drought to stay fit. Except here, we are not eating the weak, we are eating the strong. And among our upper management there are some very fat animals. They will eat your career if it will make theirs even a fraction better. And the harder you work, the more arrests you make, the more criminal contacts you have, the greater the chance you have of getting into a situation where you will be eaten. I have always felt that there is a positive correlation between the amount of good, hard police work one does, and the amount of personnel complaints one receives. Because assholes don't like going to jail, and they and their families will always piss and moan about it. And if they can find some asshole attorney to sue you, even if it's for a bullshit reason, all the better."

Akers pauses for a moment. Lets it sink in. "This job is no longer about doing the right thing," he adds. "We are more concerned about doing things right. Which means by the book, which I have seen throughout my career as not always being the best for the citizens. They tell us in the Academy that we are hired for our common sense, for our ability to make a decision in a given situation. But that is not really what they want anymore. What they want now are robots. They want a robot army that will bow to the wishes of the politicians, wishes which from what I can see are generally opposite of what is best for the citizens. So you better be mistake-free, especially if you want to promote. You could be the king of the felony arrests—catch all the murderers you want—but if you make that one mistake, smack that one asshole too hard, you will find yourself on the blacklist. We are now an organization that promotes simply on the basis of the absense of wrongdoing. We don't promote for initiative, innovation, or leadership. That's why our guys on the fast track are a bunch of dead fish. We are promoting a bunch of pencil-pushing robots, a bunch of noncops who have never really been involved in police work. And you hard workers out here, I don't know. I just hope your house is in your spouse's name."

He pauses for a moment. "I do not mean to bring you officers down," he says. "I just have to be honest with you, being new and all."

Akers finishes up. "If you get in a bad situation, if I do not burn you, someone else above me will," he says. "And then they will burn me along with you for not burning your fanny in the first place. So the job is now quite simple: Survive with your brains and your pocketbooks intact, and do a little police work on the side."

SHOOTIN' NEWTON

I am already a little frazzled being on morning watch. But I think Thompson would drive me nuts even if this were day watch. I already told you he doesn't talk. Well, he really *does not* talk! I am spending my mornings as if I were sitting in an isolation tank getting in touch with my primordial being. After three weeks with him, I feel I will soon be running naked down the street, being chased by a pack of ghetto elk like William Hurt in *Altered States*.

It gets to the point sometimes where I find myself having a monologue with him. We will go the first few hours without words. Not a word; just him looking out the window in between calls. So I will lose it, especially at about four o'clock in the morning, and begin telling him some event from my childhood or commenting on some political issue. And he just sits there, listening, like a storefront Indian. Until I ask him a question. Then, yes, he does answer. So I do have a way of checking to make sure he is still breathing. But usually, that is a very few words, and they are generally directed in a way to end the conversation. I think that I really am soon going to have to shoot Thompson—just so I can hear a little noise. Either that, or bring in a portable radio.

We get a call in Newton Division. Almost every Newton officer is tied up on a suspect barricaded inside a house armed with a rifle. They have no units available right now to handle simple radio calls. So because we share a common border with them, we are called to cover their area.

Newton Division is a very busy place. It is basically what you could "politely" term a complete shithole. It is twelve square miles of graffiti-painted warehouses and rat-infested single-family homes which appear as if they were contracted by the same outfit that built the shack towns of Tijuana. The only division worse in Los Angeles is Rampart, which is a complete nightmare, full of Central American war refugees, and really should be patrolled by an armored tank division.

Newton Division has a long history of officer-involved shootings. The area covered by the division is home to numerous refugee groups from the wars in Central America, as well as a number of prison halfway houses. There are a lot of surly citizens on its streets, citizens of the type who not only fight authority, but try to kill it. So Newton has the nickname "Shootin' Newton."

Naturally, the type of call Thompson and I get is a "Shooting in Progress."

We respond using lights and siren, and are at the scene in a little over a minute. Then we hit the street at a crawl, lights out. It is a neighborhood where two and three families live in each house. The houses are small; many of them have converted their living rooms to bedrooms, beds and dressers replacing couches and coffee tables. Some have even draped blankets over ropes to create a soft wall separating the territories of the families living within. The streets are packed with cars as are the front lawns, the green grass that once graced the quaint front yards now dusty grease spots and pitted dirt. Even though the area is predominantly single-family homes, it is as densely populated as any three-story condominium complex in the Valley.

There is a quiet over the street, like a blanket, as if some large animal has just gone crashing through a forest. We also do not see

any lights burning from the late-night insomniacs who usually populate any neighborhood. We don't even hear the usual ghetto dogs
that bark anytime they hear our police radio. It's mighty quiet. Almost too quiet.

We park a half-block from where the shooting should have taken
place. I take out the shotgun, and exit. Thompson also gets out of
the car, and I look over to him to see how he wants to approach
this problem. But for some reason, he just walks down the middle
of the sidewalk, never even returning my look, like he were on another planet or something. So I sneak down the street after him,
using the maze of cars as cover.

I am not sure why he is walking so exposed. There is possibly
a man with a gun somewhere around here. But he is the P-III, so I
do not question his tactics. I am a little confused, though.

Ahead of me, I now see a man leaning against a black Z28
Camaro. It has been modified, with thick racing slicks on the back,
and heavy rear suspension which has lifted the car to a pronounced
slant. The car is parked on the lawn of the house that per our computer should be our suspect location; a white bungalow-style house
with thick burglar bars.

The man is looking up at the sky, oblivious to our presence. He
is deep in thought. His right hand holds a cigarette. His left hand,
out of my view, is at his side, as if he were holding a beer. I sneak
up on his right, a parked car between us. At this point, Thompson
is back behind us. The man does not hear me, but he now hears my
partner, Thompson's heavy boots scratching on the dirty sidewalk.

The man half turns and focuses in on Thompson. He flicks the
cigarette out in front of him, the embers skipping brightly on the
ground. I see his profile clearly. He is Hispanic, about forty. He has
the face of a man of war, chisled, with cold-set eyes. He looks back
at Thompson as if Thompson were a minor annoyance.

There is movement beyond him, and I focus in on it. I see a
woman standing in the doorway of the bungalow behind the man.
She is watching the man intently. I dismiss her as a threat. She does
not have the body language. But her eyes show fear. There is something wrong here, and it centers around this man. He has my undivided attention.

"Sir, come over here," says Thompson. It is more of a request than a command.

Thompson stands on the sidewalk about twenty feet behind the man. His gun is still holstered. He is very casual. I still do not understand his tactics. This is supposed to be a man with a gun, and Thompson's positioning has left him open for trouble.

The man looks at Thompson, then behind him. It hits me that he is looking for other officers, appraising the situation. Thompson, thinking the man does not comprehend, tries Spanish.

"Señor, venga aquí, por favor," says Thompson.

I know the man comprehends Thompson's words, but he has also disregarded them. He is simply assessing the situation before him: one police officer standing twenty feet away, and none other around.

The man seems satisfied with his assessment, and he acts accordingly. His left leg now swings around into a shooting stance, followed by his left hand, which holds a blue steel .380-caliber semi-automatic handgun. He is going to shoot Thompson! I stand straight, shotgun level.

"Police!" I yell.

It is all I say. It's up to him now. My next reaction will be to flick my finger. My finger touches on the trigger. I can kill him now. I could articulate it. I can justify it. And if my partner were alone, he would have already opened fire.

But I don't open fire. Because the woman is still in the doorway behind him. If I shoot him, I may hit her. So I give him an extra second. He stops, the handgun not quite targeted on Thompson.

Out of the corner of my eye, I see Thompson run for cover. The man looks at me—in a most peculiar way, because I can see it in his eyes. He is actually considering the possibility of trying to shoot it out with me! Me with a twelve-gauge shotgun pointed right at him.

He is actually calculating, taking into account lag time, reflexes, how much of a target he has of me. And something else. Something that I cannot put my finger on. But I know he has experience in this type of situation from somewhere before. Somewhere in his past. This is one bad actor.

Again I consider the possibility of killing him. But the woman is still there, a blur in the background to my eyes which are focused on the suspect. She is just in what I gauge to be the target range. The shotgun spread is one foot for every ten feet. He is fifteen feet, a thin sideways target. That means a one-and-a-half-foot circle of pellets would hit him. But he's not more than a foot wide, so some pellets will miss and continue on. She is thirty feet away, standing facing me, her torso full view just beginning behind his back. That would mean a three-foot circle of pellets by the time it gets to her. So I'll have to fire just in front of him and hope some of the spray spreads out to hit him. Or shoot for his legs, which is stupid, because that won't stop him from returning fire—especially if he's on drugs.

Why she doesn't move, I don't know. We stand for a beat. I don't want to voice commands, as he may be trained to fire upon sound, lag time increasing when one is forced to speak while attempting to react. I decide to use something monosyllabic, and then shoot him, the woman taking her chances, if he does not comply.

"Now!" I snort.

His eyes are on fire. No fear in them, just hate. I now know he would try me if he had cover. He doesn't like being uncovered. But he is too exposed, his whole body available for me to fire upon. And he is standing at the middle of the car; no bumpers readily available to jump behind.

So his hand slowly opens, and the gun clatters to the ground. I then order him away from the gun, and then, after almost having to kick him, get him to lie on the ground. Thompson gets him handcuffed.

A Newton unit arrives. We find out the woman is his wife, and that they are both recent arrivals from El Salvador. He fought in the war, on which side, I do not know. This afternoon, he found out his younger brother had been arrested by the LAPD for armed robbery, and will probably be doing some serious time. So after a six-pack of beer, and a few punches on the wife, he had adjourned to the front yard with his handgun to fire a few rounds at his neighbors' residences—and await arrival of the LAPD.

We examine the gun. We find that it holds nine rounds when one is in the chamber. There are still four in it.

When we get back in the car, Thompson Milt is visibly shaken.

He is normally a tactically sound officer, and I still think he is excellent at all facets of police work. But on this date he messed up—which is all it takes on this job. One slip-up can end a career. And a life.

"I'm going through a divorce from my wife," says Thompson. "We had a custody hearing over our daughters today. It's all I've been thinking of. It ain't an excuse for what just happened. My mind was not here. I coulda got us both killed. I'm sorry."

I do not say anything. I understand. Thompson is a man who loves his family, a family that is falling apart. His eyes are real sad, and I see a hint of water. I now feel bad for being disturbed by his silence. He had a lot on his mind. So I just shrug in reply.

"Hey, the Man upstairs was watching out for us on this one," I reply.

"Let this be a lesson to you," he says. "Leave your personal life at home. A wandering mind can be deadly out here."

DEPLOYMENT PERIOD
TWELVE

Milt Thompson was scheduled to be my partner again for this DP, but the stress of his problems at home has caused him to be placed on leave. I tried calling him at home to check up on him, but all I reached was an answering machine. In true Thompson fashion, the message was but few words: "Leave a message at the beep."

Jackson is once again my partner, the result of our mutual request once I found out about Thompson's status. Jackson has just been transferred to morning watch after spending almost two years on P.M. shift. He is not happy about it.

"I only have two nights free a week," he says. "I'm gonna have a hard time keeping my women happy."

What is worse for Jackson is that Mikoshi is closed by the start of morning watch, which means no rice. But Jackson is a creature of habit, and he cannot just step right into handling radio calls. So we make one quick stop out of roll call, that being at a 7-Eleven convenience store for a cup of coffee, which of course for Jackson is drunk black.

"Coffee is bad enough for you with all that caffeine," he says. "And those sweeteners they have, I think that when they heat up they turn into a chemical that is real bad for your body. Some of them are known to cause cancer in rats."

So Jackson and I sip black coffee in the parking lot. The nights are getting colder as the city settles in for winter. It is almost the same time of year as when I started at Southwest. Now I own a jacket, though, and am prepared in case we get stuck on a perimeter.

"You're gonna be off probation soon, ain't you?" he asks.

"Yeah, one more DP and I'll be a P-Two," I reply.

"Well, if we're gonna work together this DP, you better start acting like a P-Two, 'cause I don't want to have to train you anymore."

"OK," I say, taking a sip.

"And you better start by calling me Kyle," he says. "No more of this 'sir' stuff," he says.

"All right, Kyle," I reply. "Only if you call me Bill."

"OK, Bill," he says. "Why don't you finish up that coffee, and let us go fight some crime."

We are truly working in the world's largest open-air asylum. And tonight the doctors have gone on strike. Jackson and I have had a drunken group shooting into the air; another drunken group throwing rocks at passing cars; a gas station attendant almost coming to blows with a customer in a dispute over change; and a naked man running down Rodeo Road.

(On this last one, we were fortunate enough *not* to find our suspect, although for a moment there, it seemed we might. Three different citizens, out at this hour for who knows what reason, all pointed up the street when they saw us and said, "Naked man just ran past me. If you hurry, you can catch him." We, of course, hurried. But alas, the naked man disappeared into the night. I even made Jackson smile when I said, "If we find him, and he's running, and he's naked, I ain't tackling him.")

These incidents were of course on top of the usual street robberies and domestic disputes we have been sent. *Citizens are just not behaving themselves!* We handle eight radio calls in the first four hours. I feel like a doctor at a plane crash, bouncing from one call to the next, just trying to put a Band-Aid on the situations we encounter so that we can rush off to the next call.

Then we get a call of a "battery just occurred" at the Crenshaw Family Inn, located not far from Dorsey High School. Jackson is driving, so I pull out a crime report, filling out part of it so that we can get it signed in a minimum amount of time and then move on to the next call.

I think about the location we're going to. It has a rusted, ancient metal sign near the entrance that says it's an "Inn for the Whole Family." I smirk at this, as the motel is frequented by drug dealers and prostitutes. The only family that would stay there would be a family of criminals.

Jackson parks two driveways from the motel entrance, giving us some distance from the call. "You see that?" asks Jackson. There is movement in the darkened driveway of the motel.

"Yeah," I reply.

We get out of the car. I can now tell the movements are made by a man, and he is wordlessly coming toward us. He is in the shadows of the motel, but I can tell he is not wearing a shirt. He does not speak, he just slowly comes toward us. His movements are labored, jagged. A male black, about twenty-five years old, he passes under the motel's neon sign that flashes NO VACANCY in red. His chest shimmers in the glow. It is blood-soaked.

"Kyle, he's got a big wound," I say. I pull my gun and approach him.

His neck and left shoulder are a shredded mess, inhuman looking. At first I think it's a knife wound. But at closer inspection, it looks more like a shark bite. Large strips of shoulder muscle hang down, his deltoid eviscerated, his neck swelling as if he swallowed a softball. It threatens to choke off his breathing.

"What happened?" I ask him.

He can't speak. He just looks at me, moves his mouth, but no words come out. He is trying to tell me something, something urgent. He points back into the motel courtyard, then moves his hands trying to communicate some unknown message. I do not understand what he means.

"Don't try to talk," I say calmly. "You're OK. Let's sit you down."

I look for "safe" spots where I can put my hands to steady him. He is drenched in blood, and I have long since developed a self-preservation instinct when it comes to touching people on duty who are bleeding. I find two spots I can hold and I get him on the curb. I still check my hands to be sure. Good, no blood.

Jackson is already calling for an ambulance and a backup. I watch the courtyard. No movement. I listen. It is the dead of night. The only sounds I hear are the distant vehicular drones of the Santa

Monica Freeway wafting in over the cold, thick night air from the north. I kneel next to the man, talking to him calmly, reassuring him. I also check him for weapons. For all I know, he could be a bad guy. But I do it visually, not wanting to go into his pockets for fear of blood contacts.

Soon, the rescue ambulance arrives. The paramedics have trouble treating him. He will not lie down for them, still motioning into the courtyard. I motion for him to lie back so that the paramedics can work on him. But he is trying to tell me something.

"I understand," I say, even though I don't.

This calms him down, and the paramedics lay him prone and begin to work. Jackson and I walk up the driveway to survey the motel courtyard.

A typical no-tell motel: two stories of thin rooms in an L-shape, surrounding a small parking lot. A high brick fence with barbed wire on top surrounds the other two sides. Looks more like a concentration camp than a "Family Inn."

"Uh, Officer," calls one of the paramedics. A husky blond female, she is looking at me to make sure I am listening. Her voice is a little unsteady. "Looks like a shotgun blast."

"He's also got two gunshot wounds in the back," says the other. "Like a nine mil or a three-eighty."

I do not look at them, but now slowly move closer to the building edge. It is not that I see anything, I just want some cover. I now collect my thoughts on the situation. What have we got here? A man shot with a shotgun and some other gun. So two weapons, probably at least two suspects. And where are these shooters? Unknown. Could still be around. I look at my feet. A blood trail runs past them from the wounded man into the courtyard. It leads to where he came from.

I scan the rooms and see nothing out of the ordinary, except for a room on the second floor. No lights are on in the window. But the door is just a hair open. I snap my fingers twice to get Jackson's attention. He comes over immediately.

"Upstairs." I nod. "An open door."

"Roger," says Jackson. Jackson has again called for additional units and a supervisor, but no one has been able to respond yet. Like I said, it's busy. Everyone is tied up. He tries again.

"Any further on our backup?"

"Negative, no units available," says the RTO.

"Three-A-fifty-seven, can you try Seventy-seventh Division, or Wilshire?" he replies. "Advise units we have a crime scene with possible suspects still in the area."

"Three-A-thirty-one, advise fifty-seven we'll be responding from Brotman Memorial with a fifteen-minute ETA," says a voice.

It's Jeff Wilson. They had a drive-by shooting with hits about an hour ago, and are probably just finishing their investigation. Thank goodness for hard chargers.

"Three-A-fifty-seven, also be advised Twelve-A-one is en route from Seventy-seventh Division with a ten-minute ETA," says the RTO.

Jackson stands, thinking for a moment. "We can't wait for them," he says. "There may be more victims."

He's right. I am not crazy about putting my life on the line for what I already feel are victims of a drug rip-off. Especially when this victim has gunshot wounds from two different weapons, which means at least two different suspects. And for all I know, they are still somewhere nearby. But it's part of the job. So we enter the motel courtyard.

As we head toward the stairway to the second floor, I see the motel manager watching us from behind his bulletproof glass. I go over to him.

"You see anything?" I ask quietly.

"I see nothing," he replies, his words muffled and difficult to hear. But I can tell he's from Pakistan. He has almond-colored eyes. They are full of fear. He fully grasps what has happened here. But all he says is "I was in my bed with a sound sleep over me."

"What about that guy?" I ask. I point over to the beginning of the driveway. Our victim is not visible, only the lights from the ambulance. "What room was he in?"

"At the top of the stairs, room two-oh-five," he replies. "He checked in with a girl."

"But you didn't see anything?" I ask.

"No, he just came to my window telling me to call the police," he says. "I may have also heard gunshots which awoke me."

He knows more than he is saying. But I do not have time to interrogate him. I just make a mental note.

Jackson and I climb the stairs, stone slabs held in place by a steel frame. The vibration from it resonates as we climb. I see drops of blood every other step. They reflect the dim light from a single, naked bulb that shines out over the parking lot, casting thin shadows on the asphalt. The drops of blood are in a random, chaotic pattern. Some steps are splattered, while others have a bare smattering.

The walkway of the second-floor landing is white paint stained by dirt and oil, the cleaning of the landing apparently of low priority to the motel's management. The door in question is the first, and I can see that the blood trail comes from within the room. Five drops of blood surround a small pool at the base of the door.

I stop and listen. The door is cracked barely a quarter-inch. Jackson passes me quickly at a low crawl, and he now has the other side of the door. He signals to me that he is going to push it open so that I can take a quick peek inside. I ready my flashlight and handgun and go down on one knee. Jackson pushes the door, and I pop my head in, a quick peek, then withdraw.

I close my eyes to develop the picture of what I have just seen. The snapshot clears. I see a room that is in complete disarray. A table and chair are knocked over; a double bed has all of its covers yanked off and dumped into a huge pile on the floor; clothing has been pulled from open dresser drawers and strewn about the room. It is a mess. But that is not the worst. I saw two feet coming out from the wall against which I now lean. And they are bloody and lifeless.

I inform Jackson with my hands that there is someone on the floor on the other side of my wall. He mouths to me the question, "Are they dead?" I shrug, and mouth, "I don't know."

I nod to Jackson now, an indication I am going to enter. He agrees. I take one side as Jackson takes the other, and we quickly slide around the corners, staying low, our flashlights leading our guns.

The room glows in the saberlike beams of our flashlights. There is no movement to catch my eye, no targets.

At my feet is the man attached to the feet I had seen on my

quick peek. I immediately dismiss him as a threat after only glancing at him. He is in a sitting position next to the wall air-conditioning unit, his one remaining eye looking up at the ceiling. The rest of his face and skull is up on the wall to his left. A long, linear, red smear streaks down the wall from where he must have been standing when he was shot. He is wearing a white T-shirt that has a huge red splash in the middle of it. This is not an artistic design, but the result of taking another twelve-gauge shotgun blast point-blank center mass.

The wall above the bed now catches my eye. It too is covered in blood. Our flashlights give the wall a shiny, glimmering feel; the blood looking like a black mirror. The reflections make it almost seem alive. The blood in the room gives off a strong, steamy smell, one that seems almost unnatural.

I feel the wall behind me and flip on the lights. What illuminates is now clearly a war zone. Bullet holes and blood pepper the dull brown walls of the room.

Across the room, the bathroom door is shut. Jackson motions that he is going to open it, and that I should back his play. I nod and ready myself. He takes one step toward the bathroom door, his foot landing on the big pile of covers pulled from the bed. He stops, curiously examining the pile underfoot. He reaches down and pulls them back. A woman's face is staring straight up at him. Her eyelids are wide, her pupils glazed. Her face is pulled back and tight, a mask of intense fear. Jackson lifts the covers farther, and finds that sheets against her chest are drenched and matted in blood. At first, I think she might still be alive, just in shock, her heart and brain fluttering in confusion. But it appears she may not have any heart left; just a huge, gapping hole. Jackson puts two fingers on her neck, then quickly stands up as if dismissing her, going back to the business of the bathroom door. I too put my thoughts back to the door.

Jackson pushes it open. I can now hear water running. Jackson quickly enters, flipping on the lights. I hop on the bed to follow, ready to confront whatever he's found. But before I can enter, Jackson is back at the door.

"They left the water running in the sink," he says. "Must have happened fast."

He walks past me, out the door.

"We better leave the room," he says. "Detectives will want it as fresh as we can leave it."

When we get back outside, the female paramedic calls to us. "We got to go," she says. "He's fading fast."

Jackson nods to me. "Go with them and try to get a statement," he says.

Moments later, I am in the ambulance, en route to Brotman Memorial Hospital on the eastern edge of Culver City. We have been advised to use this facility as USC County General, the largest trauma center in the city, is already full.

Like I said, people are not behaving themselves tonight.

I look back at the female paramedic who is riding in the back with our victim. Her head and shoulder cradle a radiophone and she is listening intently to someone on the other end. She sticks a needle in our victim's arm and injects a clear fluid with a steady press of her thumb. It has no instantaneous effect. Not that I expected any. Since I sat down in the ambulance, the guy hasn't made a sound. Then she catches my eye, and slowly shakes her head as if to say, "I don't think he'll make it."

When we hit the emergency bay at Brotman, the victim is quickly taken into a small room with bright circular lights and shelves full of surgical tools and bandages. Brotman is a community hospital in a nice neighborhood. It does not have the war zone "stitch 'em up and move 'em out" feel of hospitals in the South End. Older, more experienced doctors and nurses appear and attend to the victim. I am amazed when I find out he is the only patient in the emergency room. I am further amazed when a nurse approaches me and nods to an elderly, gray-bearded doctor with bifocals who is closely examining the victim's wound.

"That's Dr. Schwinn,"* she says. "He's a talented surgeon from Beverly Hills. He donates time to the ER." Then she pushes me out of the room.

Two hours later, the nurse comes into the waiting room. "Your guy is a lucky man," she says. "If anyone but Dr. Schwinn had worked on him, he'd probably not have made it. Dr. Schwinn is a specialist. He was amazing to watch. So your guy is still critical. But he is stable."

Jackson arrives an hour later, followed by a detective from South Bureau Homicide. But there is really nothing more to be done. Our guy is stable, but he is unconscious after the surgery, so there is no further information that he can give us. Because we're beyond end of watch, we call the watch commander and ask him to send a unit to relieve us. Our guy is a material witness to a double homicide, and there is a chance the bad guys may try to get him if they find out he is alive. A short time later they arrive—and we go home.

The murders at the Crenshaw Family Inn draw little acknowledgment from the local press. Only one paper does an article, and the story is short, printed on page 10 next to a story about rising fuel costs in Mexico. It was a simple and factual account which begins, "A Baldwin Hills man and woman were found shot to death last night in what police believed was a drug deal gone wrong."

The article paled in comparison to what I saw.

The black-and-white of the newspaper, no matter how eloquently the words are phrased, cannot take the place of the red and gray of a homicide scene—because one cannot write about smells like those of blood, or the howls of grieving relatives, or the intense stress and then frustration an officer feels when he first arrives at a scene and tries to bring calm to a situation filled with chaos and confusion.

With about eleven months in the field, I have been at almost fifty shooting scenes with hits, and have worked at an even dozen homicides. Still, what I saw at the Crenshaw Family Inn left a lasting impression on me.

The homicides were carried out with unusual savagery. The man who died from the head shot appears to have had the weapon in or near his mouth when the trigger was pulled. His front teeth were not broken off, which suggests the man may have willingly let the gun be placed into his mouth. So there was possibly some conversation between the suspect and the victim, the suspect ordering the victim to open his mouth, then the gun going in. Then probably more conversation. Then the fatal shot fired.

The dead woman on the floor had been tied up in the bed sheets in which we found her. This was done prior to any shooting. If she struggled, it was not fierce. She was still alive when the man had his head blown off, determined by the way some of his blood fell on the sheets around her. She was then shot a number of times, even though she was surely dead with the first blast.

Even though the homicides were exceptionally vicious, they would normally fade from our minds as they were replaced by other murders. Except that last night a similar homicide was committed in Wilshire Division. One that was equal in savagery. We have been informed by the watch commander that South Bureau Homicide is putting together a briefing for us, and that they will be in roll call soon with some suspect information. Hopefully, no more homicides will occur in the interim.

Jackson and I respond to a "man down" call. An anonymous citizen has phoned the station desk to report that he observed a man lying prone under a streetlight on the edge of a park on Harvard Boulevard. This is not an unusual occurrence at this location. The park is frequented by alcoholic and drug-addicted transients who have been known to just lie down and sleep on the sidewalk. Usually, they awake after a couple of hours and then move on, so this is not an extraordinary call—except the caller thinks that the man is not breathing.

I look at my watch. It reads "0300" hours military time exactly. I once read somewhere that the average human is in deepest sleep at three o'clock in the morning. The mind and body are at their most relaxed, the body functions slowed to a mere crawl. If your pulse were taken, it would seem you were near death. I think to myself, *Maybe this guy is just in a very, very deep sleep.*

Unfortunately, the man down is not a transient on cheap wine. He is a gang member named "G-Roc." He is lying on his back, feet on the sidewalk, his upper torso on a thin patch of brown grass, as if he were peacefully gazing at the stars. He has taken a single medium-caliber round, possibly a .380, deep in his right eye. The round appears to have been fired from about two feet away, tiny specks of black gunpowder peppering and singeing his cheek and nose. *Up close and personal,* it occurs to me.

Door-knocking the surrounding residences fails to find anyone in the area who heard or saw anything. We just get a bunch of sleepy citizens who are now scared to death because another murder has happened near their doorstep.

There is no way to track down the citizen who "found" him, the call having been placed anonymously to the front desk of Southwest Station where there is no tracing computer. Whoever "found" G-Roc does not want himself to be found.

Usually, homicides in Southwest are a little more "spectacular," with carloads of armed youths gunning down other gangsters in front of sidewalks full of witnesses. But this murder is right out of a dime novel—very little clue as to who the bad guys are or why they did this. Just a corpse and nothing else.

Jackson and I get another unit and set up a crime scene. I take one end and begin to search, flashing my light on the ground, looking for evidence like shell casings or any other blood. It is a cold autumn night, a dense chill laying a blanket over the area. The quiet is broken by the deep growl of a muscle car turning the corner down the street. I am immediately squinting into high beams. I calmly walk over to a tree, just in case this is a drive-by. Drive-by shooters have been known to return to homicide scenes and open fire on officers. Not more than a month ago, a group of gang members did a drive-by on a crime scene in the notorious Oakwood area of Pacific Division, a crime scene guarded by more than ten LAPD officers! On this scene, there are only four of us, so I am not taking any chances.

I shine my flashlight back into the high beams. They kick down to normal as the muscle car approaches. A young black woman, about twenty, with sharply curving facial features and thick, solid eyeliner, drives up in a new black 5.0 Mustang. She stops the vehicle parallel to me.

"Is he dead?" she asks.

"Yes," I reply. Her tone of voice is solemn, spoken in a way that leads me to believe she knows him. "Are you the one who called?"

"No," she says. "Someone called me and said my boyfriend was here and that he was dead. Is his name G-Roc?"

"I don't know," I reply. And I don't. At this point, he is just another dead gangster. I would not find out his gang name until later. "Who called you?"

"Just some boy G," she says. *Boy G?* That's the first time I have heard that one. But then, gangster slang changes all the time.

"Why don't you pull over here and let me get some information from you," I say.

"Let's just talk here," she says. I want to keep her wordy, so I allow it, which is a mistake. Whenever someone does not do what an officer asks, there is always a bad reason. But since I want to keep her wordy, I think this is the way to do it. So we talk in the street.

She tells me that she does not know the name of the gangster who called her. He simply told her that some gangster had shot her boyfriend in the face for no reason. But while she talks to me, there is a faint smile on her lips. She does not seem too upset. It now hits me that she's a friend of the bad guys, trying to milk the police for information.

"Why don't you park your car at the curb for me," I say again. This time I am firm. So she punches it, leaving me in a wake of dust. I am too far from our police car to give chase. Not that it would matter if the car were right next to me. No way a Chevy Caprice with 160,000 miles on it is going to catch a brand-new 5.0 Mustang. I look at the rear of her car to write down the license-plate number, but there is no plate. It has been removed. So I put out a broadcast about the vehicle, hoping a rolling unit might pick her up. But none does.

Anyway, I really don't know what I have with her. She could be one of the murderers, or she could be telling the truth. This could be her boyfriend, and she may be going to his crib to lay claim to his stash before his homies do. She could even have warrants and fear spending the night in jail. It just adds to the mystery of what is turning out to be a very bizarre string of homicides.

SERIAL KILLERS, SOUTH CENTRAL–STYLE

"Wilshire Division had a homicide two nights ago that has the same MO," says Detective Cutter. "A male black, unknown name as yet but about thirty years old, was apparently selling rock on the corner of Washington and Gramercy Place. The suspect, also a male black, medium build in his late twenties or early thirties, approached our victim from behind, shot him twice in the head, then took his money and his drugs. The suspect then drove off in an early-eighties Toyota, white or tan in color, driven by another male black. The suspects were seen from a block away, so we will not be able to ID them from photos.

"Get me FIs on any car like this one. If you can, go through the car. We're looking for a three-eighty automatic handgun—which appears to be a weapon used in all homicides—and a sawed-off pump shotgun, which was used at the Crenshaw Family Inn."

Cutter absently takes a long drag from an already short cigarette. He's been busy lately and it shows.

"Also, the double homicide at the Crenshaw Family Inn from last week may turn into a triple," he says. "Our one living victim is very critical. Somehow, he has survived a point-blank shotgun blast to the neck. He'll be severely disabled if he lives." Cutter shakes his head. "If he does live, he's gonna be booked for a one-eighty-seven we think he did in Seventy-seventh last month, which was also a drug thing. He's only been out of prison for nine months, too.

"Anyway, he did give us some info on the shooters. Wrote it out for us. We're looking for a male black, five feet eight or nine, early thirties, slender but muscular build, goes by the street name of 'E' or 'Mr. E.' He physically fits the description of our Wilshire shooter. E drives a brown or tan 1970s Plymouth Duster, unknown plate. He was accompanied by a dark-complected male black, six two to six four, two hundred fifty pounds, called 'Big Mike.' Possibly one or two other male blacks were with them. We have very little information on them other than they are male blacks, and one has a ponytail. Our victim did not see any other suspect than E or Big Mike during the shooting, but because of previous contacts the victim had with the two seen suspects, he feels either Mr. Ponytail or the other guy was waiting with a car outside.

"All of these crimes appear to be drug rip-offs. The word is that there were ten ounces of rocked-up coke in the room at the Crenshaw Family Inn, and that our victims had been dealing out of there the previous three nights. And the victim from last night"—Hoffman looks at his notes for clarity—"G-Roc, was also a known dealer."

Summing up, Hoffman says, "What we have here basically are some serial killers, South Central–style. Yeah, they're doing robberies as well. But they're killin', plain and simple. And I suspect they'll keep on doing it until they are caught."

DEPLOYMENT PERIOD THIRTEEN

"You remember me?" she asks.

Just as I was getting used to morning watch, I have been moved back to day watch. It has been hard waking up at a time when I had been going to sleep, and my mental state is something akin to that experienced during jet lag. So my mind is a little foggy, and I have to look at her for a moment.

She is skinny from smoking crack, and her black skin has a yellowish tint from what I can only guess to be the beginnings of liver failure. Then I remember her first name, which is Karen, from a battery report I took a few months ago. Her boyfriend, another cluckhead, had beaten the hell out of her because she would not give him the money she earned as a prostitute who works the streets near Adams and Western. I was surprised when she flagged us down.

"Yeah, I do," I reply. "Your boyfriend punched you in the face."

She is happy to be remembered. She also seems real nervous. "That was me," she says. "My name is Karen Johnson. But they call me Kiki."

"What's up, Kiki?" I ask.

"There was a killin' at Twenty-third Street and LaSalle the other night," she says. "I know the guy that did it."

A homicide at Twenty-third and LaSalle? This is a homicide I do not know about. I have been off for two days, and it was not mentioned today in roll call. So I look to my partner for confirmation. I am working today with the P-III who goes by the nickname of "Hondo." It's a hot day, and the thick oppsessive air is made

247

worse by waves of smoke that are rhythmically puffed from the cigar that is constantly perched on the corner of Hondo's mouth. I turn to him, trying to read his eyes, but they are faint shadows behind his dark sunglasses.

"You hear anything about this?" I ask.

He rolls the stogie around in his mouth. "Nope," he says. "I've been off for three days."

Great, two cops who don't know what's going on, I say to myself. "How do you know he did it?" I ask Kiki.

" 'Cause I was in the car wid' him," she replies. Her face now contorts. Tears well into her eyes. "All I wanted was to smoke some wid' him. Then he drivin' down the street, killin' people. Now he says he's gonna kill me."

I look over at Hondo. I can tell by his face that he believes Kiki. So do I. I open the rear door.

"Get in," I tell her.

We drive around the corner, off the main street, to where we can talk to Kiki without other cluckheads watching. Kiki is twitching, probably having smoked some rock right before she saw us. Her hands tremble as they knead the bottom portion of her faded blue sweatshirt into a ball. She is having no luck in controlling her emotions.

"Calm down," says Hondo, his tone soothing. Stoned people are very difficult to talk to. Stoned, scared people are worse.

"Who is this guy?" I ask.

"His name is Eric Buford," she says. "They call him E. He used to be a Harlem Thirty. He crazy."

I recall Eric Buford from the drive-by shooting report I did on his house a few months ago. It is not four blocks from where we stand. Kiki calling Eric a *Harlem* means something, too. Harlem 30s are what the Rollin' 30s used to be called back in the late 1970s, early 1980s. The name has changed because the newer gangsters want their own identity. But they kept a portion of the name so they can still be homies with the "original gangsters." What this means is that Buford is an OG, and maybe then some. I also notice she called him E, as in E of the Crenshaw Family Inn killings. She has my undivided interest.

"How did this killing happen?" asks Hondo.

"He was mad at this guy, I think they call him Trey," she says. "He'd tried to tell Trey that Trey would have to pay him for sellin' rock—"

"Like Eric was going to be his protection?" I ask, trying to clarify.

"Yeah," she says. " 'Cept Trey says, 'Fuck y'all, I ain't payin' you shit.' So Eric go'd to his house and got him a gun. Drove back to Trey. Saw Trey standin' out front his house, on the corner. Says, 'Yo, Trey, come here.' So Trey walk up on the car, sayin', 'What's up?' Eric go, 'This is what's up, muthafucka.' *Bam.* Shot him dead."

I look over at Hondo.

"Let's take her to the station," he says.

"No," says Kiki. "You gotta get him now. He's home, but he's gonna be leaving town soon. You don't get him now, you won't. Then he'll find out I told you, and he'll have his homies kill me."

She barely gets the last words out. She is now crying like a small child.

"I don't understand this nigger at all," she says. "Trey and he are homies from the same hood. Harlem an OG set, ya know? They shouldn't be bustin' on each other like that. It's fucked up, ya know?"

"I agree," I say. I guess I do. Hell, why not? "How close were you when he did the shooting?"

"I was sittin' in the car next to E," she says. "I just thought he was gonna scare the homie into givin' up some shit. But Trey just walked up and *bam,* without a word, E kilt him dead."

"You see the gun?" I ask.

"He used an automatic," she says. "A black gun. I think he said it was a three-eighty."

"And the car?" I ask. "What kind was it?"

"A white car," she says. "It's an old busted-up white car. I don't know what type."

I give Hondo a quick rundown on the Crenshaw Family Inn and G-Roc homicides while he rolls the stogie around his mouth. "I think we need to find this fool," says Hondo.

Hondo gets the watch commander on a tac frequency. He confirms there was a homicide at Twenty-third and LaSalle two nights ago, and tells us to stand by while he makes a few phone calls to find out which detectives are handling the case.

"Somethin' wrong with the man," she says. "This ain't the only killin' he done. He put in a lot of work for the hood. I know he kilt more than ten peoples in his lifetime."

The watch commander comes back and advises us that Robbery-Homicide Division (RHD), LAPD's unit that handles major homicide cases, is handling the Twenty-third and LaSalle case as opposed to our own South Bureau Homicide. RHD routinely takes cases from a bureau homicide unit when that team has too many homicide cases in the works. And judging by Detective Cutter's recent briefings, South Bureau Homicide must be overrun. The watch commander tells us to stand by while he contacts RHD.

"Where does he live?" I ask her. I already know the answer, having been to his place on the report call. I just want to be sure.

"Down on Hobart, just below Adams," she says. "But he don't live in the front. He lives in a house in the back, off the alley."

"He have any weapons in there?" asks Hondo.

"Yeah," she says. "He had the gun he kilt Trey with. And he's got a sawed-off shotgun. When he told me he'd kill me, he stuck it in my mouth—" She begins crying again.

"When did he do that?" asks Hondo.

"About thirty minutes ago," she wails. "I went over there for some, and he stuck a shotgun in my mouth."

What "some" is I don't know. Probably either rock or sex. Whatever it is, the memory of the gun in her mouth causes her to shake violently. It's as if she's about to have a seizure. I flip on the car's air conditioner to full blast.

"Lean forward," I say, indicating I want her to put her chin on the back of our seats as I point one of the air jets at her head. The cold air hits her sweaty face, and she calms down.

"That feels good," she says. "Thank you."

"How do you know him?" I ask.

"I have a baby by him," she says. "But that was ten years ago. I known him since high school."

"Where's the child now?" I ask.

"Boy's with my grandmother in Texas," she says. "He ain't never seen him."

"When did you last see your son?" asks Hondo.

"A year ago," she says sadly. Somewhere in that drug-induced haze that has long ago consumed her motherhood, I recognize guilt. "Too long, huh?" she adds.

"Yeah," I reply simply. "You two ever married?" I ask. A bad question. Could have just punched her in the stomach. Kiki makes a face. The thought seems repugnant to her.

"Hell, no!" she says. "He's crazy. I just had a baby wid' him ten years ago. Weren't no love or shit there. He never gave a fuck about my ass. We just got nasty one night and he wouldn't use no rubber. So we got us a baby. But he don't act like it. I jus' another ho to him. I never even talked wid' him while I was gone. I only see'd him again about a year ago, when I moved back here from Texas. I been on the streets and went to him only to see if he'd give me some money. I didn't know he'd do no shootin'."

"Did he give you any money?" I ask. "Did he help you out?"

"Only when I'd give him a piece," she says painfully. "He'd make me do things, nasty things. He a sick muthafucka . . ."

The watch commander comes back on the tac. He's sending out a supervisor and another unit to go after Buford with us. We send him a message of where to meet.

First we make a little side trip. Kiki claims she knows where the "white car" that Buford used in the Twenty-third and LaSalle killing is.

"It's registered to some Mescan," she says. "Eric bought it for one hundred dollars. Never put it in his name. He use it to do crimes."

"He doing any other crimes you know about?" asks Hondo.

"Yeah, he dealin' crack," she says.

"You don't know where he's getting it from?" asks Hondo.

"Same place the other dealers do, I guess," she says. " 'Cept he gettin' a better price."

"Why's that?" I ask.

" 'Cause he sellin' it cheap," she says. "Almost like he gettin' it for free."

Free, yes. But with a little blood spilled.

The location where the "white car" should be is just inside Wilshire Division, not far from the scene of their related homicide. It would be perfect if we could get the car. Not only would it be excellent evidence for the Twenty-third and LaSalle homicide, but it might also link up the Wilshire murder.

But it is not there.

"One of his friends may have it," she says. She nods to an empty parking space in the open-air apartment garage of a two-story, five-unit complex. "He park it there when it ain't bein' used."

I make a note of the address, then we head over to the Buford residence.

"You think they'll bust me like I was involved?" she asks.

"I don't know," I say. "Were you?"

"Like I said," she replies, "I just went to his house to get some smoke. I ain't got no reason to kill nobody. I just out on the streets livin' day to day. You know, I'm smokin'. It's all I care about, gettin' fucked up. I don't want nobody dead. Ain't no reason to it. And then he's shootin', killin' people, killin' Trey. He crazy."

"Some time in jail might save your life," says Hondo. "Get your ass dried out."

She thinks for a moment.

"Y'all probably right," she says—and nothing else.

Sergeant Gonzalez, a new sergeant from Central Bureau who stands about six feet six inches tall, meets us at Buford's with Randy Rangel and Hector Contreras, two large Hispanic officers. We send Rangel and Contreras to the back, while Hondo, the sergeant, and I door-knock the place. No one answers the front door, so the sarge and I go around one side while Hondo goes around the other. We run into Buford's mother, who is tending to her rosebushes. She does not seem surprised to see us.

"Mrs. Buford," I say, "how are you?"

"Fine," she says. She is real guarded. She knows something is up. She examines Sergeant Gonzalez and me closely. "And how are you, Officer?"

"Splendid, ma'am," I reply. "Do you remember me? I was here to take the report of your shooting."

"I remember you," she replies, her voice even, matronly. "I been through a lotta shootings. I've forgotten most of the officers I've met. But I do remember you, son. What can I do for you?"

"I was wondering if I could talk to your son Eric," I ask.

She looks at Sergeant Gonzalez's stripes, then calmly wipes her hands on her gardening apron as she shakes her head sadly. I am about to speak, but then she turns and walks away from us toward the backyard.

"Mrs. Buford," I say. She does not reply. She just opens the side gate and begins to walk to the back guesthouse where I know Buford lives. It hits me that she might be warning her son. I almost run after her, but something makes me stop. Her gait is too dignified to chase. Plus, if Eric is in there with a sawed-off shotgun, I sure as hell don't want to be caught in the middle of an open yard.

"Eric," she yells, "some friends of yours are here to see you."

She says it calmly. She bangs on his door a few times for punctuation, then turns and walks back across the yard to her own house. When she gets to the rear steps, Buford, wearing only his underwear and once again looking as sleepy as he had on our last encounter, opens the door to the guesthouse. He looks across the yard at her.

"They're around front," she says, and then wearily enters her house. She doesn't want to see anything more.

I am behind a thick bush, and Sergeant Gonzalez has flattened out against the house, so Buford cannot see us when he looks our way. He grabs some pants from near the door, puts them on, then walks over to where we are. He sees us only when he's about ten feet away.

"Eric," I say, "turn around, man. Put your hands on your head."

"Shit," he says. And that's all he says. He then tenses, like he might fight, but he takes one look at Sergeant Gonzalez, who towers above both Buford and me, and thinks better of it. He then looks back, as if he is about to run. But Rangel and Contreras are now coming in through the alley gate. He calmly turns around and is soon handcuffed.

After Buford is in custody, we notify the watch commander. Rangel and Contreras, who have their black-and-white parked in the alley behind Buford's house, transport Buford to the station. Hondo, Sergeant Gonzalez, and I then walk back out front where our black-and-whites are parked. I then realize Kiki is no longer in the backseat of our black-and-white.

"Shit" is all I can say.

In the time it took us to hook up Buford in the backyard, Kiki has disappeared to parts unknown. She had been so talkative, and so cooperative, that we didn't want to handcuff her. We felt that she would be more inclined to talk to the detectives later if she was not restrained, and that she was so petrified with fear of retaliation from Buford's homies that she *wanted* police protection.

We get in the car and cruise the area looking for her, but do not find her.

Phil Vannatter and Tom Lange, detective partners from Robbery-Homicide Division who would both later gain fame as the lead detectives in the O. J. Simpson murder trial, have been assigned to the Twenty-third and LaSalle murder. They arrive at Southwest Division each wearing a conservative sport coat over a freshly pressed white shirt, the white shirt being the only *color* traditionally worn by an RHD detective.

Vannatter carries a thick folder under one arm containing the case file for the murder. He is a bear of a man who speaks in a quiet, even tone.

"I really wish you had been able to hold on to Karen Johnson," he says. "I've been trying to get in touch with her since yesterday, but the phone number I have for her is no good."

"So you knew about her involvement in the homicide?" I ask.

"She had already called our office, but she just said she had information on the murder," he replies. "I didn't know she was in the car with Buford. That makes her a material witness to a homicide, if not an accomplice."

I then show him the field identification card I had made out on Kiki while in the car, pointing out the phone number and address she gave me.

"That's the same information I have," says Vannatter. "It's her sister's place, but Karen's hardly ever there. I guess she's out on the street a lot."

Vannatter and Lange then take Buford back into one of the station interview rooms for questioning. While they interview Buford, I run him for warrants and rap sheet on the department computers. I find that this is his *fourth* arrest for murder, although he has either been acquitted or had the charges dismissed on the previous three arrests. I tell Hondo, who is in the report-writing room having a cup of coffee with some other P-IIIs, one of whom is Tom Murrell.

"I was involved in one of those homicides," says Murrell, a tall officer with all-American looks. "Buford threw some dope dealer out a third-story window. But the jury believed him when he said the dope dealer committed suicide, that the dope dealer jumped to his death on his own."

"I'm sure Buford was just there trying to talk him down," says one of the other P-IIIs, smiling.

"Yeah, talk him down with Buford's foot on his ass," says Hondo.

The detectives finish their interview.

"We're going to book Buford for murder," says Vannatter. "We have enough to hold him, but we better find Karen Johnson; otherwise we won't have much of a case."

"You know, I think Buford is also involved in the murders at the Crenshaw Family Inn," I say.

"The Crenshaw Family Inn?" says Vannatter. "I'm not familiar with that case."

I tell him what I know. Because the LAPD has so many homicides, three different levels of homicide investigation have formed. They are separated by the complexity of the investigation, as well as notoriety. The first level is the *divisional* homicide unit consisting of patrol officers and detectives. They handle drive-by shooting homicides and simple murders that the media have little concern with and that can be solved through minor investigation. Then comes the *bureau* homicide unit, our area coming under South Bureau Homicide (SBH), which handles homicides in Seventy-seventh Street Division, Southwest Division, Southeast Division, and Harbor Division—the four divisions that make up South Bureau. Detectives who investigate for SBH take the murders that are more complex, such as drug hits, multiple murders, or domestic-violence homicides. At the top is Robbery-Homicide Division, which handles complex murders citywide, such as Mafia hits or high-profile cases like the

O. J. Simpson case. It takes a detective a long time to work his way up the ladder to RHD, and they are our best and brightest detectives.

As in any division of labor, one section may not always know what the other is doing. So Vannatter is unaware of the investigation being conducted by South Bureau Homicide. I tell him to contact Detective Hoffman, the head honcho at SBH, or Detective Lemus, who is the case detective.

"We're gonna drive over to South Bureau Homicide and talk to them," says Vannatter. "Also, Buford gave us permission to search his residence. We'll come back and get you and your partner for the search after we see what South Bureau has on Buford."

While Vannatter and Lange drive over to SBH, I get Buford booked for murder. He is still sleepy when we are standing in the booking cage, and he yawns and scratches like a cat who has just awoken from a nap. He does not seem to mind being in custody at all.

"They serve lunch yet?" he says, his only real concern being an empty stomach.

When we do the strip search, a requirement when booking for any felony arrest, he takes his clothes off before I even ask him.

"I probably know this shit better than you," he says. "I think this arrest is my thirtieth." He looks up at the ceiling, smiling. "Yes, I do believe this is my thirtieth anniversary."

He then goes through the visible search on his own, opening his mouth, lifting his arms, lifting his testicles and then showing me the bottoms of his feet.

"Yeah, I've done this thirty times," he says.

We complete the rest of the process without another word.

Hondo, Vannatter, Lange, and I go back to Buford's residence. Buford's mother is still there, and she uses her key to let us into Buford's room. She is courteous, joking lightly with Vannatter about her rosebushes, a noticeable spark in her step. She seems relieved that her son is not coming home tonight; not so much that she does not care for him, just that she does not care for the danger that hovers around him.

"He's still my son, and I love him," she says, "but he's gone bad, real bad." Lange asks her if she would like to elaborate. "No, that's your job."

We enter Eric's house—or really, Eric's space. It is a one-car garage turned into a bedroom. Decorated in a style that can best be described as early crash pad, it's a real mess. There are two ragged, musty lime-green couches with bare springs and stuffing protruding placed against two facing walls. A wood dresser against the far wall looks like it has been used for knife-throwing practice. Chips of wood litter the floor around it, and deep knicks are all over its front. Eric's bed, a single, stained mattress with a pile of covers in the center of the room, is plopped down conveniently in front of a new thirty-six-inch Mitsubishi color television with VCR that sits next to the door. On one side is a five-shelf rack-mounted stereo system with about two dozen CDs scattered around its base. That's it for furniture. Everything else is in piles: piles of cloths, piles of news-papers; piles of beer cans. The piles fill the floor space, making it difficult to maneuver, so I decide to exit and let the detectives at it. They know better what to look for, anyway.

I go back outside with Buford's mother. There is a big-rig Ken-worth truck parked in the backyard, covered by a tarp. Mrs. Buford notices me looking at it.

"My husband was a truck driver," she says. "He died three years ago. I was hoping Eric would use it. He coulda made good money truck driving."

Mrs. Buford goes on to tell me she is a retired office manager with the Department of Water and Power. She and her husband made good money. Eric Buford did not grow up in an economically deprived situation. On the contrary, both of his parents had good-paying jobs. I talk to her more, trying to find out why this guy has turned to a life of crime. She does not try to deny his crimes. She just tries to explain him.

"Eric was always smarter than most," she says. "When he was young, he got in with the Harlem boys. They always were looking up to him. Guess it made him feel like somebody. So when things went bad for the Harlems, Eric was the one they ran to so he could make it right. When they needed money, Eric was the one who'd lead them to go get some. He was just down for his boys. It's a shame. He's smart enough to have been somebody."

Her face tightens. I get the feeling that a picture of Buford as a small child has flashed through her mind.

"My other boys, they're good kids," she says, smiling. "James is making something of himself. He wants to be a deejay on the radio. Got a fine voice. And he loves music. He doesn't hang with Harlem or the Thirties anymore, and it's saving his life, 'cause he was on the wrong road for a while."

A black teenage girl, maybe nineteen, real pretty with hair pulled back in a bun, comes strolling into the backyard with Buford's rottweiler on a leash. She takes one look at me and smiles. "What's Eric done now?" she says.

Sasha* is Buford's current girlfriend. Sasha does not seem too upset when I tell her what Buford is in custody for.

"He always in some kinda shit," says Sasha. She smiles broadly, looks me in the eye, quickly adding, "And I don't know nothin' about it!"

I smile at the last comment. The dog brushes up against my uniform again, as it did when I was here four months earlier. Then it hits me. "What's the dog's name?" I ask, trying to remember.

"Gangster Jack," she says.

"Gangster Jack," I say. "Why did Eric name him Gangster Jack?"

"Because that's E's best friend," she replies.

I pull out my pocket notebook and flip through it, finding descriptions of the killers at the Crenshaw Family Inn. Suspect number one is nicknamed E, has a slender build, and is probably Buford. Suspect number two is big: six two to six four, two hundred fifty pounds. I decide to roll the dice with Sasha.

"Gangster Jack," I ask, "is a big dude, right? A Harlem who hangs up on Adams?"

"Nah," she says. "Jack a skinny muthafucka."

Then she apologizes to Mrs. Buford for swearing in front of her. Mrs. Buford dismisses her words, looking at me with curiosity. She realizes it was not an idle question, that I want to know about Jack. "Jack is very skinny," she says, her voice full of honesty and confirmation. It also silently says, *Keep trying, I'll help.*

"He sometimes is up around Adams," says Mrs. Buford. "Why, are you looking for Jack, too?"

"No," I reply. "Just trying to keep track of the OG. Does he have a ponytail?" I ask.

"Yeah, I do believe he does," says Mrs. Buford.

"But he's skinny," I say, thinking aloud.

"Eric does have some big fool who hangs around him sometimes, but I never got his name," says Mrs. Buford. She looks at me hard, to impress that she is telling the truth. "Real big. Must weigh two hundred and seventy-five pounds. And he's tall, six two or six three. But I don't know his name, because Eric just calls him G." She turns to Sasha. "But Sasha knows him, don't you, Sasha?"

"No, I don't," says Sasha. But yes, she does. I can see it in her eyes. They flicker like a moth on a flame. "Most of E's friends are skinny like him."

"What about that big old fool drives that Cadillac?" says Mrs. Buford, annoyed. "Always wears black like he's some kind of Mister Velvet. You know who I'm talking about. All three of you were just here in my house last week."

"Big Mike?" says Sasha, as if trying to say, *"Not him!"* "He ain't that big."

"Hell he ain't," says Mrs. Buford. "He's got to weigh two hundred and seventy-five pounds, Officer."

"Mike and E ain't even that close of friends," says Sasha, now trying to cover up. But the more she tries to cover up, the worse she sounds. "They just kick it sometimes."

"Girl, Mike's over here all the time," says Mrs. Buford. "Every time I go in the back they're lifting a forty together."

"Well, I don't know," says Sasha. "I don't see them together that much."

"You know Mike's last name?" I ask Sasha. But she is not going to give up anything more about her homies.

"I don't know," she says. "I don't even know if Mike's his real name. I think it just a play name."

"You mean Mike's name ain't Mike?" I ask, a little amused.

"I don't know," she says, trying to cover. "He just some boy G. I don't know him too well."

Boy G? Hey, I've heard that slang before, and it was driving a 5.0 Mustang. I look at her closely. I saw the girl with heavy eye liner in the dark for only a minute, and Sasha's not wearing any makeup, so it's hard to tell. But it could be her.

"What kind of car do you drive?" I ask her.

She looks at me curiously. Then a flicker of remembrance runs across her face. Then it is hidden.

"I ain't got no car," she says. "But I'm driving my mother's Chrysler today. It's parked out front if you want to see it."

"You know G-Roc?" I ask. "Got shot a few weeks ago?"

"No," she says. "I don't know no G-Roc." She is *lying*! I can see it in her eyes. Too bad we can't arrest on instinct.

"You're not telling me the truth," I say.

"Tell the man the truth," spits Mrs. Buford. "If you know a G-Roc, you tell the man."

But Sasha stands firm. "I don't know no G-Roc."

Mrs. Buford glares at Sasha. Then she turns to me, gives me a sympathetic look. She can't help me anymore.

"OK." I shrug.

When the detectives come out of Buford's residence, I tell them about the night at G-Roc's homicide scene, and about the information on Mike. They talk to Sasha briefly, but she has all but shut up.

"Take my ass to jail," she says to the detectives. "Otherwise, stay the fuck away from me."

They decline, and thank Mrs. Buford for her courtesy. Soon we are all in the front yard.

"We didn't find any weapons," says Vannatter. "Or any other evidence. But the place is such a mess, it would take a team of search dogs to find anything. It's an old garage, with a lot of loose wood wallboard, and a floor that has holes in it. There are a million places to hide things."

Which is a disappointment. I was hoping we would come up with the .380 auto, or at least the shotgun.

"At least we have Buford in jail," says Detective Vannatter. "Now we just have to build a case."

A thin fog still hugs the morning ground, pressing a calm over the area. The gray thickness almost makes the streets feel safe. None of the drug dealers or gang members who normally haunt the area are present, warmly holed up under whatever rock it is they inhabit. Cold seems to have an inhibiting effect on criminals. You think maybe if we refrigerated the city, all the bad guys would leave?

It is now two weeks after Eric Buford's arrest, and one week after his release. The murder charges were dropped against him. Lack of evidence: no weapon, no witnesses who will testify. Because Kiki has disappeared. Where? No one knows for sure. I only hope that she left town for Texas—because if she did not, that means that one of Buford's homies got her.

Roll call is short. The only thing of interest is that there was another murder last night, a double murder. Information on it is sketchy. It started on the corner of Raymond Avenue and Adams Boulevard, where all the OG Rollin' 30s hang out. Three male blacks drove up in a possible brown Duster and opened fire on two dealers standing on the corner. A running gun battle ensued, with shell casings being strewn down Raymond for one block to the corner of Raymond and Thirtieth Street, where both of the dealers were finally killed.

"It sounds like another killing involving Buford," says Hondo after roll call. "I'm gonna show you how we used to catch criminals."

Hondo is a man on a mission, and I barely sit in the passenger seat before he puts it in gear and drives out of the parking lot. We are two blocks from the station before I even get a chance to type communications so that I can log onto the computer.

We drive straight to the neighborhood where the killings happened, Raymond Avenue and Thirtieth Street. No breakfast, no morning cup of coffee, which is a big deal. Hondo is a man who usually needs a morning cup to wash away the cobwebs. Each day we have worked together, we have driven straight to the Boulevard Café for eggs, bacon, and coffee. But not this morning. He pulls to the curb in front of a white, cottage-style house with a heavy, black wrought-iron fence.

"Wait here," he says.

It is a fortress of a house, built to keep out the army of gangsters who own this part of Los Angeles. Even the rosebushes adorning the front yard seem to have exceptionally large thorns.

When I see these fortified homes, I half expect them to be owned by freedom fighters, men and women from the French resistance during World War II. Each home is a reclaimed area in a sort of "Vichy Los Angeles," a place where the gangsters control the streets but the people control their residences.

Hondo walks up to the gate and buzzes an intercom system that goes into the house. Soon a middle-aged black lady with curlers in her hair appears at the front door. She smiles when she sees Hondo, then, letting out a shriek, runs down the walkway to the gate.

They speak for a while, their voices too low for me to hear, idle chatter punctuated by smiles. But soon their words turn to serious discussion. She looks over at me, gauging whether I can hear her or not. She does not trust me. She continues to talk to Hondo.

They converse for some time. My rear end begins to fall asleep, so I get out and stand. Residents en route to their jobs, driving their cars with cups of coffee in hand, slow and inspect me, giving me looks as if to say, "What's happened now?" Some stop to chat, and we exchange pleasantries about the day. Soon Hondo comes back over to me.

"One of our suspects is Gangster Jack," he says, which fits in light of Eric's dog's name. "I know Jack by sight. Used to be a Harlem. If we find him, we'll find the other two."

"That lady saw the shootings?" I ask.

"Not exactly," he says. "She seen Jack and two others running up the street after all the shooting stopped. One of them sounds like it could have been Buford. The other was a skinny black man."

"So we have a witness," I say.

"We ain't got shit but knowledge," he replies, smiling. "She won't say what she saw anywhere but to me in private. She used to be a gangsterette with the Businessmen. She knows everything that is on the streets about the killings. But she is a homegirl first. She won't never tell it in court. So we're just gonna have to find Jack, and then sweat him. Or kill him."

I mull this last sentence over in my head.

"I know this Jack, too," Hondo continues. "A big-time crack smoker. Always high. He is also one cold muthafucka. I arrested him, oh, ten years ago for a mugging. Hit some old Spanish man over the head with a pipe and took his money. The man needed something like fifty stitches. She says Jack, Buford, and a cat named Big Mike always hang out together. Lately they've been stirring up all kinds of shit in the hood. Besides our killings, they've been taking rocks and money from the pooh-butts by force. And apparently they jammed one of G-Roc's runners the day he was killed. They probably killed G-Roc because he was looking to kill them."

I mull over what I've just heard. "So, basically what we have are a bunch of Harlem Thirties killing people from their own hood?" I say. "But I thought these guys were loyal to each other."

"Understand, this is killing for money and drugs, plain and simple," Hondo says. "You put money on the table, and homie goes out the window."

Yeah, yeah. I'm learning. Life on the streets ain't no rap video.

"She's seen Jack driving a tan Duster just yesterday," he adds. I look at my notes on the Crenshaw Family Inn killings, and point to the description of E. "Drives a tan Duster," I say.

We now go to the Boulevard Café and get some breakfast. Hondo seems to be computing all the information he has taken in on the case. I don't say anything to him while we eat. I just let him chew and think. He doesn't speak again until we are paying for our food.

"Jack ain't the type to put money away," he says. "He's the type who'd binge on drugs if he got some. Just go fucking wild, staying as high as he can for as long as he can. So Jack's probably hitting the pipe at some crib."

We go back to the 30s hood and start canvassing some of the rock houses for leads on Jack's whereabouts. You might think it strange that officers do not try to shut down rock houses when they know about them. The problem is, there is nothing harder to do than to shut down a rock house. You need to enter the location to make an arrest. *That means* you need probable cause for a search warrant to enter the location. *That means* you need to have surveillance on the location to get enough information to convince a judge that the location is a rock house. *That means* you would have to go undetected in the area for a number of *hours* as transactions are sporadic. But undetected surveillance by a patrol officer is nearly impossible when most of the kids in the area will dime you off in a heartbeat. And even if you do get enough information for a search warrant, you still need to serve it effectively. But these are fortified houses with fortified beehive inner sections that insulate drug sales from direct contact with the public. So most of the time there is need for either SWAT or some kind of large, well-armed entry team with the ability to explode or disable steel doors immediately. Otherwise, all the dope and money go down a toilet in about twenty seconds. Even if one does get through all of the above, you will probably only be arresting young kids or gangster girls with little or no criminal history, and thus recipients of little or no time, as the hard-core OG who own the operation usually stay out of the structure, keeping a watchful eye from a distance. And even if you do *all* of the above, and you *catch* the kids and women with the money and the dope, the house will be open the next day with other kids, women, money, and dope. So rock houses are very tough.

In front of a rock house on Catalina Avenue just north of Jefferson Boulevard, we see five Rollin' 30s, all in their late teens. The sun has now poked through the morning fog, and the drug trade, which was asleep during the morning rush hour, is now fully awake. It is odd that rock houses, which are supposed to run around the clock, slow almost to a standstill during morning rush hour—probably as some quiet protest against having to work for a living. Anyway, it is now ten, and we walk up on these gangsters.

"What's up?" says Hondo, running a hand through his gray hair.

"Not much, Hondo," almost all reply. They are all courteous to Hondo: no mad-dog looks; no disrespect. Hondo is a policeman with a reputation, a well-earned reputation. Hondo was on the fringes of the Black Panther party as a youth, still sporting a tattoo of a panther on one forearm. He then served a tour in Vietnam as an army ranger, and came back a changed man. He has been a street cop at Southwest Division since the 1970s.

"Any of you seen Gangster Jack today?" he asks. One of them, a burly teenager named C-Dawg, speaks up.

"We're looking for him ourselves," he says. "Guess you know what happened?"

"Yeah, I do," says Hondo. "He's a muthafucka out of control." Hondo lights up a big fat stogie. He absently pushes out a thick cloud.

"No doubt," says C-Dawg. "We ain't got time for that bullshit.

Nigger bustin' on his homies like that. You might as well leave us a body bag, Hondo, 'cause we gonna need something to put Jack's dead ass in."

"Yeah, don't make no bed for him at CJ," says another, referring to county jail. "He won't be usin' it."

I look at C-Dawg and the others. They are sporting big, defined weight-lifters' arms, probably from doing some time in the California Youth Authority. Real muscleheads. But I think they are full of talk. If Jack shows up with a gun, having just killed all these people, I'm sure these guys will piss in their pants. We are not talking about beating up some smaller fool, or shooting at some unarmed kid. We are talking about getting into it with a hard-core killer. An *armed* hard-core killer. You tangle with Jack, and it's to the death.

"Uh-huh," says Hondo. "I heard that. And if you find him, he's gonna kill your ass."

I think Hondo agrees with my appraisal. Hondo walks over to a pillar that holds up the house. He takes out a pen and writes on it. "You see him, you call the desk, understand?" He gives the five gangsters a cold look. I can feel their uneasiness. Hondo nods to them. We turn and get in the car. "Those boys will call us if they see him," he says.

Over the next two hours, we stop and talk with any other Rollin' 30 we see on the street, asking about Gangster Jack. Most of them have already heard about the Raymond and Thirtieth murders, but they do not seem too concerned. Most of the comments are the same: "It's fucked up." And that's about it. To most of them, it's just another day in the hood.

Then a message comes over the MDT from an officer working Southwest desk. It reads: SOMEONE JUST CALLED THE STATION. . . . HE SAYS JACK WAS JUST AT CATALINA AND ADAMS IN A BROWN DUSTER. . . . DO YOU UNDERSTAND THIS MESSAGE?

I reply in the affirmative. We go directly to Catalina and Adams. C-Dawg is out on the sidewalk in front of the rock house. A serious-looking "original gangster" in his forties, sporting a green polo shirt, sits quietly on the steps behind him. He observes us from behind deeply tinted sunglasses.

"Jack was here not ten minutes ago," says C-Dawg. "I told him what you said."

"You did, huh?" replies Hondo, smiling.

"He says, 'Fuck you, Hondo,' " says C-Dawg, smiling back.

"You know where he was going?" asks Hondo.

"No," says C-Dawg. "But he had some skinny muthafucka with him who I ain't never seen before. And they was in E's car, man."

"You mean Eric Buford's car?" I ask.

"I don't know his name," says C-Dawg. "But I know it's his brown Duster. There ain't no other piece of shit like it in South Central."

Hondo takes this in.

"They packin', Hondo," says C-Dawg. "I told them they was fucked for the killin'. If I didn't have G here, and my backup in the inside, they'd have busted caps at me."

I now look at the house. A teenager with a hard face, maybe seventeen, stands in the window just to the OG's right. I have no doubt he has an assault rifle within arm's reach.

We leave C-Dawg and drive around some more. Gangster Jack and his friend cannot be that far away from us, even at this minute. It's a distinct car, and should be easy to spot, but we don't see it. I send out an MDT message to other units, informing them of our search for the brown Duster. We even contact the air unit, asking the pilot to keep an eye out.

We spend the rest of the watch talking to people, coming up empty, forsaking taking any radio calls this day. It's now nearing the end of watch. We go by C-Dawg's rock house for the third time. Standing out in front with a large group of 30s, he meets us in the street, a look of excitement on his face.

"Yo, Hondo," says C-Dawg, "Jack says he'll be at Gold Mine at four o'clock."

Hondo nods, and we drive off. "Gold Mine" is a rock house. Two stories high, it's a blue wood and black iron fortress owned by one of the richest white families in Los Angeles, leased knowingly, I am sure, to some of the OG at an exorbitant rent. It has been raided numerous times over the years, but continues to operate at a conservative estimate of twenty thousand dollars per week. It is protected by numerous lookouts on the street, and numerous lawyers in the courtroom. And Jack wants to "meet" us there.

"What, this guy is just going to give himself up?" I ask Hondo.

A thin smile rolls across his lips. "What have you learned in your time down here?" he says. "Obviously not enough, 'cause you're missing the point. Jack ain't meeting us to give up. I mean, you saw C-Dawg's face. He knows what's coming. Jack wants to do an 'O.K. Corral' with us."

"What, a gunfight?" I ask.

"Yes," he replies simply.

I look at my watch. We have about an hour until the meeting. We drive to the station and park.

"Wait here," says Hondo, motioning me to sit tight. He goes into the station, then, moments later, pulls up behind me in an undercover car.

"Sergeant Roberts OK'd us for overtime," he says. Somehow, I get the feeling that he didn't tell the whole story, but I'm not that concerned.

I look at Hondo. He is a *tough* cop. He has seen action in a time of war, heavy action. He gives me a lot of confidence, especially if this turns violent. He throws me a set of keys. "You're driving."

It is a dark-green sedan with dull hubcaps and an interior, forward-facing, flip-down red light for cutting through traffic. It is usually used by detectives. I transfer our equipment into the plain car. Then I see Hondo pull a bulletproof vest out of his bag. He takes off his shirt and puts it on. Hondo never wears a vest.

"You're wearing a vest, right?" he asks. Probationers are required to.

"Yeah," I reply.

"I have an extra shotgun, too," he says. I'm holding the one from our patrol car in my hands, switching it from the rack in the black-and-white to the one in the plain car. Hondo points to one he has laid in the trunk. "You got rounds?"

"Plenty," I reply. "I always keep an extra box in my bag."

I take them from my bag and load up the extra gauge.

"There ain't too many officers I'd do this shit with," he says. This makes me feel good. "You been in a shooting yet?"

"No," I reply. He just nods. He already knew that.

"You'll do fine if there is one," he adds.

Soon we have ourselves and the car ready. As we drive through the lot, we see Moe Landrum from the shooting team. Hondo tells him what we've got.

"I'll meet you up there in five minutes with my partner," says Moe. He then reaches into his car and takes a booking photo out of his briefcase. "I just got this today. This is Jack's last photo. I kind of figured he had some involvement in these killings, him being so close to Buford." Hondo shows it to me, then gives it back to Moe.

Moe goes into the station. It is three forty, twenty minutes until the meet. We pull out of the lot, heading northbound on Denker.

Then, just as we are approaching Thirty-ninth Street, *"Three-T-fifteen is requesting a backup,"* says the RTO. *"Thirty-ninth and Denker on a man with a gun."*

Even though we have a pressing engagement, you never leave your partners hanging. Anyway, we are already on Denker approaching Thirty-ninth. We see the unit, a two-man black-and-white, facing westbound right at the corner, behind a . . . *brown Duster!*

Both officers, a pair of pepper-haired black traffic cops, calmly have their guns pointed at two male blacks seated in the front seat. We pull in at an angle on the Duster.

"Well, I'll be a muthafucka!" exclaims Hondo, and we are out of the car, me with a shotgun, Hondo with his laughter. Gangster Jack, hands in the air, looks over at us. He has the thin, strained face of a recently paroled con who has spent a lot of years in prison lifting weights and thinking hate.

"Driver, open your door with your hand using the outside door handle," yells one of the traffic cops, a bespectacled man with massive forearms. He holds a chrome six-inch .38 revolver, a nasty-looking weapon which I am sure is pointed centered at the back of Gangster Jack's head. Jack slowly opens the door, his hands deliberately visible, and I see a semiautomatic handgun sitting loosely in his lap.

"Gun," I say calmly, an advisement. "The driver has a gun in his lap." There is no reaction from the other officers. Just as long as his hands stay high, Jack will be all right.

His hands stay high. And he is all right. He walks backward to the traffic officers, and is soon handcuffed.

The passenger, another recent parolee, is *sitting* on a revolver. He, too, keeps his hands in sight and is also all right, soon in handcuffs without incident. I take Jack and sit him in our car for transportation to the station. He looks at my name tag.

"Dunn," he says, as if greeting an old friend. He is smiling wide. "You and Hondo been lookin' for me all day. Was on my way up to Gold Mine with my boy to meet you."

"Guess we'll have to do it some other time," I reply. I know, sounds real corny—but it's all I can come up with.

Hondo approaches me with the passenger's semiautomatic handgun in a plastic bag. I look closely at it. On the side, the caliber, .380, is stamped in the metal. "I think we got 'em," he says.

The traffic cops had stopped the brown Duster to issue them a ticket for an expired license plate registration tag. When they attempted to walk up on the car, neither Jack nor the passenger would show their hands. After asking them three times, the old-timers just assumed they were dealing with bad guys with guns, and put out a backup.

They had not heard we were looking for the Duster.

BOOBE: PART TWO

It is the last day of my probation.

A supervisor is requesting an additional unit to his location at West Boulevard and Adams. My partner, Darius Lee, and I are just returning to the division from having booked a dope pusher with diabetes at the jail ward downtown. We are almost six hours beyond our end of watch and ready to go home. But no one else is answering the supervisor's call.

"Let's take it," Darius says to me.

Once we get to the supervisor's location, we find out where all the Southwest units are. They are here. All the streets are blocked off for six blocks, cops everywhere. They have a command post set up, and the captain has even rolled from his home. We report to the supervisor who requested us.

"We have a one-eighty-seven suspect somewhere in this perimeter. You guys are going on the dog search," says the supervisor. "Go see Landrum."

Moe Landrum is standing next to a police car marked K-9. The K-9 officer stands at his open trunk putting on a bulletproof vest. Landrum is next to him, and seems a little upset.

"Moe, we're doing the dog search," says Darius. "Who's our suspect?"

"He's a male black, five eleven, one sixty-five," says Landrum. "He's a Rollin' Forty Crip, wanted for murder. That's his cousin's house right there."

I look to where he is pointing. A modest, single-story structure with a manicured front yard, it has a new convertible Chrysler in the driveway.

"The murder happened about three hours ago, a gang thing, and I came by here because we had information on the suspect," he says. "Just as I rolled up, I see the suspect coming down the front steps. He had this in his hand." Landrum holds a .25-caliber stainless-steel automatic in a plastic evidence bag. "I got out of the car and he saw me. He threw the gun and ran."

"You got a name?" asks Darius.

"His name is Mickel Addams,"* says Moe, "but he goes by the name of Boobe."

Boobe!

"I just arrested him not two months ago in a stolen car while working with Thompson," I say. I feel my heart in my throat. *Damn!* I knew he would screw up big time. He was too much of a gangster when I met him. But for some reason, I am truly bothered by being present at a manhunt for him. Between his stutter, his severe dyslexia, and his shyness, he seemed like a lost soul. But now he is a suspected murderer.

"I don't know if we got the perimeter up in time to catch him," adds Landrum.

Landrum did not. We follow the dog through the neighborhood for an hour. He picks up Boobe's scent numerous times, but we do not find him.

Boobe gave himself up at the front desk of Southwest Station the next day. I don't know what to say about this kid other than, I feel sorry for him. I don't know why. Maybe it's because I had a chance to talk to him, to see a piece of his life. I think it's human nature to care about things we know, and not to care about those things we have no knowledge of.

That is the story of fighting crime in South Central Los Angeles: People do not really care about it because they do not really know about it. Yes, they see graphic news reports of bodies lying in the streets, but they do not know the stories or the lives behind those bodies. They do not know the human beings who populate the area, and they do not know the criminal animals. They do not know the hearts of the policemen who daily commute into the area to try to carve out a piece of sanity from a piece of our world that is just completely insane.

Because they do not know, they do not care; so it just keeps getting worse.

Nothing in South Central is the way it should be. Despair is more prevalent than hope. Dreams are replaced by nightmares. Death is such an ingrained part of everyday existence that it is spoken of more than life. So it will take much more than money or social programs to heal the problems of South Central Los Angeles. It will take an almost completely new mind-set for the people who inhabit the area, and tremendous help from their neighbors in surrounding communities. Those ideals and lifestyles that have led to the rampant violence and drug abuse that are part of everyday life will somehow have to be altered and then forgotten. And those who promote those ideals and lifestyles will somehow have to be stopped.

EPILOGUE

Many of the officers I worked with in what is still a short time ago have left the department. Mike Gurr has moved to an agency in Arizona. Kent Pallister is with an agency in Alberta, Canada. Laura Gould is back in her native Indiana with a small municipal force. Sergeant Pam Roberts is now Chief of Police Pam Roberts in Perris, California.

Sergeant J. J. Reese still runs P.M. watch roll call. But Don Murphy took an early retirement. He was one of forty-four officers listed in the Christopher Commission Report as being a problem officer. It is particularly odd to find him on the list, especially in light of his work fighting police corruption in Colorado.

Phil Vannatter and Tom Lange need very little explaining. They did a great job with Eric Buford. Eric "E" Buford and Mike "Big Mike" Caldwell are both serving life sentences for the murders at the Crenshaw Family Inn. Gangster Jack was never charged with any of the murders, although as of the writing of this book, he is currently in the California prison system serving time for robbery. And the murder charges against Boobe were ultimately dropped when the shooting was deemed to be in self-defense.

I was stationed at Foothill Division when the 1992 riots began. For four nights I took rocks and bottles as well as a Molotov cocktail or two from the citizens of Los Angeles. It was the most confusing and frightening time in my life as a police officer. To see so many of my fellow citizens so desperately try to harm me and the officers I work with was beyond comprehension. The people of my city acted like animals. There is nothing else to say. I was sickened.

After the rioting had subsided, I returned to Southwest Division with one of my Foothill patrol sergeants, Jeff Bender. What I saw shocked me. It appeared that the division had been the victim of carpet bombing. All along Adams Boulevard and Jefferson Avenue businesses were looted and many of the buildings burned to the ground. Crenshaw Boulevard, where the cruisers rode, was one long sear mark in the earth.

The Blue Star Market was torched, simply because of its Korean ownership. Businesses across the street stood, spray-painted with the words "Black-owned business," this being their only protection. And according to Southwest officers, the first structure to catch fire was the Winchell's Donuts that Don Murphy and I had coffee at my first night, its association with police nutrition being its death warrant.

Many of the businesses destroyed in Southwest Division during the riots will never return. An estimated 15 percent of the jobs in the area went up in smoke for good during that troubled time. This has thrust the area into even deeper depression.

The only thing that has rebounded from the riots is the gangs. Gang membership has risen drastically. Many will say that statistics do not bear this out, that *reported* gang crime has fallen. But during the days of the riots, many of those who had cooperated with the police were either beaten or had their property damaged. Citizen involvement with the police is at an all-time low in the area. In one Department of Justice survey, it is estimated that 50 percent of crimes go unreported there. Southwest is no longer just an area that lives in fear, it is one that lives in panic.

Since I began writing this book, a number of LAPD officers have been killed in the line of duty. Two of them were boots: Tina Kerbrat, and Christy Hamilton, who was killed by rifle fire at a family dispute in Devonshire Division in February 1994. They are two boots who gave their lives for the city of Los Angeles, and to them I dedicate this book.